Chinook Concerns:

Emma Millet Luscier, Isabella Bertrand, Verne Ray

Jay Miller, PhD

Emma Millet Luscier

© 2019

FIG. 15. Designs from horn bowls (compare Field Museum specimens 19692-19698).

Foreword

Chinooks had a formidable role in the culture and history of the Northwest. With a huge population and strategic location on the Columbia, their complex language provided key words in the development of the ubiquitous trade jargon known as Chinuk Wawa. The trading network included western North America including the Southwest and Plains. Absolutely decimated by European diseases by 1830, few survivors carried on, especially at Bay Center, with Charles Cultee providing texts and data to Franz Boas around 1900, and later, to Verne Ray, two women elders, who will now be introduced:

Living sources for information given Verne Ray were Emma Millet Luscier (qwɑl'wɑnxᵘ) and Mrs. {Isabella} Bertrand (pətra'n), both at Bay Center. Emma (1861 - 1954) was notable for her intelligence and willingness to share with scholars, both Ray and John P Harrington, who joined her on bus rides through the countryside to gather place names and ethnography.

Isabella Bertrand had a Grays Harbor father, and mother named a•luɑmaks, whose own mother was a Satsop named akənsi married to o•cuwɪlɪks, whose sister was a chief as well as mother to Concomly, both of them chiefs at *qʷatsa'mts* (# 9) at the mouth of the Chinook River on Baker Bay, Washington. Her age and familiarity with the past enabled her to list common quest destinations: the top of Scarborough hill (above qʷatsa'mts village), Saddle mountain (south of Astoria), the swampy regions near Ilwaco, the head of Skamokawa river and Naselle mountain.

Emma's family included chiefs at Cowlitz, Quinault, Chinois, Tokeland, Willapa Bay, and Chinook. Her father t'łolox ~ Sam Millet's father and grandfather were chiefs at wa'qaiya•qam (# 3). Her mother qa•ktsəm was daughter of Cowlitz chief waxawa. Emma was married three times, to Frank tsa•k'to, son of chiefs at Chinois and Quinault, to Charlie Stills, and to Alex Luscier, son of an anglo and Julia.

Sam Millet's father died when he was young, leaving a wife and four children, two younger than Sam. Winter village wa'qaiya•qam providing the modern term Wahkiakum, once located across Alockman creek, about two miles north of the modern town of Cathlamet, where it relocated about 1810 after a fire.

Ike Stills was a soldier at the post near Ilwaco who married a Skagit woman, a slave insultingly named sqa•'tcitł for her tribe and formerly owned by a•'kaiak. They had many children, including Charlie.

As a girl, Emma was treated at least twice by shamans who dreamed her ailment and recovery. Word reached her father that qwaisi' dreamed that an ill Emma would be cured if placed within a traditional cradle. Sam invited the shaman to his home, thanked him, and let him pick up Emma and promise her an old style cradle the next day, when she was bound inside it with a headboard pressing down to shape here forehead. Soon, however, Sam's sister removed it, deciding she was opposed to the process. Finally, gifts went to the shaman and all who had had held the sick child.

Another shaman dreamed that Emma would be cured by piercing her ears. When word reached Sam, he invited in the shaman and other guests. As they ate breakfast, the shaman swam in the river, returned to Emma, pierced her ears around the rim and in the lobe with a hardwood needle, and threaded in buckskin thongs to keep them open. Over the next several days, everyone continued visiting, dancing, and singing. Finally, gifts were given, with the shaman receiving a gun, blanket, and other tokens. Pierced ears also assured a long life.

Verne Ray

Verne Ray, home-grown, male, and mobile, had a long career. He attended University of Washington (1924-28), studying mostly with Leslie Spier, and went on to UC Berkeley (1929-30). After Melville Jacobs joined UW in 1928, Ray returned for his MA, published as the classic <u>Sanpoil ~ Nespelem</u> (1933) in the UW series. For his PhD, he followed Spier to Yale (1936-37), financed by the building of two houses with carpentry skills learned from self-help books. His definitive PhD on Plateau Cultural Relations (1939) moved him up the UW ranks, becoming a graduate school dean (1948-54, with time at Yale) before resigning in 1966 to become expert witness for native land claims in court, based in DC. He retired to Port Townsend, and died in 2003 at the age of 98. His library and papers are at Gonzaga University in Spokane, notably not at UW. His professional academic obituary provides an appendix herein. His newspaper obituaries published in *The Seattle Times* on 20 October 2003 and his hometown *Peninsula Daily News* on 2003-10-01 add details:

> Verne F. RAY, PhD, retired professor of anthropology at the University of Washington, and pioneer ethnographer of many Pacific Northwest Indian tribes, died on 28 September in Port Townsend, Washington, at the age of 98. After retirement in 1966 he served as an expert witness and consultant for 53 Indian land claims cases. Dr. Ray was born on March 13, 1905 in Enfield, Illinois to Della Duncan and Arden Ray, but came to the state of Washington as an infant. He graduated from Franklin High School in Seattle, and received his B.A. and M.A. in anthropology from the University of Washington, and his Ph.D, from Yale University in 1937. As one of the first anthropologists at the University of Washington, he was appointed "Assistant in Anthropology, Washington State Museum" in 1930. During his tenure as a Professor he also served as head of the Anthropology Department and as Associate Dean, but since the University did not have enough money at that time for the position of Dean, he was appointed as Associate Dean. In the 1930's he was Director of the Emergency Conservation Program, U.S. Department of the Interior, on the Colville and Spokane Indian Reservations. On a leave of absence from the University from 1951 to 1954 he was Research Director of the Human Relations Area Files in New Haven, Connecticut.
>
> His anthropological interests were varied, ranging from theory and methodology to field research in the Middle East, the Valley of Mexico, and in all of the Indian tribes of the Pacific Northwest and northern California. His professional papers and books in the 1930's and 1940's were models of research for the many Indian land claims resulting from the passage of the Indian Claims Commission Act in 1946. Dr. Ray represented 44 tribes in 53 cases before the Claims Commission and other courts, winning millions of dollars for the tribes for the wrongful taking of their lands by the United States government. For the Cowlitz, it gained them recognition as a tribe by the federal government. For this achievement, the Cowlitz Tribal Council voted him an honorary member in 2000. He had many other interests, especially sailing and the building and remodeling of boats and houses. Having been rejected by the military

because of health problems during World War II, he joined the Coast Guard Auxiliary, and consequently became well acquainted with Puget Sound and the Strait of Juan de Fuca, and finally, Port Townsend, where between 1965 and 1970 he restored a four-apartment building to its single-family state of 1884 without any help. He was a life member of the Seattle Yacht Club. He was preceded in death by his daughter, La Verne Ray Fromberg and son-in-law, Gerald Fromberg. He is survived by his wife of 48 years, Dorothy Jean Ray of Port Townsend; stepson, Eric S. Thompson of Anchorage, Alaska; three grandsons, Paul Fromberg and Robert Fromberg of Evanston and Oak Park, Illinois, Steven Fromberg of Chapel Hill, North Carolina, and two great grandsons.

Retired anthropologist Verne Frederick Ray died in Port Townsend at age 98.

He came to Washington as an infant, graduated from Franklin High School in Seattle, and earned his bachelor's and master's degrees in anthropology from the University of Washington. He received his doctorate from Yale University in 1937.

As one of the first anthropologists at the University of Washington, he was appointed assistant in anthropology, Washington State Museum, in 1930.

During his tenure, he also served as head of the anthropology department and as associate dean of the graduate school.

In the 1930s, Dr. Ray was director of the emergency conservation program for the U.S. Department of the Interior on the Colville and Spokane reservations.

During a leave of absence from the university in 1951-52, he was a research director in New Haven, Conn.

Dr. Ray's professional papers and books in the 1930s and 1940s were models of research for many Indian land claims resulting from passage of the Indian Claims Commission Act in 1946. He represented 44 tribes in 53 cases before the commission and other courts, winning millions of dollars for tribes from wrongful appropriation of their lands.

This endeavor also gained recognition of the Cowlitz as a tribe by the federal government, for which the tribal council voted Dr. Ray honorary membership in 2000.

He was a life member of the Seattle Yacht Club. Although unable to serve with the military during World War II for health reasons, he became a member of the Coast Guard Auxiliary in 1965. This affiliation led to his becoming acquainted with Puget Sound and the Strait of Juan de Fuca.

Dr. Ray married Dorothy Jean Tostlebe in Seattle on Feb. 2, 1955.

He and his wife purchased a circa-1884 residence in Port Townsend that had been made into an apartment building. He restored it to single-family status by his own efforts between 1965 and 1970.

Republishing this volume enables corrections to be made to faulty production. Among these irregularities now corrected are the following:

p61 Figure 2 the weapons images are printed upside down

p35 p.v instead of proper Latin > q.v. for *quod vide* = "which see"
  idem ~ *id.* = Latin > "the same"
  loc. cit. = Latin > *loco citato* "at the place already cited"

p46 footnotes jump from #38 to #47 without notice

Chinook Traders of the Columbia River

At the emporium at the Dalles (Long Rapids) along the Columbia River, thousands of people gathered to fish and trade during summer salmon runs. Set at the gateway between the lush coast and the dry interior, this fishery intersected routes along the sea, upriver, and across land in all directions. Small items as exotic as pipestone from Minnesota, turquoise from the Southwest, galena from Montana, and copper from Alaska and the Great Lakes were traded there.

The bulk of the materials were regional, however. From the coast came dried shellfish arranged in standard units by being impaled on two-foot long sticks of salmonberry wood. Upland hunters provided mammal furs and dried meat in tule rush bags of standard size. Dried berries provided a variety of tastes and condiments. From the interior came dried roots like camas and the potato-like wapato. From further east came the skins of elk, deer, and occasional buffalo, along with dried meat. From California and Oregon to the south came slaves raided from small villages.

Local Chinooks, who managed this trade, provided dried salmon, pulverized salmon flour, dried sturgeon, dried smelt, dried seal, and canoes, which facilitated this water borne exchange. Occasional beached whales provided blubber and exceptionally large bones for tools and weapons.

Most valuable of all were tusk-like shells called dentalia (<u>*higua*</u> in Chinook WaWa or jargon) from the West Coast of Vancouver Island. Ordinarily these shellfish lived deep in the ocean. Off this shore, though, they were only a few hundred feet below the surface. Traders had marks tattooed on their arms to measure standard lengths of strung shells. They carefully appraised the quality of each.

So significant were these shells that they had a supernatural aura. According to Chinook, the insides were the food of people so tiny their mouths could only eat dentalia. After sucking out the meat, they gave the outer shell to their tiny slaves, who strung them in standard lengths to be traded by their noble masters to humans.

Practicalities of gathering these shells were much more ingenious, however. Important families of the Nuchahnuth (Nootka), over centuries, had closely guarded the secret location of dentalia beds. Landmarks along the horizon were used to triangulate a canoe so a round brush could be lowered over the side. Many handles were added on, one joined to another, until the tips rested on the bottom. Stone weights with a hole in the middle were fitted over the end of the handle and allowed to sink until they forced the bristles to close up. Then the entire apparatus was laboriously lifted to the surface, as each handle was detached. If the collector were lucky, a few shells were clutched within the brush.

In this way, dentalia were gathered for trade across all of western North America. The further from the source, the more mysterious was their origin so that they became truly wondrous items.

Even so, their mystery conformed to cultural expectations of a stratified society. The tiny people, like all other communities, were divided into ranks of freeborn and of slaves. Throughout the region, the shape of the head physically distinguished these classes. A freeborn baby was bound in a cradleboard with a sloping plank pressing against the forehead so that the skull would grow into a wide, wedge shape.

The skull of a slave child grew normally. As dentalia were the measure of standard value, slaves were the units of prestige. Every important family had several slaves, as much to indicate their social standing as to perform drudge work. Most slaves were children purchased from their captors, and raised within the household of leading families. They did tedious, sometimes distasteful, work such as getting water, firewood, and clams. If slaves had children, then they too were slaves. Most slaves were commoners taken in raids. Important people, invariably adult women, if captured, showed by their conduct that they would not perform menial tasks. They were more valuable if ransomed by their kin. In some cases, captured noblewomen married into the elite of their captors, forming a diplomatic alliance between their two communities.

Local people might also end up as slaves under unusual circumstances. Inability to pay debts, murder, or other failures to compensate would generally mean that a person had to forfeit his or her freedom, either for a stated period or for a lifetime. Orphans without kin to protect them also became slaves at the insistence of their chief, who used the purchase price for his own needs.

A slave had no standing in the community, nor any distinct identity. Their only designation was that of their tribe, which also served to insult and denigrate all these other people. The life of a slave could be forfeit at any time. Alternatively a master could free a slave or accept a price for his or her freedom. In a few cases, devious owners had male slaves act as henchmen, ambushing, poisoning, or killing rivals in secret.

When European ships arrived on the coast, slaves were sent to taste their strange food and drink their mind-altering alcohol. Since they survived the experience, and some even liked it, their masters knew that these new items were reasonably safe.

Slaves were traded far from home so that escape was virtually impossible. Most were well treated. Those who lived in elite households were well fed, although they ate by themselves because of their tainted status. Slaves who ran away only to be recaptured were punished by having their ears cut off. Even when he or she reached home, however, they still carried the stigma of having been a slave. Unless some form of rehabilitation, like a feast or potlatch with lavish gifts, were held, such a non-person would be shunned.

At the other extreme of these communities were the elite families with molded heads and prideful bearing. Their influence was only limited by their ability. Some governed because they were kind, generous, and skilled arbitrators. Others were feared because they were haughty and suspected of controlling reserves of great puwah that could render their enemies maimed or dead. It was such chiefs who had their slaves act as henchmen and poisoners.

An effective chief managed a vast network of kin, trade, and alliance, in a few instances backed by loyal warriors and bodyguards. This "muscle," however, was otherwise out of keeping within the region. Profitable free trade required wide access and unrestricted transport. Injuries or murders were quickly adjudicated by chiefs to dampen hostilities. Deep-seated antagonisms more often led to secret sorcery than to overt attacks.

Leadership passed from father to son, though Chinook kinship was characterized by considerable flexibility. People claimed as many noble ancestors as possible on both sides of the family.   Only matters of residence restricted these linkages since members of a household cooperated more fully than did other relatives. People might live in several households during a lifetime, thus cementing ties of kinship through a large network of birth, domestic, and marriage relationships.

Prestige factors influenced succession because an important leader had both slaves and many wives, and their children inherited certain privileges and restraints. A chief added to his influence by having a large family, not all of whom had the same status. The children of the senior wife had the best chance of assuming leadership roles, unless other factors and abilities intervened. Women from coastal villages outranked those upriver because coastal communities were more cosmopolitan, wealthier, and better connected. Personal ability also played a role. A wise and patient child was often groomed for leadership. An older sibling who was angry, sloppy, or careless was passed over.

Prestige was a key to successful leadership. Thus, the son of a chiefly coastal mother and a father from upriver was more entitled to lead than a man of distinguished but lesser ranked parentage. Some of these women were quite powerful, controlling vast trading privileges.

Chinook leaders coordinated activities, more than directed them. He or she would announce when the villagers would move to resource areas to take seasonal foods. Generally, a man of chiefly family initiated moves to fishing and hunting camps. Elite women led berrying and plant gathering tasks. When a beached whale was found, nothing was done until a chief indicated where the first cut was to be made and what slices would go to which people. While commoners and slaves did the actual work, they could not commence until sanctioned to do so by the chief or his representative. More a manager than a martinet, the chief and his family set the tone for transactions between people, land, and spirits. His ability was judged not so much as due to his pedigree and training, though this was important, but rather to his special relationship with tahmanawas via immortal allies over many generations. Indeed, the Chinookan word taa<u>x</u> for supernatural power ~ energy ~ force entered Chinuk WaWa as the all-purpose word for anything spiritual ~ involving spirits ~ wondrous ~ mystical.

Ordinarily punctuations should have been drastically simplified for a current reader, but that will wait until later revisions. A few clarifying additions appear between {curved brackets}.

Mạsi to Tony Johnson, Joan Wekell, Earl Davis, Nathan Reynolds, and others.

Chinook

UNIVERSITY OF WASHINGTON PUBLICATIONS
IN
ANTHROPOLOGY

Vol. 7, No. 2, pp. 29-165

LOWER CHINOOK ETHNOGRAPHIC NOTES

By

VERNE F. RAY

PUBLISHED BY
THE UNIVERSITY OF WASHINGTON
SEATTLE
1938

CONTENTS

FIGURES

TABLES

PLATES

Added Appendices

Index

PREFACE

It has been assumed since the late nineteenth century that the Lower Chinook were an extinct people. In 1890 and 1891 Dr. Boas obtained meager but invaluable ethnographic data from Charles Cultee, thought to be the sole surviving member of the group capable of furnishing reliable information. It appeared futile to hope for subsequent additions to Dr. Boas' data. It was consequently with great interest but slight credulity that I heard reports, while in the Willapa Bay region in 1930, that one or two aged Lower Chinook were yet surviving. Upon further investigation, the reports not only proved sound but led to the work upon which this paper is based. Three survivors were found but only two of them were usable as informants. The recoverable data proved discouragingly meager, though extensive enough to furnish a general setting for the culture and answer some of the significant problems. This piece of work is not presented as a complete ethnography in any sense; it pretends merely to make available those gleanings that were obtainable at this late date.

The summer of 1931 together with a part of the summer of 1936 and several brief intervening periods were spent with Lower Chinook informants. All work was undertaken for the Department of Anthropology of the University of Washington. The informants furnishing the information were principally Emma Millet Luscier (qwɑl'wɑnxᵘ) and Isabella Bertrand (pǝtra'n). Mrs. Luscier (1861 – 1954) proved to be an extremely intelligent woman and an excellent informant considering the remoteness of the culture. It was she who furnished the bulk of the material. She was still living in 1936, aged about sixty-five.

Mrs. Bertrand was considerably older. According to her daughter, Mrs. Riggs, she was born in 1843. This could not be far from correct. Mrs. Bertrand spoke no English; her daughter interpreted. She was a less facile informant than Mrs. Luscier but her greater age rendered her services of unusual value. Additional information relating to these informants will be found throughout the following pages. See especially the genealogies.

I have leaned heavily upon the earlier sources for supplementary material, particularly in the chapters on material culture. Swan's acute observations and Lewis' and Clark's extensive commentaries have been especially helpful. Of the early fur traders, Franchère is by far the most reliable. Brief observations by Gray, Boit, and Broughton are of peculiar value because these men were the first whites to visit the Chinook (1792). White contact was almost continuous from that time forward; for his reason the student interested in Chinook life should acquaint himself at least superficially with the history of the early years. [30]

In an effort to amplify further the data on material culture I corresponded with all the leading European museums as well as those in America, but the results were almost wholly negative. Apart from the small collection of Chinook specimens at the Field Museum of Natural History in Chicago nothing of consequence was unearthed. The Musee d'Ethnographic of Paris has a few weapons and the National Museum of Washington possesses unsegregated material from the Lewis and Clark expedition but neither of these collections was available at the time.

The phonetic system used herein is that described in *Phonetic Transcription of American Indian Languages.* Not all of the transcribed words are Chinookan; some are Salishan. The only native dialects spoken in the area today are Salishan, though a few Chinookan loan words are still current. Therefore I have seen fit to record whatever term the informant was able to furnish, though preferably the Chinookan form, where it seemed that such a reference might be of value.

VERNE F. RAY
New Haven, Conn. [31]

INTRODUCTION

THE LOWER CHINOOK AND THEIR NEIGHBORS

The name Chinook is derived from the Salishan term *t'sɪnu'k* of the Chehalis dialect.[1] The Chehalis appear to designate by the term a dialect group rather than an ethnic group.[2] The Chinook themselves had no designation for a larger political unit than the village;[3] therefore the application of this name or any other to a group of villages or an area is an arbitrary one, whether it be by neighboring peoples or by the ethnographer.

Yet there is reason to believe that the people of a village or villages on the north side of the Columbia river near the mouth, did use the term Chinook in self-reference in one way or another. All of the early writers speak as if the term were so used, including Captain Gray, commander of the first vessel to enter the Columbia, and his mate, John Boit. The official log book of Gray's vessel contains this entry: "At one, (from its being very squally,) we came to, about two miles from the village, *(Chinouk,)* which bore west-south-west."[4] In a contemporary journal, Boit writes: "Shifted the ship's berth to her Old Station abreast the Village *Chinoak,* command'd by a chief named *Polack.*"[5] These statements are unequivocal and the name could hardly have been heard from any but the local Chinookan-speaking peoples. Later the same year (1792) Lieutenant Broughton, commanding Vancouver's Tender *Chatham,* explored the Columbia river. Included in his report is this phrase, "the deserted village called by the natives Chenoke."[6] Thus we have a definite confirmation of self-reference. Lewis and Clark corroborate Broughton on this point. In the journal entry for November 15, 1805, Clark states that the Indians of Baker's Bay "call themselves Chinnooks," and two days later an entry reads, "the name of the nation is Chin-nook."[7] These are the first times that the term appears in the journal, though later it is frequently used. It was not until several days after these entries that the explorers were visited by a party of Chehalis Indians (November 21).[8] The village referred to by Gray, Boit, and Broughton is probably that called *qwatsa'mts* in Chinookan. By the time of Lewis and Clark "Chinook" seems to have had a wider reference. From that time forward the term came to be used in a more and more expanded sense.

These facts seem to admit of but one interpretation: Before the first appearance of the whites the term Chinook had already become established in Chinook [36] jargon as a loan word

---

[1] Cf. Boas, *Handbook,* p. 563; Boas, *Chinook Texts,* pp. 5 f.; Boas, *Kathlamet Texts,* p. 6; Hodge, pt. 1, p. 272; Pilling, q.v.

[2] Pilling refers to the use of the term Chinook by Gallatin and comments that "though based upon the speech of but a single tribe, it was adapted by him as the name of a family of languages" *(loc. cit.).*

[3] See political organization.

[4] Greenhow, p. 435.

[5] Boit, p. 248.

[6] Vancouver, vol. 2, p. 71.

[7] Thwaites, vol. 3, pp. 226, 229.

[8] *Idem,* p. 241. Lewis and Clark refer to the Chehalis as the Chiltz, Chilts, etc.

from the Chehalis Salish.[9] At first it was applied to a single village only; later it was extended to include several adjacent villages; and finally it came to denote all the Chinookan-speaking peoples of the lower Columbia and Willapa Bay. Hut the term and the successively extended applications were limited to the jargon both in use and in conception.

It seems that such a sequence of events would have developed very naturally out of the circumstances. In attempting to converse with the whites, the natives unquestionably would have used the simplest and most widely understood tongue known to them, the jargon.

As the whites required wider terms of reference than village names, the jargon term might well have been expanded; a Chinookan term would have been more resistant. Lewis and dark, acquainted with natives organized in tribes and accustomed to speaking of "nations," doubtless contributed to the extension of the term.

In the early nineteenth century Chinookan-speaking peoples occupied both sides of the Columbia river from the mouth to about fifty miles above (see map, figure 1). At that point the Klatskanie, an Athabascan-speaking people, held the south bank for a short distance, while the north bank belonged to the Cowlitz. It has been generally assumed that the Chinook speech was continuous along both sides of the river from the mouth to above The Dalles, but specific names, descriptions and locations of Klatskanie and Cowlitz villages were furnished by Mrs. Luscier, who declared that they were not merely recent encroachments.[10]

In addition to the river territory, peoples of Chinookan speech also held Willapa Bay including the northern shore. Before 1850, when the Chinook numbers were already thinning, Chehalis began to drift into the northern bay region. This resulted in a great confusion among early writers as to what people held this territory.[11] But Chinook chiefs continued to represent the various villages[12] and to the native mind it remained Chinook territory without question. My informants were unanimous and emphatic on this point, including Chehalis now living at Bay Center.

As intimated, the Salish-speaking Chehalis adjoined the Chinook on the north. To the

---

[9] This of course requires a pre-white origin for the jargon, and at the same time lends strong support to the arguments for such origin. It is true that the bulk of the voluminous literature beating Chinook Jargon favors a post-white origin but these judgments have come preponderantly from amateurs or non-linguists (for bibliography see Pilling). Gibbs points out that Vancouver's officers in 1792 found many Nutka words understood at Grays Harbor and adds that "On the arrival of Lewis and Clark at the mouth of the Columbia, in 1806 [*sic;* read 1805 the new language [jargon] from the sentences given by them, had evidently attained some form (quoted in Pilling, q.v) Alexander F. Chamberlain writes (in Hodge, pt. 1, p. 274) "there can be no doubt that the jargon existed as an intertribal medium of communication long before the advent of the whites. Dr Melville Jacobs who has made the most careful and extensive recent study of the jargon (see Jacobs, *Notes,* and *Review)* expresses complete conviction that the jargon long antedates the whites (personal communication).

[10] See villages, following. Cf. Thwaites, vol. 3, p. 295; vol. 4, p. 213.

[11] Summarized in Spier (*Tribal Distribution*).

[12] The last chief of the last remaining native village on the north side of Willapa Bay, toq, was Chinook; see villages, following, and genealogy, table 3.

east lay the Athabascan-speaking Kwalhiokwa (called sxula'umc by the Chehalis; the Willapa by Gibbs). They occupied the uplands of the Willapa Hills, approaching the bay no closer than the fork of the Willapa river. [37]

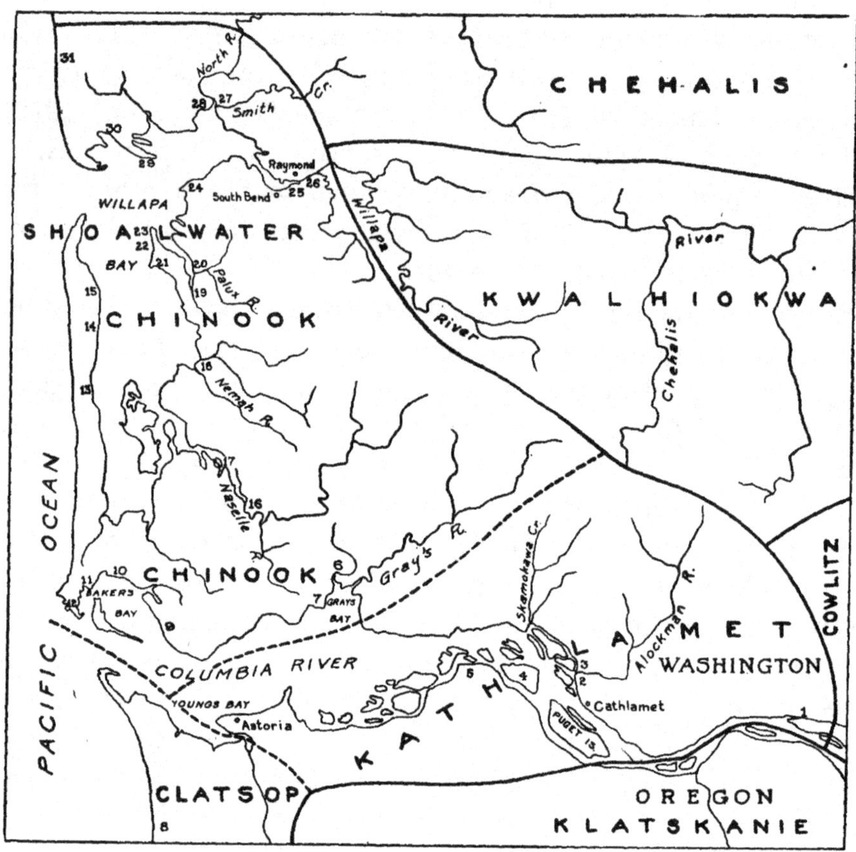

FIG. 1. Map of the territory of the Lower Chinook about 1800. Figures represent villages; see list in text. Solid lines indicate linguistic stock boundaries; broken lines indicate dialect boundaries.

The Chinook on the south side of the river near the sea have been known as the Clatsop, after the name of one of their villages. To the south of them were the Salish-speaking Tillamook. The exact boundary between the two is not known but it did not lie far south of the map border.

On the map are indicated the regional names Clatsop, Chinook, Shoalwater Chinook, and Kathlamet. These are not all of the same order or origin. Clatsop is a customary term of distinction; Chinook indicates the region to which reference is usually made by the unmodified term; Shoalwater Chinook is primarily a convenient geographic distinction; Kathlamet is first of all a dialectic division.[13]

These groups together form a single ethnic unit. Cultural differences from group to group were very slight. Constant intercourse and intermarriage occurred [38] from one part of the area to another.[14] Slight differences existing when the culture was flourishing probably

---

[13] See Boas, Kathlamet Texts.

[14] See genealogies.

8

aligned according to the divisions here named. It should be emphasized that the considerable dialectic difference between the Kathlamet and others was not by any means reflected to a comparable degree in the culture as a whole. The dialectic variation between Clatsop and Chinook was very slight. On the map the solid lines indicate differences in linguistic stock; dotted lines indicate differences of dialect.

Since the Chinookan linguistic stock is found far up the Columbia, it is necessary to be able to make exclusive reference to the, groups here discussed. For this purpose I have selected the term Lower Chinook, meaning thereby the Chinookan-speaking peoples of the lower Columbia and Willapa Bay. It is terminologically unfortunate that the Kathlamet spoke a dialect associated with the upriver peoples. But since the perspective of this paper is the general culture, it is desirable that that they be included under Lower Chinook. However, to avoid cumbersome expression, the simple term Chinook is used throughout the following pages with reference to the group as a whole, except where qualified.

The population of the peoples of the lower river was estimated by Lewis and Clark (1806) at 1,100. Gibbs considers this figure too low. Wilkes' total for 1841 is 509. After the smallpox epidemic of 1853 Gibbs estimates that sixty-six. Chinook remained on the river and thirty-four on Willapa Bay. Swan's judgment of the number on the Columbia at about the same time is one hundred.[15] The rapidity of decrease is quite apparent, though the figures are only approximate.

<h2 style="text-align:center">VILLAGES</h2>

1. ık'a'naıak. This village was located on the north side of the Columbia river at the mouth of Coal Creek Slough, or just east of Oak Point. It marked the eastern boundary of the Kathlamet; the next upriver village belonged to the Cowlitz. The settlement, though peripheral, was a large and important one. It was prominently mentioned by nearly all of the early travellers. It owed its popularity to the excellent hunting and fishing in the vicinity. The name is found in many variant renderings; Gibbs' spelling, Cooniac, is perhaps most common.

2. ılo'xumın. The north side of the Columbia, opposite Puget Island, was the site of this settlement. It was near the mouth of a small stream now called Alockman (Alochaman) creek, after the village name. It was noted for its beaver and otter hunting grounds and for its fine fishing.

3. wa'qaiya•qam. This Chinookan village name provided the modern term Wahkiakum. The settlement was located across Alockman creek opposite village number 2, about two miles north of the modern town of Cathlamet. It was moved to the site now occupied by Cathlamet around 1810, perhaps because of a fire.[16] This was a large winter settlement. It was the home of Emma Luscier's father's father. [39]

4. tä'näsılu'. This is a Chinook jargon name meaning "little ground" or "island." The reference was to the island now called Tenas Ilahee, the largest of a group of islands just below Puget Island. The villagers may have made joint use of the adjacent river bank on the Oregon

---

[15] Gibbs, *Report,* pp. 463 f; Swan, p. 110.
[16] Strong, p. 82.

side. It was famous as a fishing site, particularly for line fishing for sturgeon and smelt fishing with rake or dip net.

5. kała'amat. This is the native name which became Cathlamet in English corruption, and supplies the group and dialect designation, Kathlamet. The village was formerly located on the Oregon side of the Columbia, about four miles below Puget Island or roughly opposite modern Skamokawa. Around 1810 the remnant population of this settlement moved across the river, joining the residents of village number 3 at their new site. Not long before it had been a large and influential permanent village.[17]

6. mo'qwal. This was a large winter settlement at the mouth of Deep river on Grays Bay. (Grays Bay is in the Columbia river; it should not be confused with Grays Harbor on the Pacific, north of Willapa Bay.)

7. se'aqwal. The site of this village was the north bank of the Columbia, a short distance below village number 6. It was an all-year settlement.

8. lä't'cap. This was the village which supplied the name Clatsop, later applied to the entire group of Chinookan-speaking peoples occupying the Oregon side of the Columbia below the Kathlamet. It was but one, perhaps the largest, of a number of villages in the vicinity. The early writers speak of it, however, almost to the exclusion of all others. My informants were unable to recall the names of any of the lesser settlements. The location given on the map, near present Camp Clatsop, is based upon Lewis and Clark[18] as well as information from informants.

9. qwatsa'mts. This was the principal village of the group commonly known as the Chinook. It was situated at the mouth of Chinook river on Baker Bay, north side of the Columbia. A number of small satellite villages were clustered around it.[19]

10. ıwa'lxat. This fishing camp was situated at the mouth of the stream which now bears a corruption of its name, Wallicut river. This is the north side of the Columbia, about a mile northeast of the present Ilwaco. Fishing from the sand bar here was highly productive.

11. no•sqwalakuł, "where the trail comes out." Modern Ilwaco occupies the former site of this village. Ilwaco was named after the last chief of the village, iluwak'u'. [40]

12. noxsxa'itmıłs. This was a fishing site located where Ft. Canby now stands on Cape Disappointment. Fishing was excellent here at extreme low tide.

13. nu'patstcł, "lots of grass." This settlement stood at the present site of Nahcotta, on the peninsula opposite the mouth of Nemah river. Nahcotta took its name from a village chief, na•'kati.

14. tse'yuq, "yellow hammer." This was a large winter village situated where Oysterville is now found, on the peninsula north of Nahcotta.

15. kalawa'uus. This was an important clam-digging site on the peninsula at Oysterville

---

[17] Cf. Strong, pp. 81 f.

[18] Thwaites, vol. 3, pp. 273 f. , 282 f.

[19] Cf. Swan, p. 102.

Point. Camps were maintained for both digging and drying of clams.

16. ɪni•'sɑl (Naselle). This was a large, all-year settlement on the Naselle river where it enters the arm of the bay. It was noted for sturgeon fishing and as a hunting base.[20]

17. lɑpi•l'so', on nuq'a'lɑmil' island. The island on which this camp was situated is found in an arm of the bay below the mouth of Naselle river, near Johnson's Landing. It was a temporary settlement only.

18. ma•xᵘ. The mouth of Nemah river, below the present town of Nemah, was the site of this village. It was the place called "Mar'hoo" by Swan.[21]

19. Quer'quelin. This is Swan's oft-named village, located at the mouth of the Querquellin river which flows into the Palix river from the south, near the mouth of the latter.[22]

20. toq'pi'luks (Palix). This village, at the mouth of the Palix river, was the most important of the settlements on the small peninsula now occupied by Bay Center.[23]

21. ya'kam'noq. This was a small community situated at Sandy Point, three miles south of Goose Point. The latter is the extreme northern point at Bay Center. Winter settlement.

22. nutsxwəlso'q. The small camp of this name was found on the bay west of the town of Bay Center. In Curtis' orthography it is Nushwutsuk.[24]

23. namla'iaks. This was a small village and burial ground located at Goose Point.

24. xwa•'xots. The former settlement called Bruceport was the site of this important winter village. It was about three miles north of the mouth of the Palix river. (Swan's Whar'hoots.)[25]

25. Que-lap'ton-lilt. Swan names this village and locates it at the mouth of the Willapa river.[26] [41]

26. tsxe•'lsos. On the Willapa river, between South Bend and Raymond, is the former site of this settlement. (Curtis : Tshe'lso.)[27]

27. xa•'kəlc, "small river." This winter camp was located at the mouth of Smith creek on the northeast shore of Willapa Bay.

28. nɑxumə'nc. This was a large settlement on the west side of North river at its

---

[20] *Cf. Spier, Tribal Distributions, p. 31.*

[21] Swan, p. 211; cf. Spier, *loc. cit.*

[22] Swan, p. 211.

[23] Cf. Swan, *loc. cit.* ; Spier, *idem,* p. 30.

[24] Cf. Curtis, vol. 9, p. 173.

[25] Swan, p. 211; cf. Spier, *loc. cit.*

[26] Swan, p. 211; cf. Hodge, pt. 2, p. 955; cf. Curtis, *loc. cit.*

[27] Curtis, *loc. cit.* Cf. Spier, *loc. cit.*

mouth on the north shore of Willapa Bay.[28]

29. nukaunl.[29] The site of this village is now occupied by Tokeland. The latter took its name from the famous village chief, to'q. The settlement was large but occupied principally in winter.

30. na•'mst'cat's. This place, located between Tokeland and North Cove, was occupied principally during the winter. The site is now called Georgetown.

31. nuwi'lus. This village, situated on the coast where Grayland now stands, was the northernmost Chinookan village.

The following villages were non-Chinookan and do not appear on the map.

32. iła'tsk'anai (Klatskanie). This name referred both to the village and the river at whose mouth it was located. This was the principal point where the Athabascan-speaking Klatskanie {Swaal} touched the Columbia river. The settlement was large and thriving, being noted for salmon fishing but more particularly for the deer, elk, bear, and beaver hunting nearby. The village was most populous in winter.

33. mɑnsɛ'la'. This Cowlitz village, located where Longview, Washington, now stands, was well known for its fishing grounds.

34. awi'mani. A Cowlitz village at the mouth of Coweman river, south of Kelso, Washington.

Boas names and locates the villages of the Kathlamet as follows: "The Wā'-qa-iqam of Grey's Harbor [Gray's Bay]; the Lā'cgɛnɛmaxîx• about opposite [old] Cathlamet (on the north side); the KLā'ecaLxîx•, at the present town of Cathlamet; the Lā'qaLłala, about three miles above Oak point on the north side of the river; the Lctāmēctîx•, half a mile below the mouth of the Cowlitz river; the Lāk!ialama, at Kalama; the Tē'iaq!ōtcoē, three miles above Oak point, on the south side of the river; the KLā'gulaq, two miles below Rainier; and the KLā'moîx•, at Rainier." (Boas, *Kathlamet Texts*, p. 6.)

Two other villages on the river are also named by Boas: Tcakwayā'lxam (Chakwayalham), below Pillar Rock on the south side of the Columbia; and Lā'legak (Tlalegak), a shorter distance below Pillar Rock. (Hodge, pt. 1, p. 232; pt. 2, pp. 762,890.) [42]

Further transcriptions of village names of the Lower Chinook, by Boas, Sapir, and Olson, are brought together in the following list:

---

[28] Villages 28-30 do not accord with Curtis *(loc. cit.)*.
[29] Salish names of #29 & #30.

Common name	Chinook Name	Chehalis Name	Source	Village*
Kalama	łak !ala'ma		Sapir, in Spier, *Tribal Distribution*, p. 24	
Skilloots (mouth of Columbia river)	Sgu'lus ?		*Ibid.*	
Cooniac	Qa'niak		Boas, in Hodge, pt. 1, p. 341	1
Wahkiakum	wakXa'ikEm		Sapir, *loc. cit.*	3
Cathlamet	Kała'met		Sapir, *op. cit.*, p. 23	5
Clamoitomish (in Gray's Bay)	TlEma'itEmc		*Ibid.*	
Clatsop	la'tc !Ep		*Ibid.*	8
Gitlapshoi	GiLa'pcŏ-i	nu'pœtstcł (Luscier)	Boas, *op. cit.*, pt. 1, p. 493	13
Oysterville		Tsă'djukkw	Olson, in Spier, *Tribal Distribution*, p. 31	14
Naselle, Nisal	GiLa'lĕlam	NIsál	Boas, in Hodge, pt. 2, p. 75	16
Nemah	Nĕ'ma	Max	*Idem*, pt. 2, p. 54	18
Nayakolole	Naya'qŏlŏlĕ	Q !wĕ'qolEn	*Idem*, pt. 2, pp. 47 f.	19
Palix, Palux	Gitla'tlpĕ'leks	L !pĕ'lEqc	*Idem*, pt. 2, p. 195	20
Wharhoots	Niχwa'xŏtse	χwa'xŏts	*Idem*, pt. 2, p. 938	24
Quelaptonlilt	Niă'ktcixupenĕqē	Kula'ptEn'Et	*Idem*, pt. 2, p. 338	25
Willapa	GiLa'χwilă'pax, Gita'χwilapax	χwila'pāx	*Idem*, pt. 2, p. 956; Boas, *Kathlamet Texts*, p. 5	
Killaxthokle (probably on Willapa Bay)	GaLa'qstxoqL		Boas, in Hodge, pt. 1, p. 688	
Kwalhiokwa	TkulXiyogoa'ikc	sxula'umc (Luscier)	Boas, *Kathlamet Texts*, p. 5	

Leslie Spier has thoroughly sifted the extensive but confusing data from early sources relating to village locations on Willapa Bay. (*Tribal Distribution*, pp. 29-31.) Several of the groups identified find a ready correlation with villages included in the preceding lists, but others are distinctly supplementary. Consequently, the two sources should be used in conjunction.

PHYSICAL ENVIRONMENT

The Chinook habitat was dominated, not by the Pacific Ocean, but rather by two great connecting bodies of water, the Columbia river and Willapa Bay. The river bisects the territory from east to west; the bay in the opposite direction. The river is several miles across at the mouth and even wider a few miles inland. It forms the largest drainage in western North America. For the entire length of Lower Chinook territory it is a "drowned" river, that is, the tide is felt the entire distance, and much further. Willapa Bay is deceptive as it appears on the map. The older name, Shoalwater Bay, properly characterizes it. At low water great expanses of tide lands are exposed so that the peninsula is virtually connected with the mainland. This is especially true south of Bay Center. [43]

It was on these bodies of water that most of the villages were located and that most travelling was done. Far from being barriers, they actually facilitated communication. Travel from the river to the bay was not by the ocean route, but via Naselle river, with a short portage.

The Columbia bar was a formidable obstacle. Though the natives crossed it frequently, they did not do so more often than was necessary.[30] Wilkes comments:

"Mere description can give little idea of the terrors of the bar of the Columbia: all who have seen it have spoken of the wildness of the [marine] scene, and the

---

[30] See transportation.

incessant roar of the waters, representing it as one of the most fearful sights that can possibly meet the eye of the sailor.[31]

Almost all of the territory occupied by the Lower Chinook lay within the physiographic province of the Willapa Hills. Its characteristics are outlined by Landes:

> The Willapa Hills represent a gap or break in the long profile of the coastal chain. They have a maximum elevation of 3,000 feet and are therefore distinctly lower than the Olympics on the north and have a lower elevation than the mountains of the Oregon coast line, south of the Columbia. The Willapa Hills are sometimes described as a part of the Olympics but the two areas differ widely in both their geologic history and topographic origin. The bed rock of the Willapa Hills is composed almost wholly of tertiary sandstones and shales, but little metamorphosed, with a considerable quantity of basic igneous rocks. The strata have been folded and the tilted beds now stand at varying angles. Erosion has produced sharp ridges and deep valleys, the topographic features representing the effects of stream action when applied to rocks of varying degrees of hardness.
> A radial arrangement of the rivers and valleys is in some evidence in the Willapa Hills, although the drainage is chiefly to the west and the south. The hills are almost everywhere soil covered and in no instance do they rise above timber line. The best developed river system is that of the Willapa and its tributaries. Between the headwaters of the Willapa and Chehalis rivers there are several low divides. On their southern margin the Willapa Hills rise from the Columbia rather abruptly but on the north they gradually merge into low foothills bordering Chehalis valley. On the east they rise by slow degrees from the general level of Puget Sound Basin and on the west they decline until they merge into a belt of low sand dunes along the sea.[32]

This entire region, both coastal and upland, belongs to the Humid Transition plant life area. The Douglas fir (*Pseudotsuga mucronata*) is by far the most characteristic tree of the area as a whole. This tree varies in size according to soil conditions, but under favorable circumstances it reaches a height of 200 to 300 feet, thus dominating the landscape. The type locality for the Douglas fir is the mouth of the Columbia river. It is almost absent, however, in a narrow strip along the coast including the sand dunes mentioned above. Here the Sitka spruce (*Picea sitchensis*) takes its place. The spruce was perhaps of greater importance than the fir from the native point of view, both because of its ready availability around coastal villages and because it furnished important materials used in manufactures, particularly in basketry.

Plants associated with the Douglas fir in the uplands prominently include the shrub salal (*Gaultheria shallon*) and Oregon grape (*Berberis nervosa, B. aquifolium*), and shrubs or trees of Scouler willow (*Salix scouleriana*). A rank growth of bracken [44] fern (*Pteridium*) is also characteristic. Commonly the fir forests are of such density that the sun fails to enter. Here the

---

[31] Wilkes, vol. 4, p. 293.
[32] Landes, pp. 9 f.

salal and Oregon grape give way to a thick ground covering of mosses and shield fern (*Polystychum munitum*). The red huckleberry (*Vaccinium parvifolium*) is likewise found in this habitat.

In the valley bottoms the red alder *(Ainus oregona)* is associated with the giant cedar *(Thuga plicata).* Of lesser importance are the white fir (*Abies grandis*), large leafed maple (*Acer macrophyllum*), Oregon ash (*Fraxinus oregana*), and cottonwood (*Populus trichocarpa*). The maple and cottonwood often occur in groves. Where the bottom lands are excessively wet are found dense thickets of willows, crabapple (*Pyrus diversifolia*), and vine maple (*Acer circinatum).* Here, too, grow the devil's club (*Echinopanax horridum),* salmon berry (*Rubus spectabilis),* fetid currant (*Ribes bracteosum),* and the red-berried elder (*Sambucus callicarpa).*

Oaks (*Quercus garryana),* from which the Chinook gathered acorns, are not common but do occur in the occasional gravelly prairies. In Chehalis territory they are more abundant. The black pine (*Pinus contorta)* often borders the prairies.

The pine recurs along the sea shore in the lee of sand dunes or where the sand does not shift. The trees form dense thickets but seldom exceed thirty feet in height. Sand dunes occur only on the coast, not along the inner shore of Willapa Bay. The coast sands support a considerable variety of plants which flourish in such soil.

Every species mentioned above, with the possible exception of devil's club, was of marked economic importance to the Chinook. The variety of uses which these raw materials served is illustrated throughout the following pages. These species represent, of course, only a small percentage of those used by the Chinook, but the fact that virtually every dominant plant was subject to extensive utilization is of especial importance. Further, each species is represented in this area by a vast number of individual plants. Thus the supply of raw materials was abundant; exhaustive use of dominant species was not forced by limited occurrence. The term dominant is, of course, relative. The natives of the deserts of eastern Washington had available a larger number of distinct species of plants than did the Chinook. But there even the dominant species are relatively rare in occurrence, with exceptions, and most plants flourish through but short periods each year. Seasons are much longer in western Washington and many important plants are available throughout the year. Furthermore, the flora of the Humid Transition area is adapted to greater effective use, on the whole, than that of the Arid Transition or the Upper Sonoran zones.[33]

The fauna of the Chinook habitat was likewise rich and varied, including land, fresh water, and marine life. The Willapa Hills harbored many large mammals of marked economic value. Primary in importance in native life was the deer, of which two varieties were found. The Columbian blacktail (*Odocoilens columbianus columbianus)* is the larger of the two, a buck of good size weighing about 200 pounds. The second was the Columbian whitetail, or flagtail (0. *virginianus lencurus),* which weighs perhaps one-fifth less than the blacktail. The mouth of the Columbia river is the type locality for both, but the whitetail seems to have been the more common in the valleys, the blacktail in the mountains. [45]

The Olympic elk, or Roosevelt elk, (*Cervus canadensis rooseveiti* Merriam) was formerly abundant, and second only to the deer in importance to the Chinook. They frequented open valleys as well as the forest. A large bull of this species may weigh 1,500 pounds. Moose and

---

[33] Piper, pp. 40-47.

antelope were not known in the region.

Both the Washington snowshoe hare (*Lepus americanus washingtonii* Baird) and the Oregon brush rabbit (*Sylvilagus bachmani ubericolor*) were available and were hunted for their flesh and for their pelts which were used in making blankets. The showshoe is much the larger but was rarer; the brush rabbit is equally fine as a food animal.

The local squirrel is the orange-bellied chickaree, or Douglas squirrel (*Sciurus douglasii douglasii* Bachman) with the type locality near the mouth of the Columbia. It was sought for food purposes, as was the Townsend chipmunk (*Eutamias townsendii townsendii*). The latter is a large species, adults averaging ten inches in length. Townsend recorded Chinookan names for both (squirrel: *ap-poe-poe*; chipmunk: *quis-quis*).

The dusky bushy-tailed wood rat (*Neotoma cinerea fusca* True) was common but it is uncertain whether the Chinook sought this mischievous animal for its flesh or not. Early writers mention robes of wood rat pelts in use by the Chinook[34] but it is quite possible that the skins were rather those of the mountain beaver (*Aplodontia rufa* rufa).[35] The Oregon coast muskrat (*Fiber zibethicus occipitalis* Elliot) was present but apparently not common.

The Pacific coast beaver (*Castor canadensis pacificus* Rhoads), a fine large species, was exceedingly abundant in the lower Columbia valley. Captain Gray's ship *Columbia* carried away 300 beaver skins after but ten days on the river. The beaver was of value to the Chinook not only for its fur, but for its flesh as well.

The mountain beaver belongs to a family (*Aplodontiidae*) distinct from the beaver proper. As mentioned above, they were of great importance to the native for their pelts, but their flesh, though not choice, was yet not discarded. They were available in plentiful numbers.

The yellow-haired porcupine (*Erethizon epixanthum epixanthum* Brandt) was not common but served as food when available.

Two types of cat were relatively common, the Oregon cougar (*Felis concolor oregonensis* Rafinesque), also called mountain lion and panther, and the Oregon bobcat (*Lynx rufus fasciatus* Rafinesque). Both were valued by the Chinook, not only for their warm furs but as well for food. The cougar is a large animal, reaching eight feet or more in tip to tip length and 150 pounds in weight. The bobcat is only a fraction of this size, seldom weighing more than twenty pounds.

Another common animal was the timber wolf (*Canis tycoon gigas),* a large species, weighing about a hundred pounds. The cascade red fox (*Vulpes fulvus cascadensis)* was found throughout the territory. [46]

Fur animals given little attention by the Chinook were the weasels (*Mustela longicanda saturata,* and *Mustela cicognanii streatori).* The larger type (*saturata*) was probably quite rare; the other is very small. The mink (*Lutreola vison energumenos*) was relatively plentiful; also the martin (*Martes pennanti pacifica*).

The western otter (*Lutra canadensis pacifica)* played a great role in native economy.

---

[34] E.g., Henry (Coues, p. 749); Ross, p. 91; Fanchère, p. 243. Cf. Thwaites, vol. 3, p. 242. Boas writes of groundhog blankets (*Chinook Texts,* pp. 220, 231, 262), but there are no groundhogs, or woodchucks, in Chinook territory. Again the mountain beaver is doubtless indicated.

[35] Cf. Coues, p. 749. {See appendix}

Not so with the skunks (*Mephitis occidentalis spissigrada* and *Spilogale phenax latifrons*), though they were common enough. The local raccoon was the northwestern (*Procyon lotor pacifica*).

The Olympic black bear (*Enarctos americanus altifrontalis*) was considerably exploited by the natives. The grizzly bear did not occur in the region.[36]

The marine life of the area was even more significant to the natives than the land forms. The Columbia river and Willapa Bay constituted unsurpassed fishing and sealing grounds. The Columbia has produced more salmon than any other river in the world.[37] This fish was of primary importance to the natives, but sturgeon, trout, smelt, herring, and flatfish played each an important economic role. In addition, sea mammals including the seal, porpoise, and whale were extensively utilized.[38]

The nature and profusion of the flora and fauna suggest an equitable and humid climate. A glance at the accompanying table (Table 1) will confirm this impression. Mean minimum temperatures do not exceed seventy-two degrees F. The mean annual temperature stands at fifty to fifty-one degrees F. Thus the temperature is characterized by a very small range about a temperate mean.

Precipitation, however, is extreme. As indicated in the table, the annual rainfall varies between fifty-nine and eighty-three inches, but measuring stations have not been maintained until recently in the wettest parts of the area. For example, near the mouth of the Naselle river the annual rainfall has exceeded one hundred inches several times during recent years, sometimes reaching 140 inches, with a third of the amount falling during a single month.[39] {[47]} Thus it can well be understood that the natives favored the dryer spots for winter villages. Less than a half of one per cent of the precipitation comes in the form of snow, the normal annual fall not exceeding four inches.

Considering all of the factors discussed above, it appears probable that few areas of the world could have provided a more desirable habitat than that occupied by the Chinook. [47]

TABLE 1.[39]

METEOROLOGICAL DATA FOR REPRESENTATIVE STATIONS IN CHINOOK TERRITORY

Data	Station	Jan.	Feb.	Mar.	Apr.	May	June	July	Aug.	Sept.	Oct.	Nov.	Dec.	Ann'al
Mean Temperature[40]	North Head[42]	42.1	43.0	45.2	47.5	50.9	54.8	57.2	57.6	56.5	52.9	48.2	44.1	50.0
	South Bend[43]	40.2	42.4	44.8	48.4	53.4	57.2	61.4	61.6	59.0	52.2	46.5	41.8	50.8
Normal Precipitation[41]	North Head	8.78	7.45	5.56	4.14	2.95	2.28	0.96	1.05	2.99	5.01	8.45	9.48	59.10
	South Bend	12.71	9.75	8.81	6.32	4.22	2.91	0.97	1.55	3.72	6.77	12.42	13.20	83.35

Station	Mean Minimum Temperature[44]		Mean Maximum Temperature[44]		Normal Annual Snowfall[45] (inches)	Normal Yearly Distribution[46]				Prevailing Wind[48]
	Jan.	Aug.	Jan.	Aug.		Rainy Days	Clear Days	Partly Cloudy	Cloudy	
North Head...............	37.5	54.4	45.4	62.6	2.6	190	64	91	210	North
South Bend...............	34.6	50.4	47.4	71.8	4.0	183	116	115	134	Southwest[48]

[39] Day, *Normals of Precipitation*; Marvin and Day, *Normals of Daily Temperature*; Fisher, *Climatological Data*.
[40] North Head: 34-year period; South Bend: 35-year period. Temperature figures represent degrees Fahrenheit.
[41] North Head (combined with Ft. Canby): 50-year period; South Bend: 36-year period. Figures indicate inches.
[42] On the west side of Cape Disappointment, two miles north of the Columbia river; elevation, 211 feet. Near village number 12.
[43] See map, Figure 1; elevation, 150 feet. Near villages numbers 25 and 26.
[44] Landes, pp. 28-31.
[45] Compiled from *Climatological Data*; 15-year period.
[48] East wind is almost as common.

THE PATTERN OF SOCIETY

---

[36] Bailey, *passim*.

[37] Cobb, p. 37.

[38] See fishing and sealing.

[39] Fisher. [Actual footnotes jump here from 38 to 47!]

CLASS AND RANK

Class feeling was strong among the Lower Chinook though lines of demarcation were not rigidly drawn. The strictest dichotomy existed between definitely upper and lower classmen but there was a wide intervening zone in which classification was far from exact. This intermediate group might be termed a middle class for purposes of analysis but such terminology would not accurately reflect native attitudes. This group consisted, to their minds, of the more successful commoners and the unambitious or remote of kin of the upper class. Movement from the middle group to the upper class through acquisition of wealth and strength of personality was not uncommon. Native formulation of the possibility, however, was always in terms of movement from the lower class to the higher. The fact that in most historic examples the advances were made from this indefinite middle group does not alter the attitude. Such persons merely were further along toward the goal than unconditional commoners; their chances of success were greater though eligibility was equal.

The upper class was relatively small. It appears to have included chiefs and their families, prominent shamans, warriors, traders and others of high birth. To what extent leadership in these activities was a class prerogative and thus connected with birth is uncertain; war and trade probably belong here, shamanism definitely does not.

The upper class was loathe to associate with the lower. An upperclassman's slaves, who lived with him or nearby, probably enjoyed a greater freedom of intercourse with their masters than did lower class neighbors. Children of the two classes were not allowed to play together. Intermarriage, though far from unknown, was strongly disapproved except under unusual circumstances. If a man in the middle ground had distinguished himself through accumulation of wealth or outstanding service to a chief he might be permitted to marry into the upper class and thus take the final step in elevating himself. Under other circumstances the disapproved union would lead to the degradation of the upper class member to the level of the lower, together with their children.

Commoners were free to amass wealth and gain prestige in any way which did not infringe upon the prerogatives of the upper class. They were permitted to hold slaves and to engage in trade. Many of them worked assiduously at menial tasks that an upperclassman would have considered a disgrace to his position.

When, as the result of such industry or through an approved marriage, a man was accepted into the upper class it was sometimes made the occasion of a feast or even a potlatch at the instance of the chief. At such an event the man's accomplishments were paraded and the audience was told that he should be treated as befitted a man of his talents and new station.

A narrative recorded by Boas furnishes an example of meteoric rise from commoner to upperclassman by one who became phenomenally successful at gambling [49] as a result of obtaining a powerful guardian spirit. The account is highly over-formalized and exaggerated since it was told as a folk tale. It is the familiar story of the poor, lousy boy who achieves success in spite of his disabilities. An excerpt follows:

"Come friend, we will play." "Well," said the boy. He bought a mat. Now he won again all the property of that person. He won his canoe. Now he had won over all the common people. Next he won over the chiefs. He won first one slave and then many. Now he became a chief [upperclassman?]. He had won the property of all those people. Every day the people ate in his house. Now his elder cousin said: "Perhaps he saw a supernatural being. We will play with the accompaniment of batons. Then I shall win all his slaves. He is [too] hopeful." Then he was told:

"Your elder cousin wants to play with you." "As he likes." Now the cousins played and the people beat time with batons. They played several nights. He won the eldest brother's slaves and all his canoes. Then he played with the next brother and he won all his slaves; then he won his wives. Now the next brother said: "I want to play with you next." "No, I pity you, as you pitied me formerly." Then the Chehalis came and he won all their property. The Quenaiult came to play at disks. He won their property and their slaves. That lousy boy made everybody poor. He bought the daughters of chiefs among the Quenaiult, the Tillamook, the tribes up the river, the Cowlitz. The wives of the man who had been the lousy boy were taken from among all these tribes. If his cousins had not taken the sea-otter from him, he should not have seen the supernatural being. He saw Itc'x-ia'n. (Boas, *Chinook Texts*, p. 222.)

These new members occupied, of course, the lowermost ranks of the upper class, in company with the less aspiring members born to the class and those most distantly related to the chiefs. One might continue to climb, slowly, as time went on, but it was rare or unknown for a commoner by nativity to reach the higher ranks of the Upper class. It should be emphasized that ranking, except at the extremes, was highly informal and variable.

In addition to birth and wealth, there was yet another variable in distinctions of rank. Upriver and inland peoples were considered of lower rank than residents of the coast, the differential roughly depending upon distance, or relative distance. Thus, other things being equal, a Klatskanie chief ranked lower in the eyes of the Chinook than the chief of a Kathlamet settlement, but higher than a Clackamas chief. Not only were chiefs so differentiated, but the principal applied to other upperclassmen as well. To what extent this attitude was shared by the upriver peoples themselves is unknown, but the feeling for class distinctions extended as far inland as the Wishram.[40] In consequence of this geographical factor, when a chief had a son (or sons) by each of two or more wives, a junior son might succeed his father in the chieftainship rather than an elder half-brother if the latter were the son of a woman from further inland.[41]

Lest these considerations overbalance the picture, it should be strongly emphasized that birth was never lost sight of as the dominant factor in distinctions of class and rank. Perhaps no other aspect of Lower Chinook life approaches so closely the attitude of typical Northwest Coast peoples. The very fact of emphasis upon rank is significant, despite its lack of formality. The variance from Northwest Coast standards was in degree, not in kind. [50]

It is difficult to consider the upper class and its prerogatives apart from the office of chief and his official prerogatives. This is not the result, to my mind, of a confusion between

---

[40] Spier and Sapir, p. 211.

[41] *See* political organization.

the two or relationship such as obtained further north on the coast. That is, the chief was not merely a high ranking upperclassman enjoying power and prerogatives by virtue of that fact alone. He did not share the peculiar privileges of his position with other high ranking upperclassmen. His office was distinctly a political one. And yet, he was of necessity a high ranking upperclassman and thus enjoyed not only the rights of his office but also the privileges of his rank. It seems to me that these facts have led informants and early writers alike, or in turn, to epitomize the characteristics, prerogatives, and duties of the upper class in the person of the chief. Mrs. Luscier constantly spoke of the domination of the lower class by the chief — an instructive phrasing — but when questioned further she almost invariably extended the non-political attributes of the chief to the upper class generally. Isabella Bertrand was even more inclined to personify her remarks, particularly for the era of chief Concomly.

Consequently, the material here presented should be used in close association with that relating to chieftainship (pages 55-58). Anecdotal data of specific personal reference will be found there.

Boas provides instructive documentation relating to class and chiefly prerogatives in describing the division of a stranded whale:

> Those who found the whale do not cut it; they wait for the chief. All the people reach the whale. Then the chief takes a stick and measures the whale from the head to the tail. Then he tells the people: "You will cut here; you will cut there." It is distributed among those people. The common people cut from the tail end. When it is all cut, it is carried to the town into the houses. When the whale is measured, the chief tells the people to make the [measuring] sticks two spans and one hand width long, if the whale is large [two spans wide if the whale is smaller]. The people are told: "You cut here," and they cut the whale. Everything is done this way.[42]

Lee and Frost provide a brief remark of analogous nature with regard to game:

> "... one of the hunters went out and succeeded in bringing an elk into camp; and, according to custom, the most of it was taken to the lodge of the chief.[43][44] This statement is of special significance since it refers to the products of a single man's initiative. That the hunter was not a slave is indicated by the qualification, "most of it."

A radical privilege of chiefs and the upper class was the seizure of orphaned children to be sold as slaves to other groups. This statement by Mrs. Luscier is substantiated by early writers.[44][46]

Commoners were allowed in the audience at the potlatch but only when invited by an upperclassman. [51]

---

[42] Boas, *Chinook Texts,* p. 262.
[43] Lee and Frost, p. 283.
[44] See slavery.

SLAVERY

Slaves were held by the Chinook in considerable numbers and played a large role in the economic life. To them fell most of the laborious and disagreeable work though they often worked side by side with their masters. Emma Luscier said that there was no distinction in general type of work but that the most difficult tasks in oyster gathering, wood cutting, and fishing were assigned to slaves. Thompson states that "they appeared as well off as their masters, except their paddling the canoes, and hauling in the seine nets, in all which their masters take a share of the labor."[45] Concomly is pictured by Henry as sitting idly in the middle of his canoe while the slaves around him paddled,[46] but then he was always fond of ostentation, especially when visiting the whites. Ross speaks of each freewoman as having two, three, or more slaves in constant attendance, thus relieving her of all drudgery. He adds that in trading activities a woman was commonly followed by a "train of slaves."[47] Mrs. Luscier estimated that the average upperclassman owned two or three slaves, with chiefs possessing perhaps double that number, or even more in exceptional cases. Concomly owned ten or twelve slaves; this may represent a customary maximum. Commoners were permitted to hold slaves as well as their social superiors but of course it was seldom that a lowerclassman possessed more than one or two.

Most slaves were obtained by purchase from surrounding peoples. It is uncertain from what direction came most of the slaves so acquired. Apparently the Puget Sound region and the Willamette river valley in Oregon were particularly well represented. Both Swan and Mrs. Luscier emphasized a general northern source.[48] Slaves were an important item in trade, representing the maximum of unit value. There is no doubt that the Chinook not only possessed more slaves per capita than any surrounding people, but that their eminence as traders was largely responsible. Ross' statement that slaves were regularly bought and sold in the manner of any other article of trade[49] was substantiated by my informants. That is, slaves were not only purchased when manual assistance was needed but often merely as a "good bargain" or as a stable unit of value. In recent times the price of a slave varied between one and five hundred dollars or sometimes more. "Not infrequently a valuable canoe is added to the bargain.[50] A young female slave from Nisqually was purchased by *qe•'walaptc* about 1875 for two hundred dollars plus a considerable amount of property. The possession of a slave or slaves thus enabled one to meet any economic emergency. They might serve as payment of bride price, payment of blood-money, or might be exchanged for goods with which to give a great feast.

Second in importance as a source of slaves was raiding. One Lower Chinook village

---

[45] Tyrrell, p. 507.

[46] Coues, p. 750.

[47] Ross, p. 92. Cf. Kane, p. 182.

[48] Swan, p. 167. Gibbs makes the questionable statement that slaves were traded largely from California *(Tribes of Western Washington,* p. 188).

[49] Ross, p. 92.

[50] Swan, p. 167.

never raided another; all such activities were directed toward "outside" groups. Here the evidence as to locale is a little more specific. The Chinook, [52] Mrs. Bertrand said, took slaves from the Quinault "whenever they felt like it." This exaggerated statement is nevertheless instructive. According to Kane, slaves usually were procured from the Umpqua river (Oregon) region where they were "sometimes seized by war parties, but the children are often bought from their own people."[51] Thompson is less definite: "These people had many slaves, ... they were prisoners taken in their marauding expeditions along the seashore, most of them youths when taken."[52] When encounters occurred with foreign groups slaves were invariably taken, if possible. Thus the sources of slaves secured by force would also indicate the directions in which offensive warfare was waged. On the defensive side, the Chinook seemed to fear most the Quilleute.[53] The latter sometimes were led in their raids by Chinook slaves taken many years before, since the dangerous sand bars of the Columbia river and Willapa Bay rendered an experienced guide almost indispensable. In slave raids an attempt was always made to take captives of twelve years of age or less. No effort was ever made to enslave adult men, though women were occasionally carried away.

There existed several minor sources of slavery. Inability to pay debts or blood-money led to temporary, or sometimes permanent, slavery of debtor to creditor. The murderer of a chief [upperclassman ?] automatically became a slave, according to Mrs. Bertrand. Blood-money in such a case was never accepted [a sufficient amount rarely being available?]. A desperate gambler sometimes wagered his own body, beginning with hands, then limbs, and finally head, and with its loss came slavery. Sometimes a specified number of years was involved after which the person regained his former status.[54] In other cases a quantity of goods was named which should be considered the equivalent; if, then, by a lucky chance at gambling or through the aid of his friends the enslaved man was able to amass that amount he might immediately gain his freedom. Enslavement because of inability to pay blood-money seems to have been not uncommon. In such a case the chief called the persons involved before a gathering of villagers, where the defaulter was assigned to the complainant, and was publicly called "slave." In common with all slaves, such a person might later buy his freedom. Or sometimes the enslavement was for a stated number of years only.

A final source of slavery was the marriage of an upperclassman to a slave. Such an act degraded the freeman to the status of slave and all of the offspring of the union likewise.

Local orphans were sometimes seized by chiefs and sold as slaves, but always to some outside group. A man facing inability to pay blood-money often did likewise if an orphaned child were available among his relatives. Such action frequently caused deep resentment on the part of other persons and may have led to feuds. This practice extended to the Kalapuya. A Kalapuya slave at Bay Center had reached there in such fashion. A Kalapuya shaman had been accused of witchcraft by the doctor attending a patient supposedly the former's victim. In order to satisfy [53] the claim of the relatives of the deceased the accused shaman seized an orphaned niece and turned her over as a slave. The girl was twelve years old at the time. The

---

[51] Kane, p. 182.

[52] Tyrrell, p. 507.

[53] See raids.

[54] Parker, p. 245; Swan, p. 156.

recipients sold her and after several exchanges she reached qwatsa'mts. Her owner died some time later, leaving her free. She married a white man and moved to Bay Center before she died. She carried a great resentment for her uncle to the time of her death. At that time she was known as x̱o'x̱o (old) Maggie; formerly she had been known by the slave name, kälapu'ɹla.

This introduces two new points, freedom for slaves upon the death of masters, and distinctive slave names. With regard to the former, a number of specific examples were furnished by informants but it would be dangerous to generalize from these because all relate to a time when Chinook culture was rapidly being eradicated by white encroachment. It is certain that a master had the privilege of freeing a slave at any time that he pleased, but it is almost equally certain that this was rarely done.

Quite to the contrary, slaves often were killed at the time of the master's death. This was especially true if the deceased were a chief; seldom more than one slave was killed, however, regardless of the number owned. A slave purchased as a companion for a child was almost certain to be killed if the child died. In this case both bodies were placed in the same burial canoe. Parker relates that "the wife of Calpo, a very influential chief of the Chinook village near Cape Disappointment, on losing a daughter in the year 1829, killed two female slaves to attend her to the world of spirits, and for the particular purpose of rowing her canoe to the far off happy regions of the south"[55] Gibbs states that slaves were starved to death when their masters died, and more specifically, that Toke attempted in 1853 to kill a slave after his daughter's death, in pursuance of the girl's request.[56]

Slaves were characteristically named after the group or locality of their nativity. Thus, in the account above, kälapu'ɹla (Kalapuya); also puyɑä'lɑp (Puyallup), kwɪlii'ute (Quilleute), sqa•'tcitł (Skagit), tłä'älɑm (Klallam), and yuło' (near Port Townsend, Washington). Both men and women were subject to such designation, but sex identifying suffixes were used. Naming according to this pattern was not invariable practice; owners followed their own desires.

On the whole, slaves seem to have been well treated. As stated above, they worked together with their masters. Also they lived in the same quarters and shared very much the same food, though they ate separately. Their opinions were often sought; their ridicule was deeply felt.[57] The fact that they dared ridicule freemen is significant in itself. Ambitious and enterprising slaves were rewarded by being placed in charge of others. There was even one way by which a slave might gain freedom (in addition to the seldom achieved purchase of liberty). This was through the acquisition of shamanistic power. Such an accomplishment removed the formal stigma but the person might even afterward be taunted with the name. All slaves were allowed to seek guardian spirits and some met with marked success. Owners purchased mates for slaves reaching marriageable age. [54]

Franchère states that slaves were treated with humanity while their services were useful, but as soon as they became incapable of labor, they were neglected and allowed to perish of want, whereupon their bodies were thrown without ceremony under the stump of an old decayed tree or dragged into the woods and left.[58] Kane decries the position of the slave,

---

[55] Parker, p. 245.

[56] Gibbs, *Tribes of Western Washington*, pp. 189, 204.

[57] Cf. Franchère, p. 242.

[58] *Idem*, p. 241.

emphasizing the "power of life and death at pleasure" of the master,[59] but he was little acquainted with Lower Chinook life. Slaves were sometimes bet in gambling but there was an equal chance in an exchange of masters that it would be to the slave's advantage.[60] As an example of especially ill treatment Mrs. Luscier told of a female slave from Puget Sound named nu'tc who was owned by matél' at Oysterville. The latter not only worked the slave long and hard, even though she was very old, but beat her and threw ashes in her face when annoyed.

The punishment for a runaway slave was to have his ears cut off. If the fugitive reached his home people, seldom or never was an attempt made to bring him back. But successful escapes were rare and when the return occurred after several years there was a high probability that no welcome would be forthcoming. Most groups from which slaves were taken, themselves kept slaves; thus the stigma remained, even at home. When it was feared that a slave might run away, he was usually sold.

Some specific data follow:

A slave from near Victoria (Vancouver Island) was owned by ya'amans, chief at Naselle. He had been received by way of Puget Sound. Apparently he was Nutka, for no one on Willapa Bay understood anything of his language. He died before his owner.

A woman at qwatsa'mts owned a female slave from Puget Sound named samsa'miɛ. After her owner died she married a white man and moved to Nemah.

The slave named puyaä'lap, owned by ko'latc, became free when his master died and married a woman from Grays Harbor. He did not return home but remained with his wife's people.

The female slave named sqa•'tcitɬ, owned by a•'kaiak, was purchased by a white man (Ike Stills), a soldier at the post near Ilwaco. They were married and had many children. A son was at one time married to Mrs. Luscier.

A female slave named t'sı'ktÈ from Neah Bay (Makah) was owned by a•'itamcɨɬ of Bay Center.

The slave yuɬo', owned at qwatsa'mts, married a white man after her owner's death, and remained in the same village.

Dr. Kate (xwənxwa'nc), a Nisqually woman, brought an orphaned girl (qwa'ni') of about fifteen years of age to Oysterville under pretext of bringing her to a better place to live. There she prostituted her and later sold her to qe•'walaptc of Bay Center. This occurred about 1875.

Both the mother and father of four brothers now living at Bay Center were the slaves of the father of tai'man.

The slave named tlä'älam (Klallam) was sold by her uncle to "Old Sally" of Kathlamet. After the latter's death she married a white man. [55]

POLITICAL ORGANIZATION

---

[59] Kane, p. 182.
[60] Cf. Boas, *Chinook Texts,* p. 222.

"All of the villages form so many independent sovereignties.... Each village has its chief, but that chief does not seem to exercise a great authority over his fellow citizens." These are the words of Franchère written in 1819 with reference to the social organization of the Lower Chinook.[61] Thus these peoples are established as in basic political accord with other known groups of the region.[62] My own informants affirmed the existence of village autonomy, but pointed out that able and well-liked or greatly feared chiefs often exerted a much wider influence than might formally be indicated, though this extended power was strictly unofficial. The villages on the north side of Willapa Harbor may be taken for example. These groups were fairly small and relatively isolated. During the chieftainship of to'q at the centrally located village of nu'kaunł (#29 on map, page 37), all of the surrounding towns looked to him as leader for he was kind, generous, and a skilled arbiter. Likewise, Concomly, famed chief of qwatsa'mts (village #9 on map), was said by Mrs. Bertrand to have made his influence felt as far away as Willapa Harbor, but in this case through trade control and military strength. Such power of course must not be confused with political control, since it was of no significance in village internal affairs.

Each village had but one chief, the office normally passing from father to eldest son. However, when a chief had adult sons by wives of different social standing, the eldest son of the highest ranking wife succeeded to the office. Thus qa'tqos, whose mother was from Lower Chehalis, became chief after Concomly's death because his elder half-brother was the son of a Scappoose woman. Upriver people were considered of lower class than those of the coast. The fact that the Scappoose woman was Concomly's favorite wife was of no consequence.[63] Concomly himself obtained the chieftainship in an unusual fashion. He succeeded not his father, who was a Quinault, but his mother who had become ruler at qwatsa'mts when her father died and she had no living brothers. Such succession does not follow the formulation given by Emma Luscier (son, brother's son, sister's son), but indicates that under some circumstances a woman might become chief.[64] Several examples of normal succession may be seen in the genealogies.

The degree of control over fellow villagers that chiefs actually exerted is somewhat uncertain. Emma Luscier and Mrs. Bertrand disagreed somewhat with Franchère's observation that such control was slight. Certainly his official power was much greater than among many coastal groups.[65] Certain procedures not only were within the province of the chief, but were his distinct duty. These included the judging and peaceful settlement of quarrels, the supervision of economic movements and the direction of all activities connected with war other than strictly military maneuvers. Even these were indirectly controlled by the chief since it was he [56] who selected the war chief. The latter was usually a relative who served during the pleasure of the chief. The chief might accompany a war party, but more often he remained at

---

[61] Franchère, p. 250.

[62] See Ray, Native Villages, pp. 110-116.

[63] See class and rank.

[64] Gibbs furnishes a specific case: "Sally, the widow of Tsemahmus, a Tsinuk chief, well known on the lower Columbia, enjoys great authority among the Indians.... (*Tribes of Western Washington*, p. 185).

[65] Cf. Olson, *The Quinault Indians*, p. 95.

home "since it was so important that his life be protected." This feeling existed not only because of his importance as the village head, but particularly because the enemy would center its attack against him if he were present on the field, and would consider his death or serious injury as tantamount to victory.

In discussing the nature of chieftainship my informants repeatedly emphasized his power to appropriate the property of others for personal purposes without regard of the owner. Ross also speaks of this practice: "All property is sacred in the eye of the law, nor can anyone touch it excepting the principal chief, who is above the law, or rather he possesses an arbitrary power without any positive check, so that if he conceives a liking to anything belonging to his subjects, be it a wife or a daughter, he can take it without infringing the law; he must, nevertheless, pay for what he takes — and their laws assign a nominal value to property of every kind."[66]

It is doubtful that such appropriation was strictly a chiefly prerogative, as Ross states. Much more probably it was a privilege of any upperclassman in theory, but in practice only the chief dared assume it. Mrs. Luscier declared that the upper class could infringe as much as it pleased upon the lower classes and added that famine was unknown to the former since the food of the latter was appropriated in such a circumstance. All of her specific examples, however, were acts of chiefs. She told of seeing a chief and his party paddling down the Columbia near a fishing site. A lone fisherman had caught several sturgeon. The chief sent one of his group to take the fish, leaving the fisherman not a one. Payment was not made, nor was it customary in any similar circumstance, according to Mrs. Luscier. This contradicts Ross' unequivocal statement; it may represent more recent practice.

This practice extended to the Clatsop. One of their chiefs, kati•'di, was a particular offender and much disliked. He was constantly sending one or another of his ten sons (agents were always used in property appropriations) to seize goods , from some commoner, the penalty of resistance being death. The Chinook on the opposite side of the river became incensed at the treatment their relatives were receiving and met together at the instance of their chief to decide upon a plan of action. The Clatsop chief was in constant fear of his life and seldom left his barricaded semi-underground house. The Chinook felt that the only hope of enticing him out would be to call to him from the outside, speaking pleasantly in the manner of friends. Then when he emerged they could set upon him and kill him. Accordingly a party was organized and departed. When they arrived they were told that kati•'di was not there though he could be heard talking inside. The Chinook besieged the place for "five" days, but to no avail. Here is one example at least of a chief plotting to undermine his own privileges.

Commoners regularly but informally presented gifts to chiefs, usually of food. The chiefs probably re-distributed the goods among the upper class. In this way the commoners kept in the good graces of the chief and it is probable that summary appropriation as discussed above was by most chiefs directed only against those considered miserly. [57]

Ross' "appropriation of wife or daughter" belongs of course to an entirely different category. Mrs. Luscier declared that a chief would never think of taking a man's wife while the man was still living or when succession under the levirate was possible. Failing the levirate, however, an upper-class widow was "given" by the chief to whatever upperclassman he

---

[66] Ross, p. 88.

desired, or kept as a wife for himself. If a chief desired a particular unmarried woman as a wife for himself or his son, his request was seldom denied. Fear of consequences in the event of denial played some part,[67] but the opportunity to marry into the family of a chief was not lightly to be discarded. In any event the taking of a wife must not be confused with appropriation of property.

The political power of a chief lay definitely in the individual, not in the family to which he belonged. No common term of address existed; the title "chief" was applied to the individual only. Brothers were important in the council but not more so than other prominent upperclassmen. Sub-chiefs or dual chieftainship were unknown. Indeed, the chief was loath to delegate power in any way except to the war chief in the specific circumstance of war. The council was highly informal and relatively unimportant.

The chiefs of various villages never met together for formal council. Lives would have been in danger since relations were more often strained than amicable. Inter-village demands for blood-money or war settlements brought chiefs together but warriors from both sides were always present. These remarks must not be taken to apply to neighboring villages under normal conditions; they represent Mrs. Luscier's formulation.

Each chief was served by a spokesman selected for his ability at oratory. Various men served in this capacity, being selected upon the occasion of need. Not only lid the spokesman add strength of presentation to the words of the chief, but he served as an intermediary between classes. It was felt that the chief should not speak to the lower class directly.

A man was responsible only to the chief of the village in which he lived. As loon as a man shifted residence his political affiliations changed. When a man was visiting away from home he was liable to the chief of the village in which he was temporarily situated. This even applied, at least nominally, to a chief when in the village of another. In the case of tiny settlements intermediately located between larger villages, each with its chief, strife sometimes arose between the chiefs as to where jurisdiction ended.

It has been stated that the chief functioned as a judge and that it was his duty to keep peace in the village. Further details regarding the handling of crimes and orts are almost wholly absent. A quite formal institution of blood-money as settlement for serious torts existed, as reflected in customs connected with slavery.[68] For lesser wrongs a system of fines assessed by the chief and payable to the injured person seems to have held sway. Beyond this little can be said. [58]

Concomly, mentioned several times above as chief of qwatsa'mts, ruled during the days of Lewis and Clark and the early fur traders. There is no question but that he was an exceedingly able leader and an accomplished trader. He has become a literary figure through the repeated references to him by all early writers and his picturization in Washington Irving's Astoria.[69]

The bulk of the trade of the time was handled through Concomly's hands. He used his many slaves to advantage in the movement of goods and the contacting of prospective

---

[67] See marriage.

[68] q.v.

[69] Irving, passim. Cf. Lee and Frost, p. 65; Coues, p. 750; Kane, pp. 120 ff.; Thwaites, vols. 3-4 passim.

customers.   He married several wives (only two are shown in the genealogy) and the associations thus created proved highly profitable through his machinations.

One of Concomly's daughters married McDougall,[70] a leader in the Astor enterprise. Kane reports that upon the occasion of the marriage Concomly carpeted the path of the bride from the canoe landing on the beach to Ft. George, the scene of the ceremony, with sea otter skins, all of which went to McDougall as a dowry.[71] This is an undoubted exaggeration and not in keeping with native practice but it serves to indicate the reputed wealth of the man.

The Clatsop became envious and resentful of this village chief who looked upon the whole of the lower Columbia as his realm. They threatened forceful action and mobilized warriors on several occasions but Concomly easily frightened' them into inaction each time by threatening to bring to the field twice as many warriors; a threat which he apparently could easily have fulfilled. The chief pointed to a great rock resting on the summit of Scarborough hill overlooking qwatsa'mts village and declared, "As long as that rock remains in place no one shall question the power of me or my people!" And the rock did remain, throughout Concomly's life and that of his son. But shortly thereafter it disappeared. A party of Clatsop, aided by a number of Tillamook, toppled the rock from its position and rolled it down the hill.

Concomly apparently came into power around the beginning of the nineteenth century. He is not mentioned in 1792 by Boit; rather it is stated definitely that "the village Chinoak, [was] command'd by a chief named Polack."[72] But with the coming of Lewis and Clark in 1805 Concomly was well established in office. Scouler estimated his age at sixty in 1824.[73] If this were correct he probably became chief as he entered his thirties. He died, according to Dunn, in 1831 and was buried near Ft. George (Astoria),[74] after holding sway for perhaps thirty-five years.

---

[70] See genealogies.
[71] Kane, p. 177.
[72] Boit, p. 248.
[73] Scouler, p. 167.
[74] Dunn, pp. 131 f. See fig. 8.

WARFARE

FORMALIZED WARFARE

Warfare among the Lower Chinook was relatively infrequent and quite bloodless, but highly formalized. Slave raids and surprise attacks by distant groups, on the other hand, often led to considerable loss of life, the taking of scalps and beheading. Great care was taken to avoid a surprise attack by outsiders. If any strange canoe passed a Chinook village and failed to stop, it was promptly pursued. If the occupants were found to be friends, or if they could prove that they were bound for a friendly village on a peaceful mission, they were allowed to pass. If such were not the case, the defensive move changed to an offensive foray; the canoe was pillaged and its occupants taken, if possible, as slaves. As a result, those with malicious intent usually travelled in Chinook territory at night.

Formalized warfare was invoked among the Lower Chinook for the settlement of inter-village disputes that defied more peaceful modes of solution or in the event of persistent friction over a moot point. These conditions grew out of such incidents as inter-village murder or witchcraft,[1] insults, or abduction.[2]

A dance of incitement preceded the battle. The formal announcement is pictured by Boas:

"Open the smoke-hole of our house. Stand up there and shout. Say: 'Ah, GilLā'unaʟx! are you dead? News has come.' Thus speak twice." The younger brother did so.... He shouted twice. Now the people arose. They took their arrows, their bone clubs, and their lances. Now they went to the house of their chief."[3]

The warriors, together with shamans, took part in the dance. The former were attired in full war regalia, including armor, helmet, and face paint, and carried pecten shell rattles and weapons. Forming a circle they danced with a slight side step and sang songs of war.[4] The shamans predicted the outcome of the battle and interpreted the visions of the dancers. Boas records: "Before the people go to war they sing. If one of them sees blood, he will be killed in battle. When two see blood, they will be killed. They finish their singing. When they sing, two long planks are it down parallel to each other. All the warriors sing. They kneel [on the planks]. Now they go to war and fight."[5] Whether the warriors kneel in addition to dancing the circle, or whether the data of Scouler and Boas are contradictory, is uncertain. The dance site, according to Mrs. Luscier, was some distance removed from the village. [60]

Franchère furnishes a graphic description of the actual procedure of battle:

---

[1] Cf. shamanism.

[2] Cf. Franchère. p. 251.

[3] Boas, *Chinook Texts,* p. 231. This announcement was not in connection with war but the pattern is the same.

[4] Scouler, p. 167.

[5] Boas, *Chinook Texts,* p. 270.

Before commencing hostilities they give notice of the day when they will proceed to attack the hostile village.... They embark in their canoes, which on these occasions are paddled by the women, repair to the hostile village, enter into parley, and do all they can to terminate the affair amicably: sometimes a third party becomes mediator between the first two, and of course observes an exact neutrality. If those who seek justice do not obtain it to their satisfaction, they retire to some distance, and the combat begins, and is continued for some time with fury on both sides; but as soon as one or two men are killed, the party which has lost these, owns itself beaten and the battle ceases. If it is the people of the village attacked who are worsted, the others do not retire without receiving presents. When the conflict is postponed till the next day (for they never fight but in open daylight, as if to render nature witness of their exploits), they keep up frightful cries all night long, and, when they are sufficiently near to understand each other, defy one another by menaces, railleries, and sarcasms.... The women and children are always removed from the village before the action.

Their combats are almost all maritime: for they fight ordinarily in their pirogues, which "they take care to careen, so as to present the broadside to the enemy, and half lying down, avoid the greater part of the arrows let fly at them."[6]

The brief account by Boas agrees perfectly with Franchère but adds a further alternative if peace failed of achievement: 'When people of both parties have been killed, they stop. After some time the two parties exchange presents and make peace. When a feud has not yet been settled, they marry a woman to a man of the other town and they make peace."[7]

A war chief appointed by the political chief was in charge of such affairs. Every able-bodied man of the village was bound to accompany the party if called upon; cowardice was punished by death.[8]

A full outfit of armor was worn by the Chinook warrior. A heavy stiff vestment [clamon] of double thickness of elk skin covered the body down to the ankles; arm holes were provided, leaving the arms free. This was quite impenetrable to arrows. On the head was worn a helmet of elk skin or perhaps heavy basketry work in cedar bark or bear grass.[9] Instead of the cumbersome elk skin garment a light armor of wooden rods, twined with nettle cord, was sometimes worn. The rods were short so that the covering amounted to scarcely more than a narrow jacket but its wearer was left quite free for action. In addition, a circular shield about eighteen inches in diameter was carried. The heavy, painted elk skin of which it was constructed was rendered even more impenetrable by hardening with heat.

Weapons consisted primarily of bows and arrows[10] and clubs. The latter were fashioned of stone, bone or wood. Heavy spruce knots were used to form knobbed clubs, but some were

---

[6] Franchère, p. 251 f.

[7] Boas, loc. cit.

[8] Cf. Ross, p. 88.

[9] Dunn, p. 125.

[10] See hunting.

shaped with considerable care as shown in an illustration by Lewis and Clark (see Figure 2, A).[11]"
Here a knot served as a knob on the handle end. Bone clubs were in considerable use; pestle-shaped stone clubs were known; and also, according to Mrs. Luscier, those with round stone heads loosely fastened to a wooden handle by a covering of buckskin. [61]

The double-pointed dagger with medial handle, widespread on the Northwest Coast, was used extensively by the Chinook. These were formerly of bone, though the pattern was later copied in iron. A rough sketch by Lewis and Clark (see Figure 2, B) shows the usual asymmetry in blade length. The shorter blade was four to five inches long, the other about twice that length. The handle, which was wrapped with cord and provided with a thumb loop, was of proper size to fit the hand. These daggers were carried quite constantly and used for a multitude of purposes.[12]

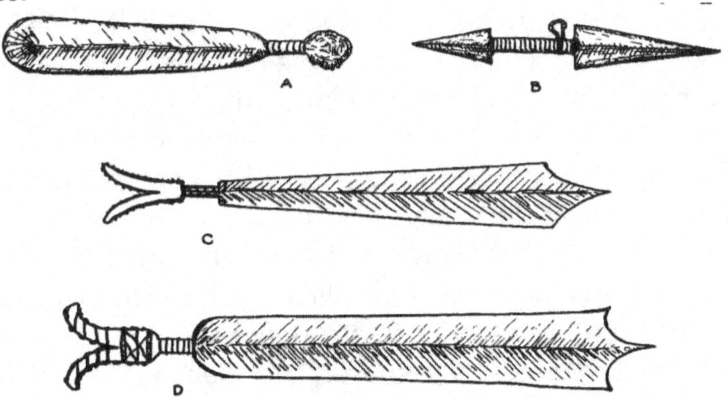

FIG. 2. Weapons. (A) Club; (B) Double dagger; (C) Short blade; (D) Long blade. After Lewis and Clark (Thwaites, *Original Journals*).
{originally printed upside down}

Double-edged weapons, sometimes as much as four feet long, are referred to by several writers by terms such as sword, sabre, and club.[13] [13] The last name suggests that these were of wood, but their actual nature and origin is altogether uncertain. Those illustrated by Lewis and Clark (see Figure 2, C, D) are described only in terms of size, three to four feet in length, four and one-half inches in width. The dimensions are given by Franchère as two and one-half feet by six inches; he adds that they rarely came into sufficiently close combat to make use of these.

Thompson describes canoes with over-decking extending ten feet from the prow on which two warriors with spears stood in battle.[14] [14]

Warriors painted their faces, their bodies where exposed, their shields and their armor. Franchère writes of "most extravagant designs" but describes only the half black, half white face painting of one war-chief.[15] Scouler mentions paints of black, red and yellow. Broughton states that, "The [Chinook] natives differed in nothing materially from those we had visited during the summer [Nutka], but in the decoration of their persons; in this respect they

---

[11] Thwaites, vol. 3, opp. p. 326.

[12] Thwaites, vol. 4, p. 24.

[13] Thwaites, vol. 3, opp. p. 326; Franchère, p. 253; Dunn, p. 124.

[14] Tyrrell, p. 507. See transportation.

[15] Franchère, p. 254.

surpassed all the other tribes with paints of different colors, feathers and ornaments."[16]
The pecten shell rattle, used in the dance, was merely a number of such shells tied to a wooden handle.[17] [62]

RAIDS

Villages were partially protected against surprise attacks with outlook posts and palisades of heavy planks set firmly in the ground, yet successful raids were far from unknown.

Boas records the story of a Quilleute raid on the Clatsop which proved particularly disastrous.[18] An account of the same incident was given me by Emma Luscier:

> A boy was returning from a guardian spirit search. Just as he was nearing Clatsop he noticed five strange canoes and many strange people. He tried to run away but the strangers pursued him. Finally he eluded them and proceeded toward Clatsop by a devious route. He arrived before daylight and warned the people. Some of them laughed at him, saying that he had been searching for spirits and had surely found them. But at daylight the village was attacked and many were killed. Shortly afterwards the Quilleute retired, carrying away many children as slaves. But the Clatsop pursued them and succeeded in killing a half of them, including the chief. As the Quilleute fled they attempted to take their captives with them but this only resulted in the Clatsop continuing the chase. To dissuade them the Quilleute threw one boy in the water and hit him over the head, killing him. But the pursuit continued. Another boy was thrown into the water and he succeeded in swimming to the Clatsop canoes. Many of the captives were thrown overboard; some were drowned but others reached their friends. The Clatsop continued the pursuit until they reached open water. Now only a few of the Quilleute remained alive so they returned. At Clatsop the body of the Quilleute chief was beheaded, scalped and elevated on a pole. The rest of the body was eviscerated.

---

[16] Vancouver, vol. 2, p. 77.
[17] Franchère, pp. 251-54; Ross, pp. 88-90; Dunn, pp. 124; Scouler, p. 167; Tyrrell, p. 507.
[18] Boas, *Chinook Texts,* pp. 273 f.

SOCIETY AND THE INDIVIDUAL

The records of customs associated with the crisis periods represent the richest of the ethnological data furnished to Dr. Boas by his informant, Charles Cultee.[1] The material is far too compact and extensive to permit either quotation or resume. It must be utilized in order to obtain the fullest picture of the life cycle. Such reference is also necessary because my information and that of Dr. Boas are not in full accord at certain points; at other points the material is supplementary.

GENEALOGIES AND NAMES

In the accompanying tables (Tables 2-7) are presented genealogies and names for practically all of the families yet living (all at Bay Center except kəlı'p) with a marked Chinook component in the ancestry. I have not attempted to analyze these since they represent, for the most part, the period of breakdown occasioned by white contact. Yet they furnish examples of village intermarriage, succession of chieftainship, intermarriage with slaves, and other data of considerable importance. In addition I have included the genealogy of one non-Chinook family of Bay Center for comparative purposes. The various lines are, of course, quite incompletely represented but the individuals that have figured most prominently in recent Chinook history are all included.

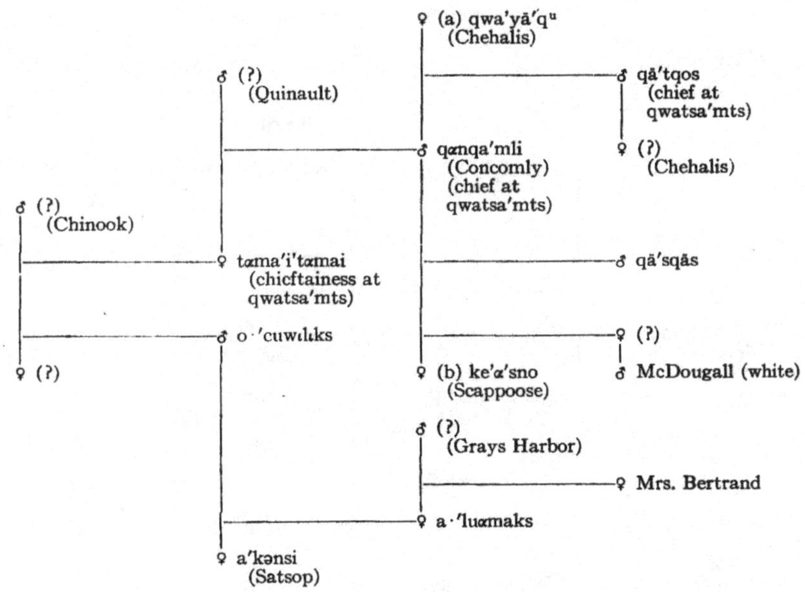

TABLE 2. Genealogy of Concomly and Mrs. Bertrand.

---

[1] Boas, *Chinook Texts,* pp. 238-58.

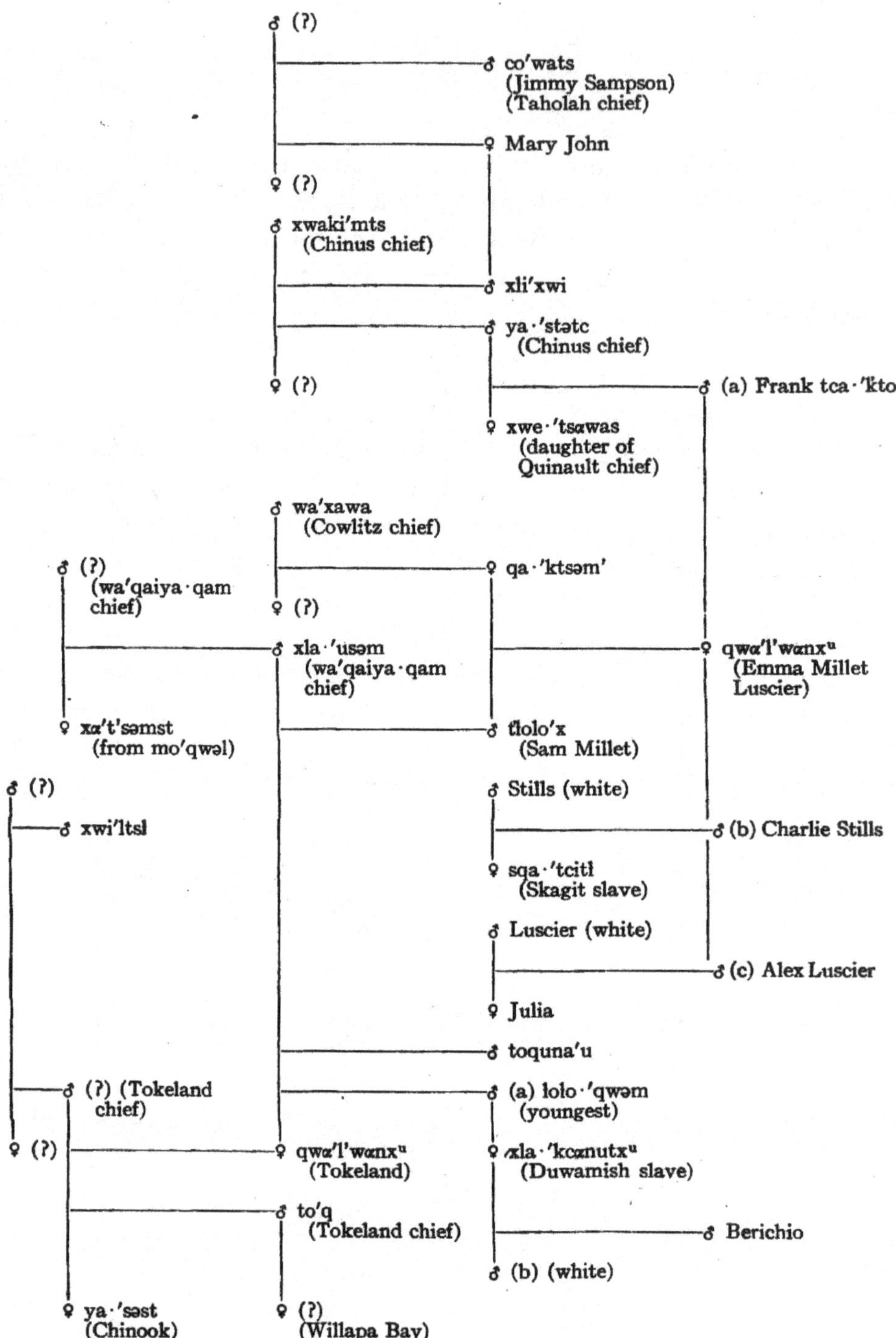

TABLE 3. Genealogy of Emma Millet Luscier.

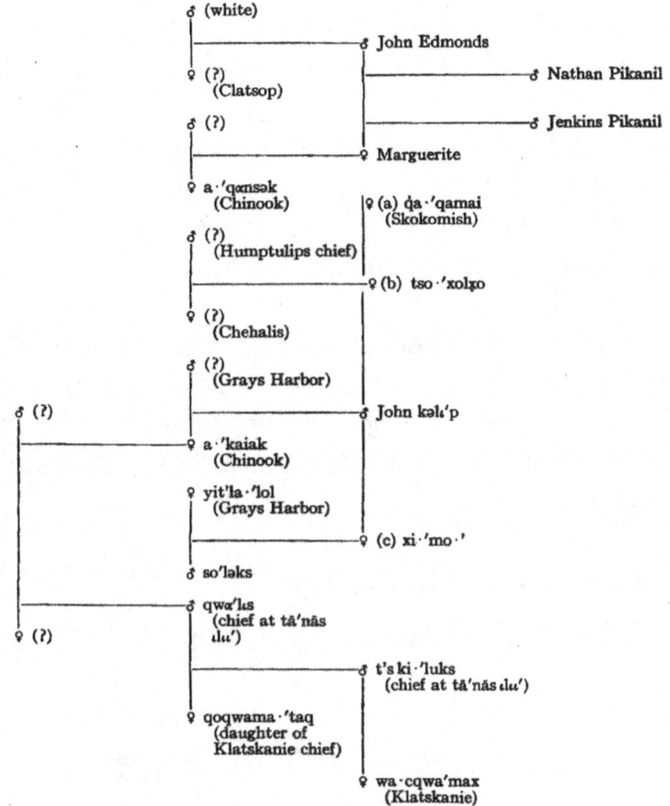

TABLE 4. Genealogy of John kəlı′p.

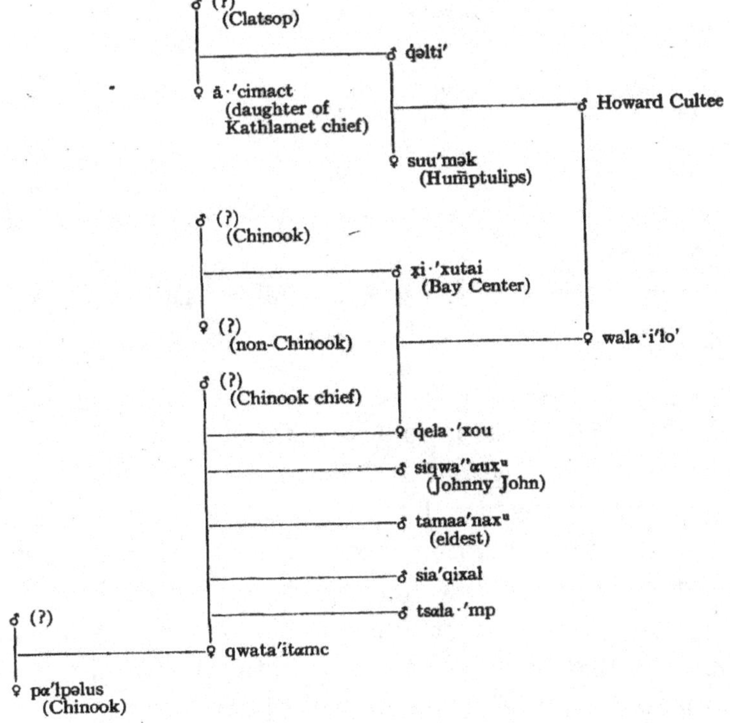

TABLE 5. Genealogy of Cultee.

TABLE 5. Genealogy of Cultee. [66]

A name was given the child at about one year of age. Arrangements for the ceremony were made by the grandparents. On the appointed day guests arrived early in the morning at the house of the parents. Singing and dancing occupied the first hours. Then the one bestowing the name selected some person to hold the child high in the air and shout out the name. The name bestowed was always an ancestral one. The father's mother usually conferred the name upon a boy; the mother's mother upon a girl. This was a coveted opportunity and a grandmother was always pleased to have a grandchild of the same sex as the parent on her side of the family.

The one holding the child also proclaimed who it was that bestowed the name and to whom it had formerly belonged. The latter was then eulogized and good wishes for the child's future were expressed. Others spoke in a similar vein, followed by more singing and dancing. Presents were then distributed and last of all, a feast was held. This was concluded early in the evening and the ceremony was over.

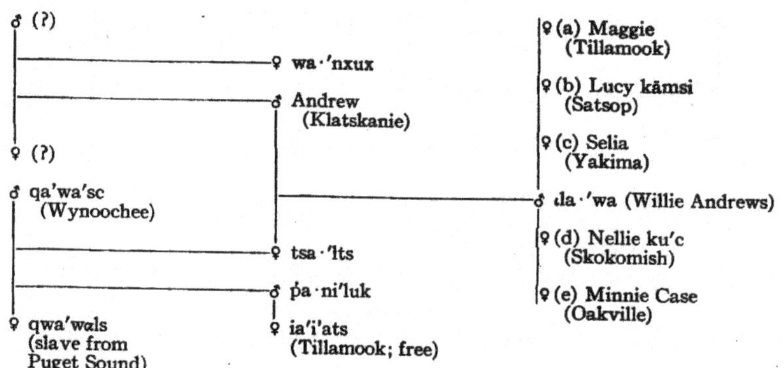

TABLE 6. Genealogy of Willie Andrews.

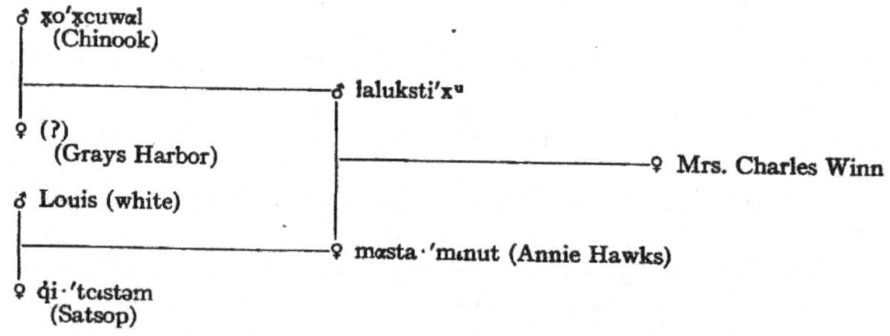

TABLE 7. Genealogy of Mrs. Charles Winn.

TABLE 7. Genealogy of Mrs. Charles Winn. [67]

Sometimes the parents changed a child's name at six or seven years of age but this was not attended by a ritual. The person himself, later in life, might change his name as he desired. This was often done at the time of an unusual experience, serious illness or the acquisition of shamanistic power. Guardian spirit or ceremonial names were commonly possessed in addition to the ancestral name. The first names were meaningful; ancestral names were not. Names were not bestowed until many years after the previous bearer had died.

PREGNANCY AND BIRTH[2]

Infants were believed to live a quite definite existence even before conception.

Mrs. Luscier's exact phrasing will convey the ideas with least distortion: "The baby's home is the sun before being born. All children come from the daylight. That is their home. If their parents do not take good care of them they think, [68] "Well, I'd better go back.' Then they get sick and die. Later, a child may take pity on its parents and decide to return. 'Maybe my parents will be better to me now.' Then the child is born again to the same mother, but is a different sex."

The prospective mother was subjected to a great number of pregnancy tabus. A few of these were as follows : She must not look at a snake, else the child would look like a reptile; she must not look upon suffering or anything ugly; after starting out the door she must not turn back or delivery would be difficult; she must not look upon a dog with unopened eyes or the child would be blind; the tumpline must not be carried around the body or the child would become entangled in the umbilical cord at birth; she must wear no beads or the child's neck would be twisted; she must not look upon a corpse or the child would faint often; she must not bathe too often or her bones would become stiff; food such as berries must not be eaten from the gathering basket but only after being transferred to a mat or dish.

The husband was subject to many restrictions also, including some of the above. Some persons were reputed to have the power of predicting the sex and longevity of the child before birth. These were not necessarily shamans.

FIG. 3. Cradle, board type. After Lewis and Clark (Thwaites, *Original Journals*).

The mother was secluded before delivery in a hut or a partitioned corner of the house. A midwife was called to assist at birth. Shamanistic assistance was sought only if delivery could not be accomplished otherwise. The midwife was a woman "who knew the right kind of medicines to give." She was sometimes a relative but more often a professional, with whom arrangements were made in advance. Her duties included attending to both the woman and the child. While the mother held to two upright posts the midwife supported her from the rear. The woman held a stick or the corner of a blanket in her mouth to avoid crying out. The child was delivered on mats covered with shredded cedar bark. The midwife cut the umbilical cord and tied it with a piece of elk sinew. The child was immediately washed in a wooden dish with warm water. Its mouth was washed out and the body rubbed with bear oil. It was then wrapped in blankets of beaver or raccoon skin. Attention was then turned to the mother. Heated rocks were placed around her bed and water poured on to produce steam. This was to make sure that all the afterbirth would pass. Her breasts were massaged, rubbed with bear grease and heated with hot [69] rocks or steamed. Her abdomen was bound with cedar bark which was later burned. The afterbirth, which was called grandmother, was turned over if it

---

[2] Cf. Boas, *op. cit.*, pp. 241-43.

were desired to reverse the sex of the next child. Then it was immediately disposed of by the midwife where it would not be found.

For five days after delivery the mother was not supposed to sleep for fear of hemorrhage. At the end of that time she was washed with medicinal water. For five more days she remained secluded and ate nothing but fish soup so that her milk might be plentiful.

FIG. 4. Examples of head flattening. (A) Young man; (B) Old man; (C) Woman. After Lewis and Clark (Thwaites, *Original Journals*).

The cradle was made immediately after birth but not before. Emma Luscier declared that cradles were made only by shamans. Two types were used; one was a flat board cradle, diagrammatically represented in a drawing by Lewis and Clark [70]

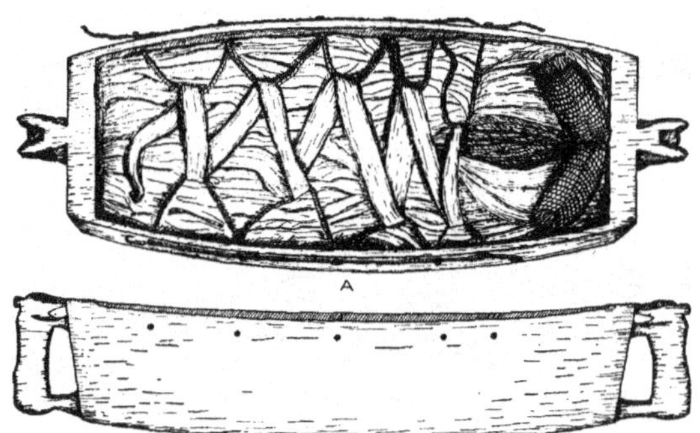

FIG. 5. Dugout cedar cradle. (A) Top view; (B) Side view.

(see Figure 3)[3] and in a portrait by Paul Kane (Plate 1.) This type of cradle was provided with a hinged flattening board which held a pan firmly against the child's head, adjustable by thongs attached to the lower part of the cradle (note: the flattening board is loosened and raised in the Kane portrait). Kane describes the cradle as follows: "Infants [are] strapped to a piece of board covered with moss or loose fibres of cedar bark, and in order to flatten the head they place a pad on the infant's forehead, on the top of which is laid a piece of smooth bark, bound by a leather band passing through holes in the board on either side, and kept tightly pressed across the' front of the head — a sort of pillow of grass or cedar fibres being placed under the back of the neck to support it. This process commences with the birth of the infant,

---

[3] Thwaites, vol. 4, opposite p. 10.

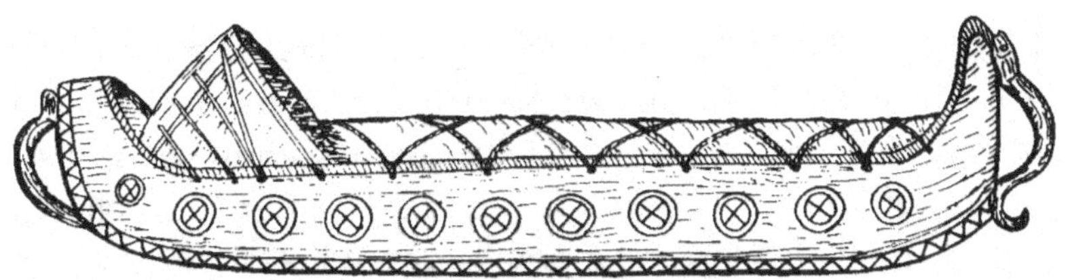

FIG. 6. Dugout cradle with hood. After Swan.

and is continued for a period from eight to twelve months .... "[4] The second type was a dugout cradle, usually of cedar. This is illustrated in Figures 5 and 6. With this cradle two basketry pads filled with thin cedar bark (Figure 7) were used to produce flattening. Their position is shown in the illustration. The pads were firmly bound in place with thongs to the side of the cradle. An openwork matting was used on the inside bottom of the dugout cradle, covered with finely shredded cedar bark, down, and fur bedding. A hood was sometimes provided consisting of a small square of matting.[5]

FIG. 7. Head flattening pad of basketry.

All children of freemen were subject to extensive head flattening. It was forbidden to slaves, being the invariable mark of the station. Flattening was doubtless carried to a greater degree and performed more consistently among the Chinook than with other peoples of the frontal flattening area. Sketches of head flattening [70] by Lewis and Clark are shown in Figure 4. The portrait by Kane (Plate 1) of a Cowlitz (?) woman shows typical flattening. An excellent photograph showing flattening is that of Charles Cultee in Boas' *Chinook Texts* (frontispiece).

A child was kept in its cradle until it was able to walk. Nursing continued for two or three years, sometimes longer.

PUBERTY[6]

At the time of puberty the girl was restricted and regulated in her activities for a period of five months. During this time she ate, slept, and worked in a partitioned corner of the house. Her time was occupied with such activities as basket-making, but a slave was assigned to provide her with food and attend her needs.

During the five days immediately following the appearance of the first menses the girl observed a complete fast and remained completely isolated from other persons.

At the same time the girl's mother or grandmother invited many old women and old

---

[4] Kane, p. 180; cf. Tyrrell, p. 506.
[5] Cf. Swan, pp. 167 f.
[6] Cf. Boas, *op. cit.,* pp. 246 f.

men to come to the house and celebrate the event. This was a simple one-day ceremony with singing, dancing and a small feast. The girl, of course, did not appear.

Following the five-day period the girl was given somewhat more freedom and was allowed a little dried salmon and grease to eat. Thereafter her food allowance was increased until she ate two regular meals each day, a small amount early in the morning and a larger quantity in the evening, but at no time was she given fresh food of any kind. If she ate anything fresh the person who had obtained the food would have been unable again to procure such articles.

At daybreak each morning the girl left the house and bathed in a pool which had been formed by damming a nearby stream at some protected spot. Before bathing she rubbed her body with rotten hemlock wood and boughs of cedar. On her return she gathered a large load of bark or wood, carrying as much as possible. This was to insure future strength and regular occurrence of the menses. If bathing was omitted a single time during the five months the period was extended.

During isolation the girl wore only cedar bark clothing. Each day she painted her face and hands with a solid covering of red. The part of the hair was also painted. But she was not allowed to comb her hair. This was done by an old woman. Two braids were plaited and fastened in a tight knot at the back of the girl's head. Dentalia were sometimes inserted in the hair. She was provided with two pointed wooden sticks with which to scratch her head.

Conversation by the girl was strictly limited. Her mother addressed her occasionally, and less often her father. In these cases she might answer but she was lot permitted to speak first. If she met another pubescent girl at the bathing pool the two conversed. Also she was visited during confinement by the girl children of the neighborhood, to whom she spoke and gave presents of her own childhood playthings, no longer proper for her to retain. [72]

If the parents travelled the girl was allowed to accompany them but her activities were highly restricted. She was supposed to keep her eyes closed; an elderly woman guided her actions. If the girl had looked at the sky it would have caused rain. To glance at a child would have caused it to become ill; or to look upon an ailing person would have magnified his illness.

At the end of the five-month period another ceremony was held, similar to the first but more elaborate. At this time the girl made her appearance and took part in the dancing and singing.

Food restrictions were not entirely lifted with this ceremony. Fresh food was avoided for a full year.

At any time after seclusion was ended the girl might avail herself of the formal mechanism for announcing her desires regarding marriage. While in the presence of older women she might sing "love songs" in which the name of the man was inserted.

Swan comments on the puberty observances as follows:

When a young girl reaches womanhood, she has to go through a process of purification, which lasts a *moon*, or month. This is simply by bathing several times a day, and rubbing the body with rotten wood procured from the hemlock-tree. They are not allowed, during this period, to eat anything that is in season, either salmon, sturgeon, shell-fish, or berries, as it is believed that, in such cases, the fish would disappear, the shell-fish would make them sick, and the berries would fall off the bushes without ripening. And should there be a southeast wind, with signs of rain, they must on no pretense, go out of the house, for *Too-lux,* the south wind, is so offended if one of these girls goes out of doors, that he sends *Hah-ness',* the thunder-bird, who shakes his wings, and causes) the roaring thunder, his eyes, the meanwhile, sending forth flashes of lightning. I never knew a thunder storm occur while I resided in the Territory but what was attributed to some girl going out during her season of purification.[7]

At each subsequent menstrual period the girl was isolated for a five-day period in the partitioned corner or in a small hut on the outside. Face painting and activities were similar to the initial period. Food tabus, however, included only fresh products.

There was no formal recognition of the puberty period in boys. It was immediately preceding puberty, however, that the most intensive searches were made for guardian spirits.

MARRIAGE[8]

Soon after a boy passed puberty his parents turned their attention to the accumulation of sufficient property so that his marriage might be arranged. Relatives were called to assist, for the amount of goods transferred was a direct reflection of the family's social position. When the amassed property was judged sufficient the boy's parents discussed the available girls of proper social rank and decided whom should be asked. The boy was sometimes consulted.

Two messengers were then dispatched to the girl's parents carrying initial presents with them. These were offered to the girl's parents together with an enumeration [73] of the further gifts if the offer be accepted. The messengers received the answer and returned. If they returned with the presents the boy's people knew the offer had been refused. Sometimes the messengers were sent back to offer even more. As soon as an affirmative answer was received immediate preparations for the wedding were made. The boy's people loaded the remaining presents in canoes, and together with the boy and many relatives, embarked for the girl's house.

A short distance from the destination, camp was made and the messengers were sent ahead to the girl's house. The party remained at the camp until the emissaries returned the next day or perhaps even later. Then the group formally approached and entered the girl's house, carrying the presents. Here they remained for two or three days, feasting, singing and dancing.

When the visitors departed the groom and bride accompanied them. Immediately thereafter the recipients of the presents called in their relatives and the presents were redistributed. The guests made their own choices, with the woman's relatives preceding the man's.

Residence was uniformly patrilocal. The next formal relations between parents of the bride and groom occurred a year later. At that time the girl's family visited the boy's, bringing

---

[7] Swan, p. 171.

[8] Cf. Boas, *op. cit.,* pp. 251 f.

with them quantities of food which they had been engaged in accumulating throughout the intervening year. An interchange of presents between the two families was made but the great bulk of food was not matched. Dancing and feasting, similar to that at the marriage ceremony, occupied two or three days, after which the guests departed.

At the time of first pregnancy, the girl was returned to her own parent's home where she remained until the child was born. Shortly afterward the mother and her child were returned to the husband's home together with another great quantity of food. Again the feast was held, the last of the three invariably accompanying marriage and the establishment of a new family.

Polygyny was practiced both by upper and lower classes. The levirate and sororate were strictly observed. Infant betrothals sometimes occurred, with the exchange of a few presents to bind the bargain.

Divorce was optional only to the husband. It was not accompanied by return if presents.

A wife's punishment for adultery was the loss of her ears or the end of her nose. The husband inflicted this punishment upon his erring wife and was privileged to ill the paramour if the case were unquestionable. According to Emma Luscier, however, the male transgressor almost always avoided the penalty by lavish gifts to the husband. The wife was sometimes sent back to her own people as a result of adultery. In such a case her relatives often carried many gifts to her husband as an inducement to take his wife back. When he acceded to this request "he knew that s wife could be trusted after that," Mrs. Luscier declared, "because her relatives had spent so much wealth on her." [74]

DEATH AND INTERMENT[9]

When a freeman died his corpse was placed in a prominent position on the bed platform where it lay in state while relatives visited and funeral arrangements were made. For an upperclassman these preparations occupied five days, for commoners a somewhat shorter time. Relatives and fellow villagers gathered as soon as news of the death was received, bringing with them gifts to be interred with the corpse and others to be presented to the chief mourners after the funeral.

During the five days all conduct was governed strictly by formal ritual. Before the arrival of the guests the corpse was washed, wrapped in blankets or furs, and placed in position. This work was delegated to young men (or women) who later were well paid. As relatives and visitors appeared they walked to the bier, looked upon the corpse, and began to wail. Chief mourners blackened their faces, wore their oldest clothing, and refrained from all routine activity. Conversation was conducted scarcely above a whisper.

At daylight each morning formal wailing commenced, all persons participating, including slaves. The wail was a monotonous chant, at times accompanied by words.[10] After a short

---

[9] Cf. Boas, *op. cit*, pp. 256-58.

[10] Swan (p. 189) presents the following as typical:

"Oh, our mother ! why did you go and leave us so sad? We can scarcely see by reason of the water that falls from our eyes.

session a slave was sent for water and a cedar bark towel. Each person washed away his tears and wiped his face with the towel. A messenger was then dispatched to a neighboring house to order the preparation of food. Meals were never prepared in the presence of the corpse. When the breakfast was I ready the mourners, except for a few, left for the other house. Later they returned but wailing was not resumed until the afternoon. It was continued from that time until sunset, but never later lest misfortune result.

At any early moment the hair of close relatives of the deceased was ceremonially cut. This was done by some close blood relative of the mourner but not a member of the immediate family. The hair was cut at the level of the lobe of the ear.

The names of all chief mourners were changed at this time,[11] accompanied by public announcement. The new names continued in use for a year or longer, sometimes indefinitely. Also all words phonetically similar to the name of the deceased were dropped. Synonyms served in lieu of the abjured terms for a long period following, ideally until the name was bestowed upon a descendent.[12] Following are [75] examples of the substitutions: t'łolo'x died, t'łu'x ("cold") was replaced by pama's; xa'wal^ux died, xa'wal^ux ("loud") was given up for t'ła'xł; la'qwask died, la'qwasək ("dance") was dropped for wa'tsyakəm. Needless to say, the name of the deceased was never mentioned.

Early on the fifth morning the corpse was prepared for interment by wrapping it, in extended position, with cattail mats and binding to it the pole with which it was to be carried. The personal possessions of the deceased and presents brought by the guests were sometimes placed alongside the body before wrapping; in other cases they were carried by the mourners to the place of interment and laid near the corpse. A few wall planks were taken out for the removal of the corpse. Two pall bearers carried the burden to the burial grounds when possible, while all the others travelled by canoe. When the corpse was transported in a canoe it was necessary to destroy the vessel. Graveyards were located on islands by preference but when this was not possible a plot bordering on the water was set aside at some distance from the village. Each village possessed its own burial ground.

Interment was invariably above the surface for all but the slaves. Two forms were

---

"Many years have you lived with us, and taught us the words of wisdom.

"You were not poor, neither are we poor, neither were you weak, but your heart and limbs were strong.

"You should have lived with us many years, and told us more of the deeds of ancient times."

Swan states that the lamentations were not begun until after the funeral but this is contradicted by explicit statements of my informants.

[11] Compare Swan (p. 189): "On those occasions they always change their own names, as they think the spirits of the dead will come back if they hear the same name called that they were accustomed to hear before death. Toke, who had lost a daughter just previous ... called himself Chehait. Heyalma, whose brother died at Russell's, called himself Cletheas. Tomhays changed his to Senequa, and Tomanawos his to Winasie. Yancumux, a brother of Tomanawos, changed his to Yakowilk."

Scouler (p. 187) writes that Concomly changed his name to Madsu when his son died.

[12] See genealogies and names.

known, canoe burial (Plate 3) and box burial (Figure 8).   Canoes were the more commonly employed but the use of boxes was not a post-white adoption. This is proved by the first white observations. Broughton writes: "The body was rolled up in deer skins, after them with mats, and then laid at full length in a wooden box, which exactly fitted it."[13]

FIG. 8. Elevated box interment. After Wilkes.

Canoes or boxes were made ready prior to the arrival of the funeral party. Oftimes a single canoe served but preferably two were employed and occasionally three, the value and number of the canoes reflected the wealth and rank of the deceased.) The vessels were scrubbed clean and sometimes repainted. They were not, apparently, made anew for the purpose. Many holes were pierced in the bottom so that rain water might escape and so that the canoe would be unfit for further [76] service. Ordinarily a burial canoe or box was raised above the ground about six feet on a staging; less commonly the lower limbs of a tree served as a support. But Henry mentions surface burial as well: "Some [were] lying on the ground covered with mats and a canoe over all; others, again, raised on stages, covered with mats, and then a canoe over the whole."[14] Those on the ground may have fallen. The staging was prepared alike for either a canoe or box. Four posts of split cedar were erected by digging holes in the ground. They were placed in pairs, separated by the width of the box or canoe, at distance determined by the length of the container. A mortise was made near the top of each post through which horizontal beams were passed connecting the pairs. Sometimes these beams were supported by trees, if conveniently located, rather than posts.

In some cases the larger of two canoes was used as the depository, the other as a cover; or this arrangement might be reversed. If three canoes were available the corpse was placed in a small one, this in a larger, and the third served as a cover. The protection for a single canoe consisted of cedars-planks. The container was not raised to position until the body was placed inside. With the corpse were deposited all objects brought by the mourners. Often these were broken or damaged at the time. Large articles, particularly baskets and bags, were hung on the canoe and staging. A man's power stick or board was either placed with the body or erected outside. No food was deposited at any time.

The canoe was lifted to the platform with poles placed underneath; direct contact with

---

[13] Vancouver, vol. 2, p. 54.
[14] Coues, p. 754.

the coffin after the corpse lay inside was avoided as far as possible. But a final covering of matting was wrapped around the canoes when once in permanent position.

A slave was often killed at the grave and buried in a shallow excavation beneath his mastery The treatment of slaves at death is discussed in the section on slavery.

After interment the mourners returned to the village where gifts were presented by the guests to the near relatives of the deceased. No feast was held. The following morning the visitors departed. Disposition was now made of any remaining personal possessions or articles intimately associated with the deceased. Guardian spirit paraphernalia were deposited deep in the woods by young men. Other articles were burned, including bed and blankets.

A house was usually deserted, at least temporarily, after a death. Sometimes it was torn down and reerected in another location. Less commonly the building was burned; this usually marked the death of a high ranking person. A slave suffering mortal illness was removed from a house so that death might not occur within.

Formal mourning continued for a year.[15] This consisted of a brief period of wailing in the early morning and another just before sunset each day. Wailing was performed, not in the house, but at some distance in the woods. Paid wailers were not employed but slaves were included. For ten days mourners did not go near the [77] water, lest a storm arise. Food tabus, observed for a month, included the principal sea products and fresh foods generally. For a year or longer bathing was abjured and the poorest of clothing worn.

The end of a widow's period of mourning was marked by a ritual which is ascribed in highly embroidered terms by Wilkes:

> At Astoria we saw one day, when there was quite a crowd of Indians at the encampment, several squaws, all dressed in their best attire. These were all more than usually attentive to their personal appearance. The principal among them was a widow, whose time of mourning for the death of her husband had just expired. Her object was to notify her friends that she was ready to receive the addresses of anyone who was in want of a wife.[16] To give such notification was, as I found on inquiry, a common custom among the Chinooks.
>
> The widow ... was attended by seven others ... and all evidently accompanied her to do honor to the occasion. Every half hour they would arrange themselves in a row, and the widow at the head, affecting a modest downcast look, would commence a chant, informing the by-standers that her period of mourning was out, that she had forgotten her deceased husband, given her grief to the winds, and was now ready to espouse another. The chant was accompanied by a small movement of the feet and body, which, with the guttural song and consequent excitement of such an exhibition, caused the fair ones to wax so warm that perspiration rolled down ear painted cheeks ...[17]

---

[15] This had been reduced to a month in Swan's time (Swan, p. 189).

[16] This is somewhat incompatible with the statements of informants that the levirate was strictly observed.

[17] Wilkes, vol. 5, pp. 117 f.

The remains of an upperclassman were reburied a year or more after death. A new canoe was made ready and guests were invited. Well paid helpers transferred the bones and raised the new container. In lieu of a new canoe the old one as sometimes repainted. Wailing accompanied these observances but a feast followed which was given over to singing and dancing. Since this ceremony usually as sponsored by a son (or daughter) of the deceased it frequently was postponed until the latter reached adulthood.[18]

[18] Cf. Thwaites, vol. 3, pp. 326; idem, vol. 4, p. 198; Swan, pp. 185-89, 191 f., 212; Franchère, pp. 250, 256 f.; Scouler, pp. 167, 176; Dunn, pp. 119 f.; Gibbs, Tribes of Western Washington, pp. 203 f.

THE GUARDIAN SPIRIT COMPLEX

THE QUEST

Both boys and girls were sent on guardian spirit quests, though the latter were in the minority. The quest was neglected completely by only a small percentage of boys, though success eventually came to perhaps but half of those keeping vigils. There were no class restrictions; indeed, slaves, orphans and the children of poor families were more successful than others.[1] "They tried harder." Possession of a strong spirit, however, did not automatically elevate one in the social scale. Accomplishments, particularly the accumulation of wealth, were the criteria, though credit might be given to the spirit for making such achievements possible.

For both boys and girls the period of vision seeking began at about ten years of age. It ended abruptly for the latter with the appearance of the first menses. Puberty theoretically marked the termination for boys likewise, but since the coming of puberty was less definitely indicated, the cessation of quests was similarly indefinite. Under no circumstances, however, might a boy seek a vision after marriage, which usually followed shortly after puberty. Virginity, on the other hand, does not seem to have been a requisite for a successful spirit search. Dr. Boas gives an account of the last minute efforts before marriage of Charles Cultee's grandfather to obtain a tutelary, though he already possessed three.[2]

The child was sent by an old man or woman, often a relative, who gave instructions and encouragement. In Emma Luscier's memory each search was limited to a single night, but repeated often, sometimes several nights in succession. Mrs. Bertrand, however, stated that the average duration was three to five nights, which corresponds with Dr. Boas' data. The one night vigil probably was a final remnant of the longer ventures of earlier times. The vision seeker embarked upon his quest early in the evening, always going alone. His destination had been specified; it was usually a body of water or a point on the beach. In the latter case the outgoing trip was to be made largely by swimming, stopping at intervals to dive, each time in sequences of five, accompanied by shouting. This was to be repeated at the destination but the return trip could be made by land. A point farther distant was named for each successive venture. If a child returned early with his hair dry ("Some children were afraid of the water") ashes were thrown on him and he was told to "go back and wash," that is, resume the quest and carry out the original instructions. The activities were not always limited to diving; sometimes rolling boulders or piling them up was included. The seeker carried a stick with identifying marks which had been given him with instructions to leave it at the destination so that his presence there might later be ascertained. The stick was deposited after diving, not before. Or perhaps he was told to bring back some object or plant only to be found near the specified goal.[3] [79]

---

[1] Cf. Boas, *Chinook Texts*, pp. 220-22.
[2] Cf. *idem,* p. 214 f.
[3] Ibid.

Children were sent on vision quests at any time during the year, but at no time were they allowed to wear clothing or to eat food while absent. Emma Luscier declared that children were sometimes forced to undertake a spirit quest as a punishment for some unapproved deed, but psychologically this would be a curious procedure.

There were traditional spots for spirit-seeking though these do not appear to have been the locales of definite spirits. Mrs. Bertrand mentioned the following as common quest destinations: the top of Scarborough hill (above *qwatsa'mts* village), Saddle mountain (south of Astoria), the swampy regions near Ilwaco, the head of Skamokawa river and Naselle mountain.

The vision-seeker was sometimes told what sort of experience he might expect and how to react. "You may hear a voice, but don't run away. Stay and listen. Then when you start home, don't run, just walk slowly. If you pass a pool or a stream, stop and swim. Dive five times. Then if you are tired, lie down, but be sure that you are on the side of the water toward home. If you hear a voice again, don't be frightened. Stay and listen. The spirit will not cross the water; it will stay on the other side.[4] It will be an animal when you first see it, but it will change and look like a man. It will tell you what power you will have and what you are to do when you are grown." (Isabella)

Emma Luscier said of her father, Sam Millet, and his quest: "When my father was very young his father died. He had only his mother to take care of him and the other three children. Two of them were younger. One day his mother said to him, 'You are old enough to go and swim now. You know what a hard time we are having. You may meet something that will help you. Then maybe you can stay in this land for a long time. You might find a good power. Now don't run away if you see anything. Stay and listen.' He went out many times. He went to Wahkiakum. He was swimming in the river thinking of what his mother had said to him. She had told him to make a fire on each side of the river when he was looking for a spirit. So he made a fire on each side. It was getting Clark. Then he went to swim. He dived five times. He swam across the river. He dived five times again. Then he went to fix the fire. He walked around the fire five times [counter-clockwise]. Then he went in the water again. He dived five times again. He swam across to the other fire. He did the same thing there. Then he stayed there all night. All at once he got sleepy. He built up the fire and then lay down. It was nearly daylight. Then someone came and talked to him. 'Oh! You're here! Look! I'm here, too! I knew you were looking for me. I knew you were looking for a spirit. I know you've had a hard time. Now I'll help you. Now I'll stand you up on your land. You'll be a good hunter. It will be easy for you to kill anything that you want to. Now after a while, when you sing, you must eat a few bracken roots.[5] The one that was talking looked like a man. But it was a bird, gray owl [?]. Before he left he told his name, *t'sastc'nəm'tc*. Then my father went home. Later he went out a few more times but he didn't get any other power." [80]

Most animals, birds, inanimate objects such as rocks and water, and such natural

---

[4] Ibid.

[5] Symbolizing the snake.

phenomena as whirlwind, thunder and clouds served as guardian spirits {taa<u>x</u>}. Animals and birds were by far the most common. Heavenly bodies and plants seldom or never became tutelaries, nor did fabricated objects. Specific spirits were not associated with particular abilities, with a few exceptions.[6] The power and talents conferred depended largely upon the nature of the vision itself. A child was expected to enter upon the vision quest without fixed spiritual or vocational objectives, but of course previous experience and personal interest played some part. A few spirits were reputed to be especially strong, including skunk ("Could he not turn away any animal, no matter how large?"), bear, cougar and thunder. Kingfisher, eagle and deer were ordinarily hunting powers, but served other functions as well.

There was no tabu against killing one's guardian animal. Indeed, those with hunting power found it easier to kill their guardian animals than others. Certain generalized favors were conferred by nearly all spirits, such as good health, wealth and long life. Emma's paternal uncle, *toquna'u*, advised vision seekers, "Be honest about looking for a power. This land will give you nothing and you will die young if you do not go. But if you do you will live long and be lucky."

When a child returned from a vision quest he told no one of his success or failure. However, if successful he was expected to sleep undisturbed all that day or longer. More important than the sleep, perhaps, was the continuance of the previous night's fast. Should this be broken during the day illness was sure to result.

Nor was any mention made of the quest experience for many years to come. Not until "maturity" (20 to 25 for women, 25 to 30 for men)[7] did the spirit return and become an active tutelary.

By far the greatest number of guardian spirits was obtained through intentional seeking. However, it was not unknown for spirits to appear unexpectedly to children while alone and away from the village.[8] Powers obtained in such a manner were quite as efficient as sought powers.

Spirit power was not ordinarily inherited but predilections were not unknown.[9] Sometimes an old man in charge of a vision seeker would send his spirit ahead for the child to find. Soon afterward he would die.[10]

Shamanistic power was acquired in the same fashion as any other power. A seeker embarking upon a quest could not know whether a successful vision might bring him shamanistic power or not. Nor was the identity of the spirit a determining factor. As Emma Luscier explained, "One person might get cougar power and become a great hunter; another might have the same spirit and become a great shaman."

In addition to conferring talents and bounties, a tutelary conveyed a song and a dance

---

[6] Cf. Boas, op. cit, p. 230.

[7] John kəlı'p had been married two or three years before his spirit returned; Emma Luscier's father was likewise married.

[8] Cf. Boas, op. cit., pp. 220-22.

[9] Cf. idem, pp. 214 f.

[10] Cf. Boas, op. cit., pp. 209, 211, 214, 221, 229 f., 236 f.; Swan, pp. 42, 174 f., 193.

to the visionary to be used at the time of initiation into the guardian spirit dance (or winter dance) and at subsequent dances. [81]

THE SPIRIT DANCE

In common with peoples along the entire length of the Columbia river, the major religious ceremony of the Lower Chinook was the guardian spirit dance. The time of the yearly dance was determined, to the native mind, by the period of spirit visitations, September until spring. Each dance occupied five days only, but many were held in various parts of Lower Chinook territory during the dance season-Dancers travelled from one to another, other activities permitting. The dances were individually sponsored by persons with guardian spirit power. According to Emma Luscier, sponsorship occurred only upon the occasion of initial spirit return, which would limit the number of ceremonies greatly. This seems doubtful; at least in older times the possession of spirit power must have been the only prerequisite to dance sponsorship.

A close spiritual bond existed between men and their tutelaries only during this ceremonial period. At other times, the relationship was real, but remote. A person first became aware of his spirit's presence through an illness which could be cured only by singing one's spirit song and dancing one's spirit dance. This might be done at any spirit dance, or, theoretically, without formal ceremony at one's own home. Shamanistic diagnosis was necessary only upon initial return, at which time the illness was much more serious, and the symptoms far from uniform. When a shaman diagnosed a case as spirit illness, his words were in effect an announcement of an initiation dance. As soon as the news spread about, an audience began to assemble. The patient was placed, reclining, at the extreme opposite point from the door so that he could see all who entered and all who danced.

Immediately upon the shaman's announcement of spirit illness the patient selected an old man, proficient and experienced, to prepare his "power sticks." These poles, two in number, were. to be used in beating upon a horizontally suspended, elevated plank drum. The old man searched for two straight cedar poles, about three inches in diameter, and as much as ten feet long. The poles were prepared exactly according to the instructions given by the patient. Sometimes they were left round, others were squared. The bark was always removed and the poles painted, one red, the other black. About a third of the length from the top were tied frayed cedar bark, deer dew hoofs, brightly colored feathers (those of a small bird called *t'se'uq*, particularly), or other pendants according to the patient's directions. The poles were prepared outside to be brought in in ceremonial procession. The shaman announced to the assemblage that the first step in the patient's cure was to be performed. All left the house and prepared to re-enter in single file. The shaman led the procession, followed by two drummers, young men named by the patient, who carried the poles. The dancers and audience followed in turn. As the procession entered, all were dancing and singing to the accompaniment of circular hand drums. They encircled the fires, counter-clockwise, five times and then, upon a signal from the patient, sat down. The drummers took their proper positions at the foot of the patient's bed, sitting and holding the poles vertically so that the upper ends might be beaten against the plank drum. The hand holds on the sticks were often wrapped with shredded cedar bark to protect the drummers' hands. This was especially necessary [82] since they were expected to remain at their posts until exhausted, fasting all the while. Mrs. Luscier declared that strong drummers might continue for as much as three days without sleep! They were well paid by the patient for their services.

As each visitor arrived, he entered the house singing his spirit song. if he possessed one. The patient listened intently to these, one after another, until he heard one which "satisfied him," relieved his illness. This indicated that the person singing possessed the same spirit as the patient. The latter then for the first time sang his own original song, the one which he had received from his guardian spirit at the time of the quest years before. He did not leave his bed, however. Indeed, he remained there for the entire five-day duration of the initiation dance. The person whose song had "released" the patient, remained near at hand throughout the remainder of the ceremony as aid to the initiate, but he did not supplant the shaman or treat the patient in any way. He was well paid.

Sometimes (often, Mrs. Luscier said), no one appeared whose song would appease the patient, who became more and more ill as a result. In such an event, messengers were sent to bring new guests, sometimes from far away. One time a cousin of Mrs. Luscier lost consciousness at his initiation. Visitors were called from as far as Georgetown and Westport. Finally, someone was found whose spirit was the same. A woman named Maggie nearly died under similar circumstances. Sometimes no amount of searching availed. The patient then died. Shamanistic treatment was of no value in such cases.

After the initiate had sung his new song, the shaman announced the nature of the power and the circumstances under which it was obtained. During the initiation period the patient did rot speak of his spirit, but talked freely of it afterward. Each request made by the patient was announced to the audience by the shaman. He was not served by a speaker.

The uniform procedure during the remainder of the ceremony consisted of spirit singing and dancing by all of those possessed of power. The song was begun by its possessor, hut soon the audience joined him. Even those guests who were without guardian spirits aided the singing, though they did not dance. They also, along with others, beat time with short cedar sticks on any board or log available. Soon after the song was started, the singer began to dance- Sometimes the songs and dances were requested by the initiate; at other times they were spontaneous, or rather, in response to the "call" of one's spirit. Dancing proceeded continuously throughout the five days and nights. Dancers served by relays to allow time for sleep.

Variant procedure, interspersed with the dances, included ritual compliance with requests of the initiate, and performances of power by the dancers. The most common request by the patient was that others join him in singing his song. He never sang alone; it would have made him more ill. Often, however, he made less usual requests, reflecting, often symbolically, his guardian spirit experience. He might ask that a fur robe of a particular animal be put over him. Or he might wish that his blanket be covered with down, or painted a specified color. He might request that his face be painted in a directed manner. Legs and arms were sometimes colored solidly, or with five alternating bands of red and black, at the patient's request [83] (but other parts of the body were never painted). The forelocks of the hair might be cut so as to fall in five segments on the forehead. (After the initiation, these usually were cut off evenly.) If the execution of any of these requests necessitated leaving the house, all of the guests went out and returned with the article in the same ritual manner as for the "power sticks."

During the five days, the initiate was allowed water in limited quantities only, and this had to be taken from other than the regular water supply. The ritual procedure mentioned above was followed in this case, too. All drank water along with the patient. A complete fast was observed by the initiate, except when broken ritually. If his spirit "requested" a certain kind of food, he conveyed the desire to the shaman, who led all of t-he assemblage in search of it. A considerable quantity had to be obtained, for the initiate never ate alone; others ate the same kind of food at the same time. After the food was brought in in the usual ritual manner, five small pieces were given to the patient, five pieces each to all others. The initiate chewed on each piece for a while, then gazed at it a few moments, after which he threw it in the fire, thus feeding his spirit.

Before each request such as those above, the patient sang his song, aided by his guests.

Sleep was tabu to the novice during the ceremony. Lincoln Jim slept during his initiation, and everyone said that he would die young, which he did.

Shamanistic or power performances, though a part of the dance program, seem to have been relatively unimportant.[11] Foremost were the dances with "power sticks" and "power boards." The former were similar (or identical) to those used for drumming, but smaller. The latter were made of flat cedar boards, diamond shaped, with rounded points, and painted. The designs were simple geometric and semi-realistic figures, symbolic of one's guardian spirit. Both types were used similarly, but the hoards served the further purpose of display (in the house) at non-ceremonial times. Some were fairly elaborate, with shell inlays as well as painting. Emma Luscier suggested that the boards were the more common in older times, the sticks, recently.[12] John kəlı'p owned one of each type. At dances he would hand one to a dancer, whereupon the latter would be powerless to let it go. It would shake in his hands while he danced around (led by the board ?) until relieved of it by kəlı'p.

These sticks also were used in ritual searches for lost articles and drowned persons. The typical procedure is illustrated in the case where Mary John, a shaman, was called upon (during a dance ?) to solve the mystery of a certain man's disappearance. She gave her stick to one of those present, and then began to sing. Soon the stick started shaking and drawing the holder along. "Follow me," the dancer said, and the others complied, singing. He led them to the water's edge and cried, "Put me in a canoe, quickly. He has drowned." A canoe was brought, and after a short journey, directed by the man holding the stick, the spot where the drowning occurred was found and the body recovered. (Luscier) [84]

Power demonstrations also included the performance of tricks such as holding red hot stones and "swallowing" snakes. Sam Millet's spirit was an owl, and like the owl he was able to

---

[11] Cf. the secret society.

[12] Cf. p. 126.

swallow snakes. During a dance he often sent several boys out to "bring back some bracken root." But instead of bracken, they found a snake at the place indicated. (This symbolism originated in Millet's spirit quest vision.[13]) Upon receiving the snake, Sam twined it around his neck and head, then "swallowed" it.

After three year's blindness, John kəlı'p regained his sight (during a dance ?) in a demonstration of the power of his spirit, owl.

Sometimes a novice's spirit indicated during the dance that the group should move to some other place for the completion of the ceremony. During Dixie James' initiation, the procedure was halted and everyone moved to Jamestown. About thirty adults were present, requiring four canoes to transport them and their children. The group travelled by water to Georgetown where they loaded the canoes into wagons and took them to Westport (Washington). At Westport, travel by canoe was resumed to the destination. The four canoes were paddled abreast so that the ceremonial singing and drumming could proceed uninterrupted. At Jamestown, the group went to the house of "old *tcımu's*." This destination had been selected because tcmu's possessed a power similar to that of James. After resumption of the ceremony at the new location, James asked *tcımu's* for dried salmon to eat. This had been a part of his spirit's instructions.

The head of the household in which dances were held provided food for the gathering, but the initiate defrayed the expenses in all cases, aided if necessary by his relatives. In the example above, Dixie Jim gave *tcımu's* many presents including a gun and blankets, and Sam Millet, one of the party, gave him a canoe.

Feasting was not a part of the ceremonial procedure prior to the last day. In fact, eating in the dance house was prohibited except in company with the initiate as outlined above. Laughing was also tabu, lest the patient become more ill.

The termination of the ceremony on the morning of the fifth day was marked by a great feast and the distribution of the presents. The principal food to be served was named by the novice as dictated by his spirit. The shaman, in turn, dispatched certain persons to a definite place where the raw food would be found. Regardless of whom was sent, or the nature of the product, it was found at the point indicated and obtained without difficulty.

During the preceding days, presents had been accumulating in some depository outside the dance house. These were supplied by the dancers, and others if they desired, but particularly by the initiate and his relatives. When the food was ready for the feast, all of the dancers, with the exception of a few of the younger ones, left to return with the presents. Those remaining did so to continue the singing. At the depository the shaman gave each person the article that he was to carry inside, and designated his place in the line. When all was ready, the procession re-entered the dance house, each person dancing, singing and conspicuously displaying the article he carried. It was necessary that the novice be able to see clearly, from his [85] position opposite the door, each of the presents. After the procession had encircled the fires five Limes, the presents were hung on the poles previously placed across the room for the purpose.

In the meantime, the food had been brought in and the feast followed. The novice ate from his bed ; he did not arise until the guests had disbanded.

---

[13] See the Quest.

After the meal, the presents were distributed by someone named by the initiate. The articles were removed from the poles one at a time and the name of a guest was called. The recipient walked over to receive the present. The last article remaining was taken by the distributor. Those of high social position, shamans, good dancers, and aides of the initiate, were given the best presents, but the distribution seems to have been fairly democratic.

Following the presentation, the novice started his song and all joined and danced for a few moments. With this finale, the ceremony was officially ended and he novice arose from his bed. However, guests often remained for several days of informal visiting and singing.

Batons or power sticks were stored after the dance, except the more elaborateness ones which were kept upon display. Sometimes, they were used to beat an accompaniment to informal family spirit singing. There were no restrictions upon the use of the common power sticks subsequent to the initiation. They might be used by anyone with spirit power.

Informal spirit singing was not limited to the winter ceremonial season. When man was ill or in dire need of help of any kind, he would sing and "wish" for his guardian spirit to come. When Sam Millet was fatally ill, he sang and tried to bring his spirit to him, "but it wouldn't come near."

SHAMANISM

Shamanistic power was obtained by the guardian spirit quest in a manner similar to any other power. However, mere reception of the power from the spirit did not alone lead to practice. It was necessary for the aspirant to go through period of training lasting about five years. As soon as it was felt by a practicing shaman that, a young person had acquired the proper power and aspired to become a doctor, he was taken in charge for training. The details of the training are quite known except that the student accompanied his instructor when the latter attended patients. Gradually the novice was permitted to take part in the treatments, until he finally performed alone. For a period then he handled treatments alone but always with his mentor in attendance. During this period he received no pay. When he was judged ready to practice alone an initiation was held at the next winter dance. At this time the persons who had been cured by the new shaman claimed his abilities. The initiate danced and sang his spirit songs, and took his place with the other shamans.

Apparently the training period came after the initial spirit return.[14] Whereas initiation was held immediately for one with ordinary power, it seems to have been deferred for the shamanistic neophyte. Or perhaps two somewhat similar ceremonies [86] were held, one at the beginning and one after the training period. This seems to have been the arrangement in at least some instances.

Informants claimed that the mentor received no pay for his services. "It was an honor!" But it seems probable that he at least received some compensation from the patients of the novice during the period when the latter received no pay.

All shamans were general practitioners, but some were better able to treat certain diseases because of the characteristics of their tutelaries. Others built up reputations of

---

[14] See the spirit dance.

proficiency in specific circumstances. Child-birth was one of these cases.

When a shaman was needed a messenger was sent, always with presents, to request aid. If no initial gifts were offered the shaman seldom accepted the call. If the presents were judged sufficient the shaman returned with the messenger. He took no paraphernalia with him.

Upon arrival at the patient's house the shaman was presented with food. When he had finished eating he went to the patient's bedside, sat down, and invited those who desired to sing to join him. The audience gathered at the bedside, bringing poles to be used in beating time on the floor or ceiling."[15] The shaman started singing and others immediately joined, drumming with the sticks. After two or three songs the shaman announced that he had diagnosed the trouble. The patient was not questioned, nor did the shaman touch the sick man during diagnosis.

Illness was considered the result of the intrusion of a foreign object, either inadvertently or through the agency of a malignant shaman, soul loss, or natural causes. The last category was not subject to shamanistic treatment.[16] If the diagnosis indicated an intrusive object the treatment was by rubbing, aspersion, drawing out with the hands, or sucking. Where no malicious cause was indicated one or more of the first three methods was used. If witchcraft were involved, sucking was the only adequate treatment. If the soul were lost it was sought by clairvoyant methods.

When the object was removed by drawing the hands over the patient's body, then clasping them together, the "sickness" so removed was invisible. Disposal was accomplished merely by rubbing the hands together, then throwing the arms in the air. But if sucking were required the removal was more difficult and disposal more involved. No tube was used in the procedure; the mouth was placed directly against the patient's body. This was usually in the region of the stomach. Treatment was completed only with the removal of some concrete object such as a piece of bone, or often a bit of blood. After showing the audience that which had been removed, the shaman asked what disposal should be made of it. The reply was, "Drown him," "Burn him," or perhaps, "Shoot him." If drowning were requested the object was immersed in water; if burning, it was thrown in the fire; if shooting, it was pressed on the point of an arrow.

Sometimes the shaman failed in the attempted removal. He could only succeed if his power were stronger than that of the shaman causing the affliction. In such an event a second shaman was called. The first remained but did not assist the newcomer. [87]

When a person was near death from the effects of witchcraft he became possessed and talked as if he were the responsible shaman. "I'm so-and-so; I'm so-and-so," he cried; "you can't put me down. I'm sorry for you but it's your own fault. I'll win the fight."

Such revelation often led to the death of the shaman thus indicated at the hands of the relatives of the patient if the latter died. Feuds sometimes started in this way but public

---

[15] Cf. p. 81; Dunn, pp. 118 f.
[16] Cf. Swan, p. 182.

opinion was usually on the side of the avengers.[17]

Shamans were occasionally hired to inflict witchcraft but the price charged was always very high and only the strongest of practitioners were willing to accept the responsibility.

A shaman sometimes dreamed of the procedure necessary to effect a cure, especially for children. The subject of the dream was not always a patient of the shaman. In such a case he made public the identity of the person indicated so that the latter might hear of the event and solicit his services. Thus while Emma Luscier was suffering from illness as an infant a shaman (qwaisi') dreamed that she would not recover unless she were placed in an old style cradle. Emma's father heard of this through a third person and called the doctor immediately. Upon his arrival the doctor was thanked profusely and led to the patient. He picked up the child, talked to her about the cradle she "wanted," and promised to make it the next day. When the cradle was ready he placed the child in it and secured the head board in place. (The board was later removed by Emma's paternal aunt who was opposed to the practice.) The parents then provided a small feast for the visitors that had assembled. Gifts were presented, not only to the shaman, but to all who had held the child during her illness.

At another time when Emma was ill a shaman dreamed that piercing her ears would lead to recovery. In a circuitous fashion Emma's father heard of the dream and sent for the doctor. Guests were invited at the same time. When the doctor appeared he reiterated his vision and announced that the patient would have died very soon without the piercing but as a result of it she would live to a very old age. The guests had arrived early in the morning. While they ate breakfast the shaman went to the river to swim. Upon returning he proceeded to his task immediately, using a hardwood needle to make holes around the rim and in the lobe of each ear. The holes were kept open with thongs of buckskin. The shaman and guests remained for two or three days of informal visiting, dancing and singing. Upon departure all guests received small presents. The shaman was given a gun, a blanket, and another article or two.

Shamans received payment whether a cure was effected or not, but the amount charged was greater in the case of a cure. The doctor made his own demands; this was in addition to the initial presents. Most shamans were quite rich but they were expected to give large presents at the winter dances.

The shaman was not served by a spokesman. Some shamans smoked before and during the treatment but this was not general. Children were kept away while the shaman practiced, lest they become ill. The aid of the shaman was often solicited in finding lost articles or persons. [88] Female shamans were said to be as numerous as male.

Dr. Boas furnishes a full and rich account of the elaborate shamanistic procedure when illness was diagnosed as soul loss.[18] For its supplementary worth I present below the data given by my informants:

If a person became badly frightened his soul departed and illness resulted, of a general and diffuse nature. Sometimes the soul could be found and returned to the patient by a single

---

[17] Cf. Scouler, pp. 165 f.

[18] Boas, *op. cit.*, pp. 205-10.

doctor but more often several were required. In this case they worked together and the treatment took on the aspect of a ceremony.

Such treatment occurred not at the bedside but in the middle of the room. The assisting singers formed a large circle around the shamans. All sang after the leadership of the doctors who began their individual songs, one after another. As before, the assistant singers beat time with sticks. Soon the shamans began to peer into space and to walk about, apparently at random. They were seeking the lost soul. They followed its trail from place to place on this earth. They addressed the soul, hoping it would hear and requested it to return by urging that it was not yet time to go to the land of the dead. Sometimes the spirit was found not far away, in which case it was easy to turn it around and start it back toward the patient.

The stronger doctors "saw better" than the others. From time to time they conferred together and announced their findings to the audience.

The shamans often came near the land of the dead. The ground became sandy and the footsteps of the soul were easy to follow. Presently a great river was reached where a canoe awaited. This was the canoe that souls used to reach the other world. If the river had already been crossed there was no hope of bringing the soul back and the patient invariably died. The shamans could not use the canoe to continue the pursuit because return would have been equally impossible for them, once the river was crossed. But though the soul were found on the very banks of the stream, return was yet possible if the shamans were strong enough. Even if it had drunk water from the river it might be captured but in such a case the face of the patient became paralyzed. The shamans encircled the soul and "gathered it in," the strongest one clasping it in his hands. It felt like a pulsing or beating in his hands. The audience was addressed and success was announced, whereupon the soul was "rubbed back" into the patient's body. Immediately a change could be seen. Very soon he completely recovered.

Sometimes the shamans followed false clues in the search. A group of doctors once thought they were following a large herd of elk which had lured away the soul of the patient, a great hunter. They saw the huge eyes of the elk shining in the dark. But when they approached closer they found it was a lone snail. Later they followed a clue that led only to a pile of rotten wood. In this case success was never achieved; the patient, Alek Smith, died.

The soul hunting ritual always lasted the entire night. The soul could not be returned to the patient until dawn. If it were found earlier it was held by the shaman until the proper time. In the meantime the doctors conferred, then suddenly someone was pointed out and told that his soul had departed. The person indicated [89] then begged that a search be made and offered presents to the practitioner, whereupon a similar ceremony was enacted.

Predictions of coming events were sometimes made by the shamans during he search. At one time, about 1875, Dr. Jack (*tsaa'x̱*) spoke out, saying, "I feel sorry for the oysters; I feel sorry for the people. All the oysters will die. The people will have to leave this country. The people will have to leave or they will die. There will be nothing to eat. A great storm will come; all the oysters will be killed." Later in the winter, while the tide was out, the mud flats froze and killed all the oysters. They were very scarce for the next thirty years.

The shaman who participated in the search for a soul was well rewarded, but the procedure was not without its dangers. A weak shaman might mistake the soul of another for that of his patient, in which event he would suffer loss of his own soul.

THE SECRET SOCIETY

Only one order of the Northwest Coast secret society[19] reached the Chinook. Even this arrived at a very late date. Mrs. Bertrand explained that Concomly had purchased a slave from one of the northern groups (Stikine ?) for the specific purpose of learning the form of the society.[20] Knowledge of the society much more probably reached the Chinook via the Quinault, where a two-order organization was present,[21] but Mrs. Bertrand's statement is significant as a reflection of native recognition of the recency of the society.

The society, despite its lack of age, was well integrated with guardian spirit practices. The strength of the latter may have speeded the process of amalgamation. The society could not have come to the Chinook so integrated for such organization was not at all characteristic of the Quinault, to say nothing of groups further north.

Eligibility to membership depended upon two factors, upper class status and the possession of a "secret society guardian spirit." The latter phrasing merely implied spirit instruction to join the society plus the conveyance of the necessary type of power. Such power was obtained in exactly the same fashion as any other.[22] It consisted of the ability to inflict self-torture, followed by miraculous recovery. Spirits became somewhat specific, however, with black bear foremost and cougar and skunk secondary. When a boy returned from a spirit quest in which he obtained "secret society power" he confided the fact to his mentor but to no one else.[23] For three days the boy was supposed to sleep, after which the mentor arranged a feast of celebration, which friends and relatives attended, at which time public announcement was made that the lad had acquired power which would lead to initiation in the secret society at a later time. This was not an elaborate affair; it lasted but one day. The object was to make known and celebrate the important acquisition [90] which the boy had made. The lad himself participated in the feast,[24] which broke the fast he had maintained during the quest.

At this time the boy was assigned for training to some member of the secret society with similar power. For several years the novice received informal instruction. During the same period he accumulated with the help of his parents the property necessary for his formal initiation, and even more important, the payment due his mentor for the period of tutelage. The latter was the closest approach to an initiation fee. In some cases the amount demanded was small but more often it imposed a considerable burden on the initiate. Mrs. Bertrand suggested an equivalence of two hundred dollars as an average.

---

[19] Cf. Gunther, *Klallam,* pp. 281-88; Olson, *Quinault,* pp. 120-23.

[20] Of course a slave could not have known the details of the society unless he had formerly been an upperclassman.

[21] Olson, *loc. cit.*

[22] See the quest.

[23] Cf. p. 80.

[24] Cf. the quest and the spirit dance.

Prior to the public initiation a number of private rehearsals before society members was held. If the boy failed to perform properly he was further instructed, made to fast in order that he might recall spirit injunctions and obtain enlightenment on the cause of his failures. Then another trial was held. When success was achieved the public performance was arranged. The externals of this affair were identical with the guardian spirit initiation described above. The dance house was provided with a partition in one end behind which the novice and his attendants remained.   No uninitiated person was allowed in this room under any circumstances. During the first two days the initiate did not appear; spirit singing and dancing in the outer room occupied guests during this period.

On the evening of the second day the initiate appeared dressed only in a breech cloth. Accompanying him were the attendants, dressed in the skins of various animals. The novice danced, jumped, and imitated his spirit as he moved with swift motions around the room. The particular color of his performance was determined by his specific power. At the initiation of Concomly's son (grandson ?) about 1860, which was witnessed by Mrs. Bertrand, he appeared dramatically with blood flowing from his mouth. His spirit being black bear, he walked on all fours and imitated the actions of a wounded bear. He moved from one to another of the "strong ones" showing them that he actually was wounded. Then suddenly he clapped his hands before his mouth, removed them, and the bleeding was gone.

In other cases the performer, with power derived from a "burst of flame," walked over live coals or "stood still in the middle of the fire." Sometimes the initiate slashed his arms or body while the others watched, then performed an instantaneous self-cure. Dunn writes of seeing many Clatsop showing scars, sometimes several in number, where a dagger had been plunged through the folds of skin on the stomach. He furthermore witnessed the act.[25]

After the performance the initiate ran to the nearest body of water, plunged in, and then returned to the inner room where he was expected to sleep until the next night's appearance. The performances continued for three nights, after which ordinary spirit singing and dancing were resumed for a day or two. The ceremony was terminated with a feast but apparently without distribution of presents. [91]

For the duration of the ceremony the novice observed a complete fast. Upon its termination he absented himself from community life for several days or as long as a month, during which he wandered alone along the beach and through the woods. Thereafter his place in the society was stable; the achievement of distinction within the group depended upon the same factors of character and initiative that operated on the outside.

Sometimes more than one novice was initiated to the society at the same time. This did not change the form of the ceremony; the individuals merely performed concurrently. But these ceremonies of joint admission did not occur often. Only a small percentage of the population were members of the society.

Ceremonies occasionally were held for purposes other than initiation. In one instance an enmity existed between two members of the society. A gathering was arranged wherein one was expected to prove his superiority over the other and thus end the friction. One of the

---

[25] Dunn, p. 128.

pair was a man, the other a woman. The former had been quite generally suspected of witchcraft. He possessed "knife power" and caused others to become wounded. The woman's power, which permitted her to find lost or hidden objects, was phrased as hunting power and symbolized by a bow and arrow. She had not yet been a victim of the man's witchcraft but clairvoyant powers enabled her to divine his intentions. At the ceremony he hid his knife, with the point directed toward her, while she was in the inner room. She then danced out with bow and arrow in hand in imitation of a hunter. She began to search for objects in the room, all the while singing that her bow and arrows were much further-reaching in their power than his knife. An intentionally hidden object being much more difficult to find than one accidentally lost, she first recovered various articles of the latter nature. But soon the knife was brought to light and thrust into a board of the wall. The woman then shot at it with her bow and arrows, hitting it time after time without an exception. Next she retired to the inner room while the knife was again hidden, this time in the sand by the fire. The woman reappeared wearing a blindfold. Without removing it she turned toward the fire and shot the knife out of the sand. Again it was hidden, during her absence, and this time she lay flat on the floor while shooting, but hit the knife nevertheless. Under such disgrace the man gave up entirely and lost his power "as usually happened when one was publicly humiliated."

There is much that is instructive in this account but little that might not well have fitted into the traditional spirit dance performances. The presence of a woman in the secret society, here indicated, was not anomalous. Women were quite as eligible as men though decidedly in the minority.

Mrs. Bertrand spoke very vaguely of secret society performances in which "the experiences of people long ago" were dramatized. Scenes were reenacted in pantomime and songs were sung in which the audience joined. Masks were worn by the actors, who were quite numerous. Other accessories included spears and arrows. This resembles somewhat the shamanistic performance in which lost souls were sought. But it is doubtful that Mrs. Bertrand would have confused the shamans with these "actor people." More specific statements could not be elicited. [92] Mrs. Riggs, the interpreter, was unable to help. Masks were likewise worn, Mrs. Bertrand asserted, at the society initiations. She was unable to furnish any details of form, but stated that they represented guardian spirits.

The audience of the society was unrestricted; any one who wished might attend the performances. Sometimes the exhibitions were outdoors with the audience arranged in a semicircle. In such case the entire house was restricted to members.

The society was well represented over Lower Chinook territory. Concomly's son's initiation took place at a Clatsop town near present Astoria; the power contest recounted above occurred near Bay Center; one group centered opposite Astoria, and another at the mouth of the Naselle river. Performances were often attended by visitors from Quilleute and Chehalis; the Quinault were not welcome.

The Chinookan name for the secret society was not remembered, but it was associated with the Nutka term *ło'kwali*.

FEASTING AND GIFT-GIVING

Among the Lower Chinook the complex known as the potlatch existed only in the most superficial sense. Formal invitation of guests and the familiar ceremonial approach were the most specific features related to the elaborate secular affairs of the more northern coast. All of the signification of the typical potlatch was absent. Presents were distributed but return was in no sense obligatory, to say nothing of return with interest. If the supply of gifts were limited the upperclassmen were favored, but if there were plenty all received share and share alike![1] Songs were sung but they were exclusively guardian spirit songs; wealth songs were wholly unknown. Leadership in the singing and dancing was limited to those with spirit power; wealth or social status was no substitute. Ceremonial grouping was based on village affiliation, not wealth or lineage. Demonstration of superiority by the hosts and the shaming of guests was limited to such neutral demonstrations as grossness of appetite, and even here the hosts dared not go too far.

Indeed, there exists a real question as to whether it is justifiable to segregate under a separate term those practices having to do with feasting and gift-giving, especially when that term is one as fraught with meaning as the word potlatch. Linguistic evidence is of little assistance because of the stock difference between the Chinook and all the peoples to the north. Boas used the term potlatch but it must be remembered that this is a Chinook jargon word with little specific meaning in native speech {= "to give, giving"} and that Boas conversed with Charles Cultee, his informant, only in Chinook jargon.[2] Both Mrs. Luscier and Mrs. Bertrand used the term with ease, but they applied it to the spirit dance, the secret society, the puberty ceremony, and secular feasting with indifference. In Boas' texts the word is used in connection with the puberty ceremony also. It seems to refer to any celebration with feasting and gift-giving.

A further bit of evidence, which should not receive too much weight because of its negative nature, is this: The early writers consistently fail to mention the potlatch either by name or description. And yet reference is repeatedly found in the comparable literature for, say, Puget Sound.

With this caution we may proceed to a description of the practices in question. A summary of Boas' excellent account will furnish a basis:

> Four, five, or six messengers are sent to invite the guests, including one who has a guardian spirit. When people hear the latter singing they know they are to be invited. The messengers proceed from town to town, then return. Those invited from furthest away start first; those nearer wait for them, so that all may arrive at the same time. When they near the destination they put their canoes side by side and lay planks across. Upon these they dance. Their faces are painted red, their hair is strewn with down. Women wear dentalia, ear and hair ornaments, and necklaces. Men wear head ornaments and blacken their faces. Shamans carry batons. They sing, and finally land. They tell a woman she is to be head dancer; she

---

[1] Boas, *Chinook Texts,* pp. 269.

[2] Idem, *p. 6.*

replies that she dare not. A good dancer, man or woman, is made head dancer. Now they enter the house dancing. When a woman bends her head while dancing, another one raises it and is paid. A person out of rhythm must sit at the side. All those who have guardian spirits sing. The people of one town finish dancing; another town begins. Small towns dance together. [94]

If the host has too little food, two youths are sent to seek aid of relatives. They all come, bringing food and dancing on the canoes. When they bring dry salmon, five men hold it in their mouths while they enter dancing. When they bring roots, five men carry them on their backs as they enter dancing.

After they dance five days they receive presents. One man is asked to stand near the host to name the people. First he names a chief of one town. When the host is liberal, he gives the man who calls out names a blanket or long dentalia. After one town is finished, another one receives presents. If a present is dragged the man is called back. Both men and women receive presents. Women receive each a fathom of short dentalia. Only men are given long dentalia. Common men receive short dentalia. If a chief has many dentalia, then every one receives two fathoms of short dentalia.[3]

Emma Luscier's account agreed in all details with this description, except that she did not mention the grouping by villages and stated that those who brought the most food received the largest gifts. Also, she suggested that all guests brought food when they first appeared. It would seem that if the Chinook had any feeling for insult, those asked only in case more food was needed would have resented it.

The visitors arranged to arrive in the late afternoon. One representative of the host was sent to receive them at the beach. All others of the host's family and local guests remained indoors and silent until after the guests had entered and begun to dance. Then all joined in the activities. Dancing proceeded for a short while. In the meantime men of the local village were busy preparing food for the ensuing meal. The cooking was done on the outside or in a neighboring house. Food brought by the guests had been left outside for the purpose. At the same time young men of the village were engaged in beaching and covering the canoes of the visitors and in putting away the baggage they had brought along.

When the meal was ready special mats were laid down in the dance house and the food was brought in and served. When all had finished eating, the utensils and mats were removed and dancing was resumed. A dance was begun by an individual starting to sing his spirit song. After a moment others joined the song, its owner began to dance and others followed. A dance lasted several minutes, followed by a brief intermission until some other person began to sing.

Dances lasted most of the night; the days were given over to sleeping, gambling and visiting. As many visitors as possible slept in the dance house, which was simply the house of the host. Others were accommodated by friends and villagers living nearby. Three meals were served each day; all were of about the same size. It is uncertain whether meals were served at night or not, but a person might ask for food at any time he desired. Such requests were somewhat formalized; when one requested food, all were served.

---

[3] *Idem,* pp. 268 f.

Upon one occasion (at *qwatsa'mts* about 1880; hostess was *ka•'alas*) the local villagers attempted to outdo the visitors, the Clatsop, in an eating bout. Immediately after the evening meal a canoe was brought in, two large rocks were placed in the bottom, and then it was half filled with salmon eggs. Thereupon the visitors were invited to start eating. The Clatsop did their best but could only reduce the quantity sufficiently to expose the tops of the rocks. The hosts then began and ate until the eggs were almost gone, a much larger quantity than their opponents had [95] consumed. Then they chided the Clatsop for their small appetites. This angered a visiting shaman (asxaia'xan). He retorted that they could hardly be expected to show their appetites just after a large meal. Furthermore, he threatened to "poison" the eggs and split the canoe wide open. At this his friends rushed to him and begged him not to start any trouble. He was finally dissuaded and left the dance house. Then the hosts ate the remaining eggs and the young men lifted the canoe high above their heads while exclaiming over the victory.

On the fifth morning the presents were hung over an elevated pole in the dance house. At this time the leading men among the guests formally thanked the hosts for their hospitality. The gifts were thereupon distributed, the guests being called in order of their importance. The man selected to hand out the articles was a relative of the host. Every person received something; those most generous in bringing food were particularly favored. No great preference was shown for chiefs. With the end of the distribution, the guests departed for home.

All relatives of the host ordinarily aided him in amassing the presents.

"Potlatches" were held in summer or fall, never in winter since good weather was desired. The last one at Bay Center was about 1890; the last on the Columbia was ten or more years before.

Not all such affairs were of five days duration or of the magnitude implied here. Feasting and gift-giving on a small scale often accompanied ceremonies such as those at puberty and marriage. Indeed, there seems to have been a wide latitude of combination.

The question arises: why segregate these practices from the guardian spirit performances, since the most specialized feature was spirit singing and dancing? The answer is two-fold: First, the Chinook themselves made a distinction. They seemed to feel that this was a basic and generalized pattern of social activity, a framework into which might be fitted any specialized or distinctly categorized procedure. This framework was not essential to the integrity of certain specific practices; as a result the aspects were separable, producing a false impression of analogy. Thus the guardian spirit dance was distinctly fitted into the framework, so well fitted, indeed, that it had become virtually inseparable. But to call one a function or analogue of the other would do violence to native theory.

Objective differences constitute the second factor. The guardian spirit dance was invariably held during the winter season. This was the time of spirit visitation, initiations and shamanistic performances. The "potlatch" was held in summer or fall and none of these features entered into it. Yet we still have to account for the guardian spirit nature of the songs. It may be suggested that these songs had in some way come to serve a double function. With spirit visitation they furnished the core of the sacred performances of the winter season. Without these visitations they served, in the absence of any other cycle, as purely social songs constituting a content adaptable to the groundwork of feasting and gift-giving. Adequate interpretation would demand a consideration of historical factors. Especially would this be so since the Chinook were exposed both to the area of the typical potlatch and to the Plateau with its highly integrated complex of the spirit dance together with feasting and gift-giving. [96]

DIVERSIONS

GAMES AND GAMBLING

Most popular of all games among men was that played with discs of wood or bone which were concealed in shredded cedar bark while being manipulated, then thrown out on a mat. Swan describes the game as follows:

A mat is first placed on the floor, with the centre raised up so as to form a small ridge, which is kept in its place by four wooden pins stuck through the mat into the ground. Two persons play at this game, who are seated at each end of the mat. Each player has ten discs of wood, two inches in diameter, and a little over an eighth of an inch thick, resembling the men used in playing backgammon, but much larger. The only distinguishing feature about these men, or wheels, is the different manner the edges are colored. There are but two pieces of value; one has the edge blackened entirely round, and the other is perfectly plain, while the others have different quantities of color on them, varying from the black to the white. These discs are then enclosed in a quantity of the inner bark of the cedar, pounded very fine, and called tupsoe. The player, after twisting and shuffling them up in all sorts of forms, separates them into two equal parts, both being enveloped in the tupsoe. These are then rapidly moved about on the mat from side to side, the other player keeping his eyes most intently fixed upon them all the time. He has bet either on the black or the white one, and now, to win, has to point out which of the two parcels contains it. As soon as he makes his selection, which is done by a gesture of his hand, the parcel is opened, and each piece is rolled down the mat to the ridge in the centre. He can thus see the edges of all, and he knows whether he has lost or won. They will play at this game sometimes for weeks, particularly during the winter season, only leaving off to sleep a little, or eat.[1]

Swan limits the participants to two but Ross states that six persons took part, three on a side.[2]

The stick game was also played but apparently less extensively. Both men and women participated. Two pairs of bones were used, one of each pair being marked with a narrow band tied around the middle. Sections of bear or deer bone of fairly small size served. Twelve counters were employed. Short sticks were used to beat on a board as an accompaniment to

---

[1] Swan, pp. 157 f.
[2] Cf. Boas, *Chinook Texts,* p. 220; Ross, pp. 90 f.; Wilkes, vol. 5, p. 117.

the singing.

Another game, often played by inter-village groups, consisted of hiding one or two small objects, such as pieces of bone, seeds, or pebbles, in first one hand and then another. These were thrown back and forth with such dexterity that the guessers found it difficult to follow the movements. When the objects were finally placed, the player held forth his clenched hands and the guesser touched one or the other. The opposing players were arranged in two rows facing each other. Players alternated in holding the objects, and first one and then another of the opponents attempted to guess correctly. The objects shifted sides when the guess was successful. Singing and beating with sticks accompanied the playing as in the preceding game.[3]

The favorite game among women was that played with dice made with beaver teeth. Four teeth with distinctive markings were employed. They were shaken in [97] the hands, then thrown on a mat and the count reckoned. Only two women participated.[4]

The games above were accompanied by considerable betting but several games were played for sport alone. These included the hoop and pole and shinny. The latter was often played as an inter-village game. Only men took part. The ball was a knot of yew wood; the sticks were also of yew. Douglas mentions a sport in which the object was to shoot arrows through six-inch hoops of grass as they were thrown in the air.[5]

Several laughing games were played. In one of these each side stood behind two piles of sand spaced about a hundred feet. One side was made up of girls, the other of boys. Sticks were erected in the sand piles and each side dared the other to come and take the marker. As one side started out the other jeered and laughed, trying to make those approaching laugh. If they succeeded the losers had to retire behind their sand pile and the others came forward.

Swimming, jumping, and foot races were popular pastimes of children. Swan provides a number of interesting sidelights on children's activities:

> The boys were fond of making canoes either from flags, which were twisted so as to form a sort of boat, or from chips, on which they would hoist a leaf for a sail, and start them off on voyages down the creek. Sometimes a lad with more ingenuity than the rest would carve out a pretty model of a canoe from a cedar stick; and I have seen boys, with little canoes which they had made, scarce three feet long, fearlessly paddle about the water in these little cockles, which seemed ready at any moment to sink.

> Sometimes the boys would catch a lot of minnows, and then the girls would join them, and, having made a little fire and a miniature rack for smoking fish, would imitate the manner of curing salmon, which, when done, were served up as a repast. The girls were very fond of making rag babies and dressing up clam-shells like children.[6]

---

[3] Cf. Swan, p. 158; Thwaites, vol. 3, pp. 274 f.; *idem*, vol. 4, pp. 37-39; Wilkes, vol. 5, p. 117.

[4] *Cf.* Ross, p. 93; Swan, p. 158.

[5] Douglas, p. 261.

[6] Swan, pp. 198 f.

SMOKING

A native species of tobacco was planted and cultivated by the Chinook The authority for this statement is none less than the botanist Douglas, who writes:

"The *Nicotiana* is never sowed by the Indians near the villages lest it should be pulled and used before it comes to perfect maturity; they select for its cultivation an open place in the wood, where they burn a dead tree or stump, and strewing ashes over the ground, plant the tobacco there." An informant explained to him that the wood ashes invariably made the tobacco grow very large.[7]

Kinnikinnick for smoking was made by crumbling dried leaves of bearberry (*Arctostaphylos uva-ursi*).

Smoke was invariably swallowed, as indicated by Lewis and Clark:

"The Clatsops, Chinooks and others inhabiting the coast and the country in this neighborhood are excessively fond of smoking tobacco. In the act of smoking they appear to swallow it as they draw it from the pipe, and for many draughts together you will not perceive the smoke which they take from the pipe; in the same manner also [98] they inhale it in their lungs until they become surcharged with the vapor when they puff it out to a great distance through their nostrils and mouth.... "[8]

Broughton comments (1792) that "The inhabitants are universally addicted to smoking" and describes the pipe as the elbow variety with ornamented hardwood bowl and a stem of elderberry wood two feet long.[9]

---

[7] Douglas, pp. 269, 278.

[8] Thwaites, vol. 3, p. 322; cf. Douglas, pp. 254.

[9] Vancouver, vol. 2, p. 77.

COMMERCE

TRADE

A thorough-going occupation with commerce dominated Chinook life. Within the territory three great streams of travel fused. Coastwise travel from both the north and the south centered here. Traders from the interior using the great Columbia waterway necessarily looked upon the mouth of the river as the point where the riches of the coast might be obtained. The fourth route, less important than the other three, led from the interior of Washington through the Cascade passes. Other routes, of still lesser importance individually, were numerous; cumulatively they added significantly to the commercial importance of the mouth of the Columbia. Full advantage of these conditions was taken by the Chinook who became the middlemen in all transactions. But even more significant was the fact that there came to be concentrated here a store of goods from divers sources which was available to the occasional trader at any time. Furthermore, a slow infiltration of goods, passed from one people to another without great travel, constituted a great share of the stock possessed by the Chinook, and such variety and quantity was not to be found at any other locality within a large area. A still further factor was the richness of the Chinook habitat itself which allowed a greater production of economic goods than was necessary for local consumption.[1]

The selection of this point as the center of early fur trading activities was, merely a reflection of the commercial importance of the site in native life.[2] A further key to the extent of pre-Columbian trading activities is the Chinook jargon which apparently had its center of development here. This "unique and beautifully satisfactory means of communication between the speakers of a hundred or more mutually unintelligible Pacific Northwest languages"[3] seems to have been an aboriginal development largely in response to the needs of commerce.[4]

The Chinook gradually came to feel, it appears, that trade was an end in itself. At least it is certain that they took great satisfaction in driving a bargain. Lewis declares that "they are great hagglers in trade and if they conceive you anxious to purchase will be a whole day bargaining for a handful of roots.... I find that they invariably refuse the price first offered them and afterwards very frequently accept a smaller quantity of the same article."[5]

In evaluating commerce as an aspect of Chinook culture one must not overlook its prestige value. It permitted them to exert a widespread influence of a sort which did not often lead to conflict. It resulted in both the group and many of its members becoming known and discussed over a wide area,[6] whereas intervening peoples might be unknown and of no interest. It led to a high contempt for groups that [100] were "just poor people" (that is, had little to trade) and a consequent bolstering of their own self-confidence.

---

[1] See physical environment.

[2] The first American commercial settlement on the Pacific was that established here by the Astor enterprise.

[3] Jacobs, *Chinook Jargon,* p. 27.

[4] See the Lower Chinook and their neighbors.

[5] Thwaites, vol. 3, p. 311.

[6] Cf. p. 58.

The dentalium shell *(Dentalium pretiosum* Nuttall) was the standard medium of evaluation and exchange. It was itself an imported article, not being found south of the Strait of Juan de Fuca.[7] The degree to which monetary formalization had been carried is indicated by Ross:

> The circulating medium in use among these people is a small white shell called higua ... and may he found of all lengths, between three inches down to one-fourth of an inch, and increases or decreases in value according to the number required to make a fathom, by which measure they are invariably sold. Thirty to a fathom are held equal in value to three fathoms of forty, or four to fifty, and so on. So high are the higua prized, that I have seen six of 2½ inches long refused for a new gun. But of late, since the whites came among them, the beaver skin called enna, has been) added to the currency; so that, by these two articles, which form the medium of trade, all property is valued, and all exchange fixed and determined. An Indian, in buying an article, invariably asks ... how many higua? or, how many beaver skins is it?[8]

The sizes of the units in which goods were sold was also highly standardized and baskets serving as containers were conveyed in any transaction along with their contents. Such units are described in the section on basketry.[9]

From the Strait of Juan de Fuca came no item of greater importance than dentalia. The quantities of these shells imported by the Chinook must have been tremendous, for not only did they use a great quantity in the daily routine of trade, but they also furnished the bulk of the supply used in the southern Plateau and western Oregon. Though the shells of exceptional length maintained an exceptionally high market value, indicating their rarity, the price dropped rapidly for those of shorter length, reflecting a corresponding increase in quantity.

From Willapa Bay to the mouth of the river steadily flowed large quantities of dried shell-fish. These were arranged on sticks of salmonberry wood, each about two feet long. From the Kwalhiokwa the Willapa Bay people received furs of the larger animals and dried meat packed in tule bags. A portion of these goods was kept for home consumption but much of it found its way, along with the shell-fish, to the Columbia river. The bay people furnished the Kwalhiokwa with shell-fish likewise; and again, with goods first received from the Columbia. Home products of the Columbia, which were distributed in all directions, included dried salmon, pulverized salmon, dried sturgeon, dried smelt, dried seal meat, blubber, and canoes. Dried berries were also a local product but the river people probably received more of them from the bay and upriver than they supplied. All of the other products here named flowed in greater quantity away from the river than toward it. Some, especially blubber and canoes, were almost exclusively exports. The upriver groups brought, above all, wapato and camas to

---

[7] The Chinook explained that the people who gathered dentalia were very small and had tiny mouths. They gathered the dentalia for food, which they sucked out of the shells. Then the slaves strung the shells as a pastime.

[8] Ross, pp. 95 f. Cf. Franchère, pp. 244 f.

[9] *See basketry and matting.*

the coastal people. These foods were highly prized on the coast and were imported in great quantities. Other important westward-moving products included dressed elk and deer skins and dried meat. Interior [101] traders returned with dentalia, blubber, dried seal meat and shell-fish, and an occasional sea otter skin. Slaves moved in all directions, but less upriver than up and down the coast.[10]

Information concerning the market value of various products differs considerably, as might be expected since several periods are involved and because the supply of many products became rapidly depleted after the coming of the whites. Dunn states that forty dentalia to a fathom constituted a fixed standard of reference, and that shells measuring fifty to a fathom were worth little over half as much,[11] while Ross (see above) places the ratio at four to three and uses thirty to a fathom as point of reference. Mrs. Luscier furnished a different method of reckoning, with a standard of fifty beads to a string, the value being judged in terms of the number of beads in excess of a fathom. Henry writes that one dentalium was held equal in value to forty or more grains of large China beads, and that one fathom (what size shells ?) was equated to three Hudson's Bay blankets of the two and one-half point quality.[12] One fathom of the longest shells, according to Franchère, was worth ten beaver skins.[13] Mrs. Luscier stated that fifty shells measuring ten over a fathom was equal to a mountain goat wool blanket; or if twenty over a fathom, two such blankets. In turn, one goat wool blanket might be traded for one unit of pulverized dried salmon. One basket of ordinary dried salmon equalled several baskets of dried clams. Lewis and Clark bought two sea otter skins for a belt of blue beads[14] in 1806 but a few years later Henry states that two such skins were equal to forty-eight beavers.[15]

The quantity of goods on hand at any one time is indicated by the huge supply of furs taken away by Gray's vessel in 1792[16] and by the whole of the fur trade literature. Henry, for example, speaks of Concomly bringing a hundred large salmon on one day; followed by another hundred, together with ducks and geese, brought by Concomly's son a few days later.[17] White contact of course stimulated trade but there is no doubt but that it was extensively developed in wholly aboriginal times.

TRANSPORTATION

Without adequate transportation Chinook commerce could not have existed on so great a scale. But transportation played a large part in the daily lives of these people as well. With an expanse of several miles of water separating the north and south banks of the Columbia, and a

---

[10] Cf. Thwaites, vol. 3, pp. 208, 265, 293 f., 296 f., 338; vol. 4, pp. 6 f., 10 f., 200, 215.

[11] Dunn, p. 134.

[12] Coues, p. 753.

[13] Franchère, p. 245.

[14] 'Thwaites, vol. 3, p. 238.

[15] Couse, p. 753.

[16] *See* hunting.

[17] Coues, pp. 750, 768.

long bay bisecting the territory in the other direction. Water travel loomed all important.
Travel from any Chinook village to any other one was possible by water alone. To reach the
Willapa Bay villages from the Columbia river, however, would have necessitated crossing the
extremely dangerous Columbia bar and traveling far to the north before entering the bay (see
map, page 37). But this route was almost never taken though the canoes were perfectly [102]
capable of making it. Instead, a very short portage was made from the Columbia to the south
fork of the Naselle river, which permitted entering Willapa Bay after) but a brief trip.

The canoes of the Chinook were of several types (Figures 9, 10), each an admirable
solution of a special problem.[18] But unfortunately we have little information as the the details
of manufacture, use, and specialization. Lewis and Clark furnish the most extensive
descriptions:

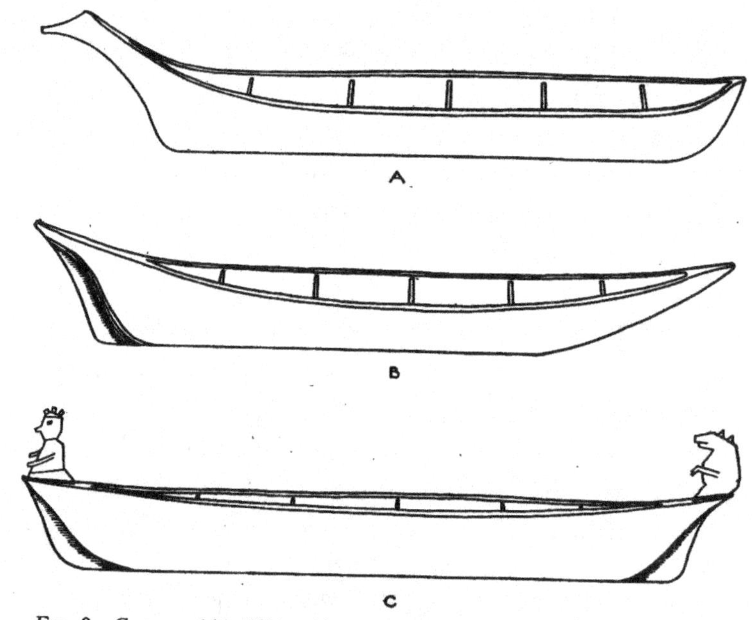

FIG. 9. Canoes. (A) "Chinook" or Nutka type; (B) Cutwater type;
(C) Double cutwater type, with raised figures. See text.

The canoes of the natives inhabiting the lower portion of the Columbia River [are
made] remarkably neat, light, and well adapted for riding high waves. I have seen
the natives near the coast riding waves with safety and apparently without concern
where I should have thought it impossible for any vessel of the same size to [have]
lived a minute. They are built of white cedar *[Thuja plicata]* ... but sometimes of the
fir *[Pseudolsuga mucronata]*. They are cut out of a solid stick of timber, the
gunwales at the upper edge fold over outwards and are about five-eighths of an
inch thick and four or five broad, and stand horizontally forming a kind of rim to the
canoe to prevent the water beating into it. They are all furnished with more or less
crossbars in proportion to the size of the canoe. These bars are round sticks about
half the size of a man's arm, which are inserted through holes made in either side of

____

[18] See Waterman and Coffin, p.15.

the canoe just below the rim of the gunwale and further secured with strings of way tape; these crossbars serve to lift and manage the canoe on land. When the natives land they invariably take their canoes on shore, unless they are heavily laden, and then even, if they remain all night, they discharge their loads and take their canoes on shore. Some of the large canoes are upwards of fifty feet long and will carry from eight to ten thousand pounds or from twenty to thirty persons and some of them, particularly on the sea coast, are waxed [oiled and pitched), painted and ornamented with curious images at bow and stern; those [103] images sometimes rise to the height of five feet; the pedestals on which these images are fixed are sometimes cut out of the solid stick with the canoe, and the imagery is formed of separate small pieces of timber firmly united with tenons and mortices ... When the natives are engaged in navigating their canoes one sits in the stern and steers with a paddle. The others sit by pairs and paddle over the gunwale next [to] them; they all kneel in the bottom of the canoe and sit on their feet.[19]

Franchère furnishes these remarks:

The bows terminate in a very elongated point, running out four or five feet from the water line. It constitutes a separate piece, very ingeniously attached, and serves to break the surf in landing, or the wave on a rough sea. In landing they put the canoe round, so as to strike the beach stern on. Their oars or paddles are made of ash, and are about five feet long, with a broad blade, in the shape of an inverted crescent, and a cross at the top, like the handle of a crutch.... All their canoes are painted red, and are fancifully decorated.[20]

In an attempt to isolate the fundamentally different canoe types a number of difficulties are encountered. Superficially five forms may be distinguished. The so-called "Chinook" or Nutka canoe of wide distribution on the coast of Washington and British Columbia[21] is recognizable here, but despite the name the canoe used by the Chinook varies considerably from the type. According to Olson this craft "is pointed at both ends, the prow projects upward and forward and, except on small canoes, is a separate piece. The stem is vertical and raised above the level of the gunwales, the upper portion in all larger canoes being a separate piece. The cross-section is angular, the bottom being almost flat."[22] The conformity of the Chinook variant (Figure 9, A) is reasonably close with the exception of the stem characteristics. This was undercut rather than straight and was not, at least ordinarily, surmounted by an extra piece. The Willapa Bay variant may have been more typical in this respect than the canoes of the Columbia.[23][23]

---

[19] Thwaites, vol 4, pp. 30 f., Cf. Ross, pp. 97 f.

[20] Franchère, pp. 246 f.

[21] See Olson, *Adze, Canoe and House Types,* pp. 19-22.

[22] *Idem,* p. 19.

[23] Swan pictures canoes outside a native house (see Plate 4) which correspond closely with the type. But Swan was quite well acquainted with the typical Nutka canoe, having purchased

The second type (Figure 9, B) varied from the preceding in that the undercut prow was replaced by a board type cutwater with vertical edge. This was an integral part, being shaped from the main log, but the sides were parallel and the thickness only about an inch. It varied in depth or projection from nine to eleven inches. The stem was sharply undercut.[24]

Each end of the third form (Figure 9, C) was provided with the vertical, narrow cutwater; otherwise the structural characteristics were similar to the second type. In addition, both prow and stern {of image canoe} were usually surmounted with large carved figures (as mentioned by Lewis and Clark in the passage above).[25] This is an unusual and exaggerated feature but substantial agreement is found in the descriptions of various early writers. For example, Ross states that the canoes were provided "with a human face or a white-headed eagle, as large as life, carved on the prow, and raised high in [104] front."[26] Thompson writes of three-foot projections above the gunwales, but more surprisingly, of over-decking extending ten feet back of the prow.[27]

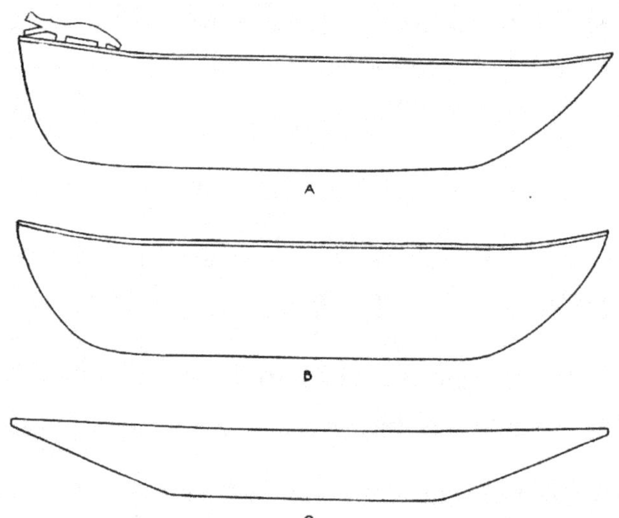

FIG. 10. Canoe profiles. (A) River canoe; (B) Sealing canoe; (C) Shovel nose canoe. (Compare Field Museum specimens 19860, 19861.)

The next type may be termed the hunting canoe. It occurred in two fairly distinct variants. The river form (Figure 10, A) was almost vertical at the prow but sharply undercut at the stem. The sealing form (Figure 10, B) was linearly more symmetrical, with both prow and stern undercut, and was wider amidships. This type is related to Swan's "71tz canoe."[28] Sometimes the prow was surmounted with a small, carved figure.

---

one from a Quinault (Swan, pp. 78 f.). Also, trade canoes may well have been present in the bay. Yet he does speak of separate stem pieces (p. 81) on local canoes.

[24] *Thwaites, vol. 4, pp. 31 f.*

[25] *Ibid.*

[26] Ross, pp. 97 f.

[27] Tyrrell, p. 507.

[28] Swan, p. 80.

In the shovel-nose (Figure 10, c), the final type, we have a form which is quite unambiguous. The Chinook took great care, however, even in the manufacture of this humble canoe, so that it varied from the comparable craft of adjacent peoples more in excellence of workmanship than in fundamental design.

Swan provides a description of the manufacture of a canoe which he witnessed:

The manufacture of a canoe is a work of great moment with these Indians. It is not every man among them that can make a canoe, but some are, like our white mechanics, more expert than their neighbors. A suitable tree is first selected, which in all cases is the cedar, and then cut down. This job was formerly a formidable one, as the tree was chipped around with stone chisels, after the fashion adopted by beavers, and looks as if gnawed off. At present, however, they understand the use of the axe, and many are expert choppers. When the tree is down, it is first stripped [105] of its bark, then cut off into the desired length, and the upper part split off with little wedges, till it is reduced to about two thirds the original height of the log. The bows and stern are then chopped into a rough shape, and enough cut out of the inside to lighten it so that it can be easily turned. When all is ready, the log is turned bottom up, and the Indian goes to work to fashion it out. This he does with no instrument of measurement but his eye, and so correct is that, that when he has done his hewing no one could detect the least defect. When the outside is formed and rough-hewn, the log is again turned, and the inside cut out with the axe. This operation was formerly done by fire, but the process was slow and tedious. During the chopping the Indian frequently ascertains the thickness of the sides by placing one hand on the outside and the other on the inside. The canoe is now again turned bottom up, and the whole smoothed off with a peculiar-shaped chisel, used something after the manner of a cooper's adze. This is a very tiresome job, and takes a long time. Then the inside is finished, and the canoe now has to be stretched into shape. It is first nearly filled with water, into which hot stones are thrown, and a fire at the same time of bark is built outside. This in a short time renders the wood so supple that the centre can be spread open at the top from six inches to a foot. This is kept in place by sticks or stretchers, similar to the method of a boat's thwarts. The ends of these stretchers are fastened by means of withes made from the taper ends of cedar limbs, twisted and used instead of cords. When all is finished, the water is emptied out, and then the stem and head-pieces are put on. These are carved from separate sticks, and are fastened on by means of withes and wooden pegs or tree-nails. After the inside is finished to the satisfaction of the maker, the canoe is again turned, and the charred part, occasioned by the bark fire, is rubbed with stones to make the bottom as smooth as possible, when the whole outside is painted over with a black mixture made of burned rushes and whale oil. The inside is also painted red with a mixture of red ochre and oil. The edges all round are studded with little shells, which arc the valve joint of the common snail...."[29]

---

[29] *Idem,* pp. 80-82.

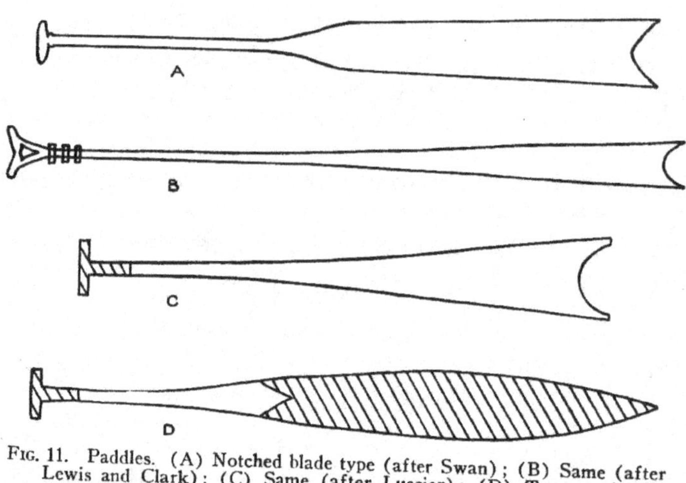

FIG. 11. Paddles. (A) Notched Made type (after Swan); (B) Same (after
Lewis and Clark); (C) Same (after Luscier); (D) Type used with shovel nose
canoe. Shading represents painting.

The inlaid shells characterized all of the finer canoes.[30] Gunwales were not always
integral; sometimes separate strips were applied. Harpoon rests and seine net frames were
provided. Mats or boards were laid on the bottom of the canoe to protect occupants from
water which might seep in. Mat sails were used but not ones of [106] plank. The sail was
supported by a mast set in a block type socket and steadied by halyards. It was erected only
when a tail wind was blowing.

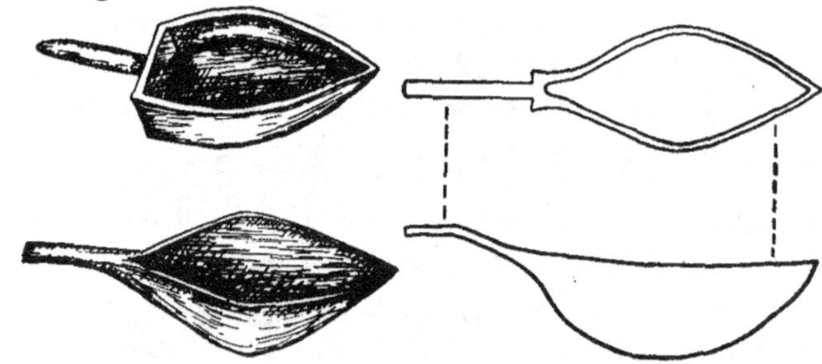

FIG. 12. Canoe bailers, three types.

Paddles were of two basic types, one with a notched blade (Figure 11, A, B, C) and
another with pointed blade (Figure 11, D). The latter was used with the shovel-nose canoe; the
notched type served for all others. Both were provided with crutch-type handles; sometimes
this was an integral part of the paddle, otherwise it was a separately applied piece. Handles
were occasionally wrapped with hide. Paddles were made of yew wood and finished by oiling,
charring or painting. The notched blade paddle varied considerably in proportions, as indicated
in the illustrations.

Bailers (Figure 12) were invariably of wood in a handled ladle shape but the exact shape
of these was subject to measurable variation also. Three typical variants are figured.

Canoe travel was the only mode of transportation utilized by the Chinook. Horses were
never accepted. Snow seldom fell[31] and snowshoes were unknown.

---

[30] *Cf.* Thwaites, vol. 4, p. 199; Gibbs, *Tribes of Western Washington, p. 216.*
[31] See Table 1.

FISHING AND SEALING

FISHING

Pushing was the principal economic pursuit of the Chinook, providing a plentiful supply of food both for consumption and for trade. The salmon was by far the most important fish but other species figured very prominently. Sturgeon (*Acipenser transmontanus),* a much favored fish, was doubly important because a single catch provided a huge supply of food. The steelhead trout (*Saimo gairdneri),* classed with the salmon by the natives, was taken in large numbers. (The candlefish or eulachon (*Thaleichthys pacificus)* and the smelt (*Spirinchus thaleichthys* ?) were in great demand for the oil they produced. The California herring (*Clupea pallasii)* and the California sardine (*Sardinia caerulea),* which were very abundant, were taken in great quantities with the herring rake.

Though the Pacific ocean formed the entire western boundary of the Chinook, little or no ocean fishing was done.[1] Willapa Bay and the Columbia river furnished far better fishing grounds; they were more productive, more accessible and less dangerous. The river was unsurpassed for salmon fishing; the bay produced a large percentage of the shellfish which formed so important a part of the economy. Sturgeon, candlefish, and herring were obtained with equal facility in either body of water.

Five species of salmon (*Oncorhynchus)* enter the Columbia river for spawning. The largest and most valuable is the chinook or king salmon (*0. tschawytscha).* The average weight is twenty-two pounds but the maximum size exceeds a hundred pounds. The flesh is commonly a deep red though sometimes it is white. Three runs occur in the Columbia: the first from January to March; the second and choicest, from May till early July; the last beginning in late July and continuing until early October. The blueback or sockeye salmon (*0. nerka)* enters the Columbia with the spring run of Chinook. This is a much smaller fish, averaging about five pounds and not exceeding twelve. The silver or coho salmon (0. *kisutch)* is not much larger on the average but sometimes reaches a weight of thirty pounds. This species runs from July until November but does not long remain near the mouth of the river. The humpback salmon (0. *gorbuscha) is* the smallest species, weighing from three to eleven pounds with an average of four pounds. This fish is not very abundant in the Columbia. The dog or chum salmon (0. *keta)* averages eight pounds in weight but attains a maximum of twice that. The run is late, occurring from middle August until late in November.

Steelhead trout are found in the Columbia river in greater abundance than anywhere else in their range. The flesh is of excellent quality and the size of the fish recommends it, the average being above ten pounds and the maximum about forty-five pounds.[2]

The most productive method of salmon fishing used by the Chinook was that using the sieve net (Plate 4). The nets were woven of twine made of imported nettle [108] (*Urtica lyallii),* Indian hemp, or spruce root fiber. These seines were straight webs using stick type floats of

---

[1] But cf. Franchère, p. 245 f.
[2] Cobb, pp. 6-11, 25.

cedar and round stone weights of about one pound each. The latter were grooved and attached with twisted withes of cedar woven to the base-rope of the net. Seines were sometimes of huge size, varying from one to six hundred feet in length and from seven to sixteen feet in width. A small seine was operated by three men. At high water, just before the tide began to ebb, two of the fishermen coiled the net into a frame which rested on the gunwales at the stern of the canoe. They then paddled upstream, staying near the shore where the current was not strong. At a selected point the canoemen threw a towline, with a wooden float attached, to the third fisherman who was stationed at the proper point on shore. The canoemen now paddled quickly into the current of the stream, amplified by the ebbing tide, and let out the net as they moved along. When all the net was out the attached towline was fastened to the canoe and the fishermen paddled ashore. During this procedure the canoe drifted downstream about an eighth of a mile, the man on shore walking apace while carrying the towline he had received. The three fishermen, all now on shore, carefully hauled in the seine taking care that none of the ensnared fish could jump over before being clubbed. Considerable skill was required to accomplish this. An exceptional haul brought in a hundred fish; an average was perhaps forty. The larger seines required more than three men to handle them.[3]

Salmon were also taken with a conical bag net carried between two canoes. More commonly, however, this type of net was used for sturgeon. They were designed to take but one of these huge fish at a time. At the lower end or point of the bag a lure was often attached, consisting of some bright object such as a bunch of feathers. A small straight web was also used for sturgeon.

A second method of taking salmon utilized dams or weirs across the small streams emptying into the Columbia. When dams were used they were built diagonally across the stream and consisted of rocks, brush, and earth. In the larger streams weirs were placed straight across. Stakes driven in the stream bed provided support for removable weir fencing woven of small willow withes. If the stream were used for transportation a canoe gate was provided in the form of a moveable section. With dams and weirs small auxiliary traps were sometimes used but more often the impediment merely served to concentrate the fish so that they might more easily be taken with dip nets or spear. Spear staging was occasionally built in connection with the weir but more often the spearing was done from the banks or by wading in.

Spearing salmon from canoes was a third important means of obtaining these fish. The canoe was allowed to drift downstream while the fisherman watched intently for the salmon. The spear he used was either single or double pronged, the latter more commonly.

The two-pronged spear consisted of a fir shaft fourteen to eighteen feet in length to which were fastened the diverging foreshafts which held the points. Each fore-shaft was about twelve inches long. The three pieces were bevelled at the point of juncture so that the proper angles would result when the parts were bound together with spruce root wrappings and pitch. Each point consisted of three parts, a flattened [109] point of elk bone or hardwood and two butt barbs of elk horn. The point and barbs were bevelled, fitted together, and made secure by careful wrapping fixed with pitch. The butt formed by the barbs contained a cupped socket

---

[3] Swan, pp. 104-107; Cf. Coues, p. 753; Dunn, p. 138; Douglas, p. 269.

which fitted the tapered end of the foreshaft. From the point to the main shaft loosely hung a strong cord made fast at either end. The single pointed spear was identical except that no foreshaft was required; the point fitted the tapered end of the main shaft.

The spear was thrust, not thrown. When a fish was speared the points came loose from the foreshafts but remained attached to the main shaft by the cords. The fish was then played by manipulating the shaft.[4]

Still another method of taking salmon was through the use of dip nets and staging. In the spring before the river level rose channels were dug near the shore. These were made of proper width and depth to accommodate a dip net. A staging was then erected and made variable in height so that it might be adjusted to changes in water level. The edge of the staging was aligned with the inner edge of the channel. When the water filled the channel and the fish began to swim through, the fisherman stood on the staging and carried his dip net the length of the channel, moving it with the current. The dip net consisted of a circular hoop of vine maple (*Acer circinatum*) attached to a handle of fir from twelve to fifteen feet in length. The bag was woven of Indian hemp cord.[5] The vertical dip net was also used.

Line and hook fishing was used most commonly for sturgeon (in addition to seining, described above). The hook was made of hardwood in two pieces bound together with string and pitch so that an acute-angled, V-shaped implement was produced. The line was fastened to one extremity; the opposite one, which was turned slightly inward and sharpened, served both as point and barb. The line permanently fastened to the hook was short; in use it was tied to another line of the required length. This was quite heavy when used for sturgeon and of a strong fiber such as spruce root or cedar bark.[6] Hooks, and also nets, were rubbed with wild celery root to attract the fish.

Swan furnishes a graphic account of sturgeon fishing:

> As soon as the sturgeon feels the hook, away he starts like an arrow, and the canoe goes whizzing and spinning along at a fearful rate, and requires a good deal of dexterous management to prevent being turned over. As the fish slackens speed, the Indian hauls in the line, and by perseverance at last tires the fish so that it is hauled to the surface of the water, and stunned by a blow on the head or nose with a heavy club carried for the purpose. The trouble now is to get he sturgeon into the canoe, for sometimes these fish weigh from three to four hundred pounds,[7] and ire from twelve to fifteen feet long. The Indian contrives to get the sturgeon's head over the gun-whale of the canoe, and with a peculiar twist suddenly jerks the fish in without any apparent difficulty.... Sometimes an Indian will catch two or three great

---

[4] Cf. Swan, pp. 38-40.

[5] Douglas, pp. 267 f.

[6] Cf. Dunn, pp. 134 f.; Thwaites, pp. 351 f.

[7] Swan is conservative in this estimate. The species found here *(Acipenser transmontanus)* is he largest of the sturgeons. Ross (p. 94) states that one brought to the trading post measured thirteen feet and nine inches in length and weighed 1,130 pounds. Douglas (p. 269) mentions four to five hundred pounds as average weights. Jordan's *Check List* (p. 34) gives the record size as nineteen hundred pounds; this fish was taken at Astoria.

sturgeon during one tide, for they generally begin to fish as the tide begins to flood, when the sturgeon follow up in the shoal water to feed.... The Indians prefer them to salmon, but it is much more difficult to take them.[8] [110]

Small fish were speared from the banks of streams or from canoes with multiple wooden spears used against the current.[9] Flatfish, such as the flounder (*Platickthys stellatus* ?) were caught by wading barefoot into the water and feeling them out with the feet. As soon as the fish was felt it was quickly stepped on, then grasped and thrown far on shore. The rough backs of the fish prevented them from slipping from under the feet. Fish caught in this manner sometimes weighed as much as twenty pounds. This method of fishing was looked upon as a sport and a laughing group' usually participated.[10]

Smelt, eulachon, and herring were caught in a number of ways. The herring rake, presumably made with bone teeth, and the dip net were favorite methods.[11] Ross states that the eulachon "enters the river in immense shoals, in the spring of the year. The ulichans are generally an article of trade with the distant tribes, as they are caught only at the entrance of the large rivers. To prepare them for a distant market, they are laid side by side, head and tail alternately, and then a thread run through both extremities links them together, in which state they are dried, smoked, and sold by the fathom, hence they have obtained the name of fathom-fish."[12]

Despite the abundance of fresh fish, those which were cast dead upon the beach were used also. A native searching for such fish intimated to Clark that sturgeon might be obtained in this way.[13]

FIRST SALMON CEREMONY

The first salmon ceremony[14] was observed for the first of the Chinook salmon and a similar rite was held for the first sturgeon. The ritual treatment continued for several days. Mrs. Luscier was indefinite on this point but Ross places the duration at about ten days[15] while Gibbs states that the rules were abated with the ripening of the salmon berries.[16]

The fisherman obtaining the first salmon immediately sent messengers to notify all of the villagers of the event. The latter gathered immediately at the house of the fisherman; it was he who acted as ritualist. In the meantime sand had been placed in the mouth of the salmon, as soon as it was brought to shore, in order to insure success in later fishing. When brought to the house the fish was cleaned by rubbing it with moss; under no circumstances was

---

[8] Swan, pp. 245 f.

[9] Dunn, p. 139.

[10] Swan, p. 83.

[11] Cf. Boas, *Chinook Texts,* p. 231.

[12] Ross, pp. 94 f.

[13] Thwaites, vol. 3, p. 276.

[14] *See Gunther,* Analysis of the First Salmon Ceremony, & A Further Analysis.

[15] Ross, p. 97.

[16] Gibbs, *Tribes of Western Washington,* p. 196.

it washed with water.

Those assembled now decided how the fish was to be cooked. If it were to be boiled it was broken into pieces with the hands; a knife was never used. The head and tail were broken from the body, then the body was broken open so that the heart might be removed. This was thrown immediately into the fire. The eyes were removed and swallowed whole, "to avoid bad luck in the future." The same was [111] done with the point of the nose. The intestines were not removed, but all parts were now placed in an oblong container of alder and boiled.

If the salmon were roasted it was cut lengthwise down the back with a mussel shell knife. The backbone and intestines were removed, together with the heart, and carefully placed in the fire. The head and tail remained attached to the body. The fish was then roasted in the usual manner, except that only alder wood was used for the fire. When cooked the fish was broken apart and a portion given to all present, including the children and the fisherman. Girls near puberty were not allowed to partake, but neither were they permitted to attend the ceremony.

The greatest care was taken to ensure that the fish be cut only lengthwise, never crosswise; and to ascertain that proper disposition was made of the heart. The breach of these rules would have been the most serious possible, in the second case "especially if a dog got hold of the heart."

Every morsel of the fish was eaten. Care was taken that the head be eaten from the nose toward the back, never in the opposite direction. Also, no part was allowed to remain uneaten after sunset. Even though many fish were caught during the day, all were consumed before sundown.

When the salmon was boiled a soup remained; especially rich since the fish had been broken up. This was eagerly drunk from spoons of horn, bone or shell. The eyes and nose part of the salmon to be roasted were eaten in the same way as with the salmon for boiling. If any vestige of the bones remained in the fire they were carefully buried.

The strength of these beliefs is indicated by the fact that early white traders were unable to obtain salmon from the natives in the early spring before solemnly promising not to cut it crosswise and to consume all they received each day before sunset. To insure proper treatment of the heart it was removed before transferring the fish.

The account above, furnished by Mrs. Luscier, differs in some respects from statements found in the early literature. Often it is stated that the first salmon must invariably be roasted. This was perhaps the result of instructions received from the natives when first fish were presented to them. Roasting was simple; the procedure in the boiling process was more complicated and involved non-removal of the intestines. Gibbs states that the heart was roasted; this statement is doubtless based on his having seen the heart placed in the fire. He adds that particular parts were eaten with the rise and fall of the tide; that the first salmon was eaten by a shaman, the second by the household; and that dancing accompanied the ceremony. Swan corroborates the dance feature but states that it had been discontinued in his time. Mrs. Luscier denied that any dancing accompanied the ceremony. It is doubtful that the first was eaten only by a shaman.[17]

---

[17] Ross, p. 97; Gibbs, loc. cit., Swan, pp. 107 f.; Dunn, p. 121; Lee and Frost, pp. 300 f.; Franchère, pp. 260 f.

The first fish caught by a boy was never eaten by him but always given to others, though not necessarily to old persons.

If salmon berries (yɪ'tɑwa') were abundant in the spring it was thought to insure a plentiful supply of salmon. [112]

SHELL-FISHING

The wide expanses of tide flats exposed with each ebb tide in Willapa Bay constituted a shell-fish grounds hard to surpass. Pull advantage of the resource was taken by the Chinook, both for the satisfaction of immediate needs, for storage, and for trade.

In addition to the usual varieties of shell-fish available along the north Pacific coast, the bay produced the native oyster (*Ostrea lurida expansa*) in large quantities. This is, however, a small oyster (about an inch in diameter) and was less favored by the natives than the clams, some of which attain huge size. The giant panope (*Panope generosa*) or geoduck, for example, reaches seven or eight inches in shell length, and the mud clam (*Mactra calilliformis*) is scarcely smaller. But the cockles (*Cardium corbis* and others) were perhaps of greatest importance, with the macoma (*Macoma nasuta* and others), the hard-shelled clam (*Venerupis staminta*) and the razor clam (*Solen sicarius* and *Siliqua patula*) all playing important roles.

Clams were dug by removing the sand covering with the hands or by the use of large wooden digging sticks with tapered points and cupped blades (Figure 13, A, B). These varied in length from two feet to more than four feet.

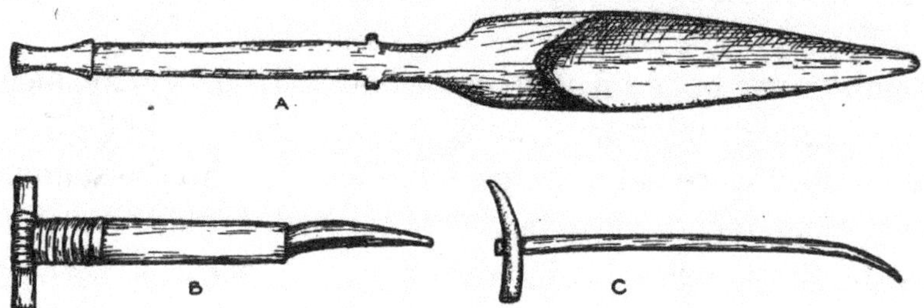

Fɪɢ. 13. Digging sticks. (A) For shell-fish, large (after Field Museum specimen 19099) ; (B) For shell-fish, small (compare Field Museum specimen 19814) ; (C) For root digging.

FIG. 13. Digging sticks. (A) For shell-fish, large (after Field Museum specimen 19099); (B) For shell-fish, smelt (compare Field Museum specimen 19814); (C) For root digging.

Swan furnishes a description of the methods of cooking and drying clams. The mud clam (also geoduck and others ?) is opened with a knife, and the clams stuck on skewers holding about two dozen; these are then washed clean, drained, and dried in smoke. The *clolum* [hard shell clam] is opened by being heaped on stones previously heated, then covered with sea weed and mats. The water contained in the clam runs down on the hot stones, causing steam which ... soon cooks the whole pile, containing usually from ten to twenty bushels. From twenty minutes to three-quarters of an hour are generally occupied in performing the operation, and the coverings are then removed. The shells, now being opened, are easily separated, and the meat stuck on skewers ... and dried in the smoke. These dried clams are a great article of trade with the Indians of the interior, and quantities are annually carried from Shoal-water [Willapa] Bay up the Columbia.[18] [113]

Mussels (*Mytrilus edulis, M. californianus,* and others) were collected though not in quantity to compare with the clams. Barnacles were plentiful but were not eaten. A small crab was gathered in large numbers to be boiled and eaten, shells and all.[19]

But more important was the large crab which was abundant in spring and early summer. The shell was broken off and only the claw part retained.[20]

SEALING AND WHALING

Sea mammals of several species were utilized by the Chinook for both food and clothing. The availability of these animals must not be judged in terms of conditions today when most of the species are almost extinct. So far as the Chinook were concerned the supply was literally inexhaustible.

The fur seal (*Callorhinus alascensis*) was found off the coast during its migrant season from December until spring. Male and female varied greatly in size; the former weighing five hundred to seven hundred pounds but the female only one-fifth as much. The huge Steller's sea lion (*Eumetopias jubata*) appeared not only on the rocks of the coast but also in the Columbia river for the entire length of Lower Chinook territory. The sea lion is a highly social animal and congregates in large numbers. Males weigh fifteen hundred to two thousand pounds, the females about half as much. The California sea lion (*Zaiophus californianus*) is considerably smaller, the bulls not exceeding one thousand pounds. These are (and were ?) less common off Chinook territory than the Steller's species. The hair seal (*Phoca richardii richardii*) was one of the most important of the aquatic mammals for the Chinook. They were found basking on the beaches, sometimes in small groups but not in colonies. Males and females were of about the same size, varying in weight between sixty and one hundred pounds. They were found far up the Columbia and because of their smaller size were of course much more easily taken than the large seals.[21]

We turn again to Swan for our best description of hunting the hair seal:

> The staff of the spear was about twenty feet long, made of fir or yew. The head of the spear, made like a salmon spear, but larger, was attached to a line thirty fathoms long.... [The native would] proceed to some sand island to the leeward of the seals, who are always, at low tide, seen basking in the sun, particularly in the spring, when the young ones are about. Having fastened his canoe and divested himself of his clothes, with one end of the line fastened round his body, and the rest coiled up on his left arm, he goes into the water, with the spear firmly grasped in his right hand, and floating just under the surface of the water. No part of his person, except the face and top of his head, could be seen, and the hair floating round made him look very much like a seal. Cautiously and slowly he gets between

---

[18] Swan, pp. 85 f.

[19] Swan, pp. 86 f.

[20] Swan, p. 82.

[21] Bailey, pp. 330-36.

the seal and the deep water; then wading ashore, careful to keep his body submerged till he is near enough, he suddenly rises up, and, darting his spear into the body of the animal, runs back on the sand, and setting his heels firmly, braces himself for the contest. He lets but little line out at first, and if he is the strongest, easily gains the mastery. But with a large old male a fierce battle ensues, and it is sometimes attended with the loss of the line; but generally the old fellow comes out victorious. When the animal is dead the first thing is to [114] stop up the spear-hole with a wooden plug, or a bunch of grass or fern, which is always carried in the canoe for the purpose....

As soon as the animal was brought ashore, the following process was invariably adopted. A couple of round logs, eight or ten inches in diameter, were laid parallel to each other, a foot or two apart, and between them kindled a brisk fire of dry chips. The seal is then laid across the logs over the blaze, and, commencing at the nose, the whole body is rolled over and over till all the hair is thoroughly singed off. The skin, which is by this process pretty well roasted, is scraped clean with a shell or knife. The blubber is next cut off in strips, which are boiled in water, and oil skimmed off with shells. After it has settled and cooled, it is poured into a bottle (as they call it), made of the paunch of the animal blown up like a bladder, and dried. In every lodge may be seen these bladder-like bottles, and the more an Indian has the greater his wealth. The meat, which is dark, is boiled with the blood, which they are particular to save, and, when cooked, is tender, and not very unpalatable.... The oil is eaten freely with all their food, and, when freshly boiled, is as sweet and free from fishy flavor as lard.[22]

The sea otter (*Enhydra lutris nereis*) furnished the Chinook with many fine robes and blankets. The animals are highly gregarious and formerly were very abundant and easily caught because of their timidity. They were found only in and near the salt water. The length of the male is five or six feet, the weight fifty to seventy-five pounds.[23] All of the early writers speak of sea otter robes in use by the Chinook but it is not certain whether they used the flesh for food or not.

The whale was greatly valued by the Chinook and highly formal regulations for the disposal of a stranded animal were enforced.[24] Yet it is not definitely known whether any but dead and stranded whales were taken. A statement by Clark, writing at Fort Clatsop, is quite ambiguous: "The whale is sometimes pursued, harpooned, and taken by the Indians of this coast; though I believe it is much more frequently killed by running on the rocks of the coast to S.S.W. in violent storms, and thrown on different parts of the coast by the winds and tide. In either case the Indians preserve and eat the blubber and oil.... "[25] It may have been that Clark had heard of whaling by the Quinault, and that the expression "this coast" was intended in a very general sense; yet the reference in the same sentence to "the rocks of the coast to S.S.W."

----

[22] *Swan, pp. 84 f., 83 f.*
[23] *Bailey, pp. 302-305.*
[24] *See class and rank.*
[25] *Thwaites, vol. 4, p. 161.*

is suggestive.[26] [26] In any event there was a number of species to be found in considerable abundance off the mouth of the Columbia. The California gray whale (*Rhachianectes glaucus*) was estimated to have numbered thirty to forty thousand on the southern California coast in the winters of 1853 to 1856. These same individuals migrated to the northern waters in the summers. The male of the California whale reaches forty-four feet in length. The Pollack whale (*Balaenoptera borealis*) was likewise common. It is somewhat larger than the preceding species. The Pacific humpback whale (*Megaptera versabilis*) was once quite abundant. The male measures about fifty feet in length. The valuable sperm whale (*Physeter catodon*) was doubtless cast up on the beach occasionally. Other whales were known to the vicinity but were relatively uncommon.[27] [115]

Boas records a number of customs and tabus associated with the whale: When the Clatsop found a whale its discoverers indicated their claim by tying straps or kelp to the animal; then others were called but they did not cut where the straps had been placed. Those who came last received the lower side of the animal. Portions removed were not recut (immediately?). If a drifting whale were seen by a menstruating woman, a murderer, or one who had cohabited the preceding night, it drifted out to sea again. But one who had cohabited might paddle his canoe to the seaward of the whale and prevent it from drifting away.

"When the people are starving, a person who has a supernatural helper of the sea sings to bring a whale. No woman who has her regular menses enters, and no young man; else a person might see the singing who has cohabited the preceding night. Therefore, also, no woman must enter, as she might become menstruant in the house where they sing. Only old people, boys, and young girls help sing. For five days he sings. Then a youth is sent and told to look seaward. Five times he is sent; then, indeed, he finds a whale adrift. When a man who has cohabited the pre-, ceding night enters the house in which the singing goes on, the supernatural helper vanishes at once. Thus also when a menstruant woman enters. The singer is covered with down. He places a pole upright on the beach and says: 'Here a whale Y will drift ashore,' and, indeed, it drifts ashore there after he has sung five days."[28]

Many species of dolphin and porpoise occur in Chinook waters but most important to the natives were the striped porpoise (*Lagenorhynchus obliquidens*) and the Pacific killer (*Orcinus rectipinnd*). Lewis and Clark comment:[29] "The porpoise is common on this coast and

---

[26] These remarks of Lewis and Clark may be significant: "On these hats they work various figures... These figures are faint representations of whales, the canoes, and harpooners striking them." (Thwaites. vol. 4, p. 24.)

[27] *Bailey, pp. 336-45.*

[28] Boas, *Chinook Texts*, pp. 262 f.

[29] Thwaites, vol. 4, p. 163.

as far up the river as the water is brackish. The Indians gig [spear] them and always eat the flesh of this fish when they can procure it.... "

HUNTING[1]

The extent to which the Chinook engaged in hunting is perhaps best indicated by an entry in the Boit log of the ship *Columbia,* the first vessel to enter the river which bears its name: "The Indians are very numerous, and appear'd very civil (not even offering to steal). During our stay [of ten days] we collected 150 otter, 300 beaver, and twice that number of other land furs.... the woods [abound] with plenty of moose [elk] and deer, the skins of which was brought to us in great plenty."[22] This can leave no doubt but that the Chinook depended to a large extent upon game as well as fish for a livelihood and that they were well supplied with the furs of land mammals adaptable to clothing and blankets. It should be remembered that the thousand or more pelts carried away by the *Columbia* were part of a normal domestic supply. Quantity accumulation for sale to white traders had not yet begun.[3]

Mammals were hunted both by individuals and by groups. A talented hunter served as leader for group ventures. The object was to surround the game and drive it toward a favorable spot for the bowmen. Each man was assigned to his position; those most expert with the bow and arrow were stationed at the point of concentration. This was always on land; game was never driven into the water. This method of hunting was most commonly used for deer and elk. Strong writes of elaborately planned group hunting in which "long lines of skirmishers drove the frightened deer into the enclosures or pitfalls."[4]

Pitfalls were an important method of taking game including the deer and elk. Lewis and Clark write of pits for elk, "some of them a cube of twelve or fourteen feet. These were placed on habitual trails at points where fallen logs crossed the paths. They were covered with slender boughs of trees and moss. In attempting to jump the log the animal fell into the pit. Similar pitfalls, but smaller, were used for a large variety of small mammals."[5]

Small animals were sought by individual hunters but the deer and elk were taken by lone stalking also. As the hunter crept closer and closer to his prey he dropped any articles of clothing that he was wearing so that the animal would be less apt to get his scent. An arrow was not shot until the hunter had come sufficiently close to the animal so that there was little chance of missing, or failing to inflict a mortal wound.[6]

Bears were hunted both by stalking and by smoking them out of their places of hibernation; in either case the bow and arrow were used.

Antelopes were not found closer to Lower Chinook territory than The Dalles, but Lewis and Clark state that "When the salmon begin to decline in the latter end [117] of summer and

---

[1] See physical environment.
[2] Boit, p. 248.
[3] But cf. Franchère, pp. 245 f.
[4] Strong, p. 25.
[5] Thwaites, vol. 3, p. 347.
[6] Strong, pp. 27-31.

autumn the natives leave the river, at least a majority, and remove to the plains at some distance for the purpose of hunting the antelope."[7]

Beaver were hunted at night and taken with harpoons. Rabbits were obtained by the use of nets but it is uncertain whether ducks were caught with elevated nets or not. They were, however, shot with the bow and arrows and killed with stones.[8] A canoe blind was used to aid the approach to water fowl. Green boughs covered the canoe and its occupants giving the appearance of floating brushwood. The paddle was not used; the canoe was allowed to float.[9][B] Snipe were felled with a brush "whip." Snares were known but not extensively used.

A small dog was used in hunting elk, according to Lewis and Clark.[10] Henry saw no dogs at the Ft. Clatsop native village[11] but it is probable that they were present but indoors, since they were allowed free run of the house. Whether dogs were kept for wool to be used in weaving blankets is quite uncertain. Dogs were customarily named.

The sinew-backed bow served most extensively in hunting and war but the simple bow was made also. The backed bow averaged two and one-half feet in length; the width at the center was about two inches, from which point it tapered gradually to the ends which were about a half inch wide and very thin. The material was the heart of the cedar. The back of the bow was built up with elk sinew laid in sturgeon gelatin glue. Bow strings were of three-ply elk sinew. The self bow was painted black on the back, red on the inside.

Arrows were of two types, simple and fore-shafted. The over-all length of the latter was about two feet. The main shaft was of soft wood and measured about four-fifths of the entire arrow length. In one end was provided a cupped mortise to receive the tenon of the foreshaft. The latter was smaller in diameter than the main shaft and made of harder wood. The two shafts were securely fastened together with a wrapping of sinew. Sinew likewise bound the head to the foreshaft and the feathers to the main shaft. The head was of stone with a wide-angled point.[12]

Yew wood was favored for the foreshaft of the compound arrow and also for the simple arrow. The latter was probably self-pointed in most cases. Shafts were straightened with a perforated wooden straightener and polished with scouring rush {Equisetum hyemale). Feathering was double with tangential placement. Feathers were trimmed and preferably of the red-shafted woodpecker {Colaptes cafer collaris). Sinew wrapping of the butt served the double purpose of securing the feathers and insuring against splitting. Point materials included obsidian, flint, and bone. Those of bone were multiple-barbed.

The quiver was usually the skin of a young bear or wolf cut and sewed so that an opening was provided on the side.[13] It was carried at the side. [118]

The beaver harpoon was foreshafted and the point barbed. A decoy for elk hunting was

---

[7] Thwaites, vol. 4, p. 95.

[8] Cf. Boas, *Chinook Texts,* p. 230.

[9] Strong, p. 22.

[10] Thwaites, vol. 4, p. 39.

[11] Coues, p. 772.

[12] Thwaites, vol. 3, pp. 346 f.

[13] *Idem,* p. 347.

made of the head of the animal[14] (see Plate 2). An elderberry whistle was made to be used as a deer and elk call.

Included in the animals hunted for food were the following: elk, deer, bear, bobcat, cougar, raccoon, beaver, squirrel, mink, mountain beaver, rabbit and porcupine. Among the animals and birds available but not eaten were wolf, raven, seagull, crow, owl, eagle, reptiles, eels, turtles, and frogs.

The first game taken by a boy was tabu to him. To eat of this would cause ill luck at a later time. It was rather given to the older people who made a small feast of it. Also, when a young boy was searching for his first game he made sure to eat nothing from the time he arose until after he returned.

Boas recounts a series of tabus:

A menstruating woman must not take the head of an elk. Women do not eat the tongue; only men eat it. They do not break the bones of the forelegs. They are carried far away, else a menstruating woman might see them. When such a woman eats the feet and hoofs, the hunter will be unlucky. When she steps over an elk's head, she will be sick with dropsy. Just so a girl who has just reached maturity. She does not look at an elk, else she will be sick with dropsy. When a hunter is unsuccessful, his child must not go near the water. When it goes near the water, it will fall sick and die at once. When he goes hunting, his wife and children sit motionless. His wife must not go anywhere. When his children make noise, one of them will fall sick if the hunter is unsuccessful.[15] "

It is stated that these tabus apply specifically to the elk but Mrs. Luscier extended all such observances to the deer as well. She reiterated a number of these restrictions, adding that the hunter's wife sometimes remained in bed throughout his absence and in no case did she comb her hair. The hunter always ate the heart of an animal he killed. It was not necessary that the game be brought in the house by a route other than the doorway. Bones were either buried or burned.

My informants knew nothing of a bear ceremony.

Skins were commonly tanned with the fur adhering. Buckskin was very little used, if at all. But skins were sometimes smoked, using fir bark as fuel. The tanning and graining apparatus included the scraping and stretching frame (for both large and small skins), mussel shell knife and scraper, wooden scraper and bevelled wooden grainer.

---

[14] Wilkes, vol. 4, p. 322.
[15] Boas, *Chinook Texts*, p. 265.

VEGETAL FOODS

Vegetal products played no small part in Chinook economics. Though sea food was plentiful and used in great variety, yet a balanced diet was achieved by a generous use of roots, stems and berries.[1] It is difficult to say which was felt to be the more important vegetal food, roots or berries. Perhaps no such contrast should be attempted; the two were distinctly supplementary. In point of gross quantity roots probably outweighed berries; stems ran a close third. In speaking of roots, Lewis and Clark state that they "furnish a considerable proportion of the subsistence... " and that they were highly valued and disposed of sparingly.[2]

ROOTS

The most extensively utilized roots were those of the lupine, bracken fern, horsetail rush, and edible thistle. In addition the wapato was imported in large quantities. This root was found only in one corner of Lower Chinook territory, the south side of the Columbia river opposite and above Puget Island. Therefore most of the roots were obtained by trade, principally from the Klatskanie. The extent to which camas was used is uncertain. One species is found widespread in western Washington but its use by the natives is mentioned only by Swan. Among most groups having access to camas it is very fully used. Edible roots were available to the Chinook over a very long season, so that drying and storage for winter use was not particularly demanded. Yet as indicated below, a number of roots were regularly gathered and dried in sufficient quantity so that a considerable variety of such food was at hand at any time of the year.

Roots were dug with a dibble or digging stick (Figure 13, c) consisting of a wooden shaft and crutch-type handle of elk or deer antler. Because of its hardness and durability, yew was preferred as shaft wood. Shafts were either straight or slightly curved near the point, and sometimes a bit flattened. The greatly flattened or cupped clam digging sticks (Figure 13, A, B) were occasionally used for root digging in sandy soil.

The principal roots are briefly described and discussed below:

1. Seashore Lupine (*Lupinus littoralis*). The farinaceous root of this plant is highly nutritive, resembling somewhat the sweet potato in taste. Under the name of licorice it is repeatedly mentioned by Lewis and Clark as an important native food. It grows abundantly and to large size in the deep sandy soil along the river. It was prepared for food by roasting in hot embers, then pounded slightly to loosen the edible portion from the fibrous center spine, which was discarded.[3] [120]

2. Bracken Fern (*Pteris aquilina lanuginose {now* Pteridium aquilinum*}*). This plant grows in great profusion in open uplands and among sparse timber. "The root is horizontal, sometimes a little diverging or obliquely descending, frequently dividing itself as it proceeds into two equal branches and shooting up a number of stems; it lies about four inches beneath

---

[1] Cf. Swan, pp. 87 f.
[2] Thwaites, vol. 3, pp. 362, 292.
[3] Cf. Thwaites, vol. 3, pp. 229 f., 292, 362; vol. 4, pp. 6 f., 10 f.; Douglas, p. 256.

the surface.... The root is cylindric, with few or no radicles, and from the size of a goose quill to that of a man's finger; the center of the root is divided into two equal parts by a strong flat and white ligament like a piece of thin tape. On either side of this there is a white substance which when roasted in the embers is much like wheat dough and not very unlike it in flavor; ... the natives eat it very voraciously.... "[4]

3. Horsetail Rush (*Equisetum telmateid {now Equsietum telmateia* ssp. *braunii}*). "The root of the rush used by the natives is a solid bulb about one inch in length and usually as thick as a man's thumb, of an ovate form depressed on two or more sides, covered with a thin black rind. The pulp is white, brittle and easily masticated either raw or roasted. The latter is the way in which it is most usually prepared for use.... It grows in greatest abundance along the sea coast in the sandy grounds...."[5]

4. Edible Thistle (*Carduus edulis {now Cirsium edule}*). The root of this thistle is a "perpendicular fusiform and possesses from two to four radicles; is from nine to fifteen inches in length and about the size of a man's thumb; the rind somewhat rough and of a brown color; the consistence when first taken from the earth is white and nearly as crisp as a carrot; when prepared for use [in the earth oven] it becomes black, and is more sugary than any fruit or root that I have met with in use among the natives; ... this root is sometimes eaten with train-oil also, at other times pounded fine and mixed with cold water, until reduced to the consistency of gruel.... "[6]

5. Wapato, or Arrowhead (*Sagittaria latifolia*). "The most valuable of all their roots is foreign to this neighborhood [Ft. Clatsop]." Lewis and Clark thus evaluate the wapato and add that it formed the principal article of trade between the upriver peoples and those on the coast.[7] The root is found in marshy or swampy places. It was collected by wading barefoot into the marsh and feeling out the bulbs with the feet. Large quantities were obtained in this way in a short time.

6. Camas (*Camassia quamash*). "This root, which resembles an onion in appearance, is a species of lily, found in moist places on the prairies. After the plant has done flowering, ... which is usually in September and October, the root is dug up by the {women} ~~squaws~~, who go out in parties for the purpose, and are generally absent several days. After sufficient has been collected, the leaves and loose outhusks are removed, and the whole roasted on hot stones [121] ... as follows: A large pile of dry wood is made, on the top of which a quantity of stones are piled; fire is then applied, and kept up till all the wood is burned, leaving nothing but the hot stones and ashes. Fem leaves are then laid on the stones, and on these mats are placed; the camas roots are then placed on the mats, and spread level; water is then thrown over them, and immediately they are covered with mats, blankets, and the whole covered up with sand, every care being taken to keep in all the steam. This heap is allowed to remain till it is cold, ... twelve to twenty-four hours. The roots then are soft and very sweet, much like a baked

---

[4] Thwaites, vol. 4, p. 5. Cf. *idem*, vol. 3, p. 362; Swan, p. 88.
[5] Thwaites, vol. 4, pp. 7-9. Cf. *idem*, vol. 3, p. 362; Swan, p. 88.
[6] Thwaites, vol. 4, pp. 3, 6 f. Cf. *idem*, vol. 3, pp. 242, 292, 362.
[7] Thwaites, vol. 4, p. 7. Cf. *idem*, vol. 3, p. 208; Swan, p. 90; Douglas, p. 256.

sweet potato. The natives preserve them by pressing them into loaves, which, when eaten, are cut in slices like pudding."[8]

7. Cattail (*Typha latifolia*). Cattail root was eaten raw.[9]

8. Skunk Cabbage (*Lysichiton camtschatcense* {now *Lysitchiton americanus*}. The root was eaten after boiling. It was not highly prized.[10]

[no 9?]

10. Cow Parsnip (*Heracleum lanafum* {now *Heracleum maximum*}). The root as well as the stem of this plant was utilized.

FRUIT

A great variety of berries ripen in rapid succession from spring until winter in Lower Chinook territory. First to appear is the salmon berry, followed shortly by strawberries in great quantities. Then one after another become available blueberries, red huckleberries, blackberries, gooseberries, currant, and, in August, salal berries. This fruit is available until December. In the meantime the crab-apple ripens, followed by cranberries. Finally, a fruit called shotberry ripens, the last of the season.

"As the season advances and the fruits ripen," writes Swan, "great quantities are used as food, to the exclusion of fish and meats."

The following list is far from exhaustive, but includes the principal species.

11. Salmon Berry (*Rubus spectabilis*). This species occurs in two forms, most commonly with yellow or "salmon-colored" berries, the other with nearly black fruit. Whether the common name is derived from the color of the former, or from the fact that the fruit first ripens when the salmon appear in the Columbia for spawning (May, June), is uncertain. These berries were eaten raw.[11]

12. Strawberry (*Fragaria* sp.). Strawberries of several species were gathered and eaten without further preparation.

13. Blueberry (*Vaccinium ovatum* {now *Vaccinium ovalifolium* Alaska Oval-leaf Blueberry}). This deep purple berry "terminates bluntly with a kind of cap or cover at the end ... they are attached separately to the sides of the boughs of the shrub by a very short stem hanging underneath the same and are frequently placed very near each other on the same bough; [122] it is a full bearer. The berry is easily gathered as it separates from the bough readily, while the leaf is strongly affixed. The shrub which produces this fruit rises to the height of six or eight feet, sometimes grows on the high lands but most generally in the swampy or marshy grounds; it is evergreen ... The natives either eat these berries when ripe immediately from the bushes or dried in the sun ... for winter use, when they either eat them in their dried state or boil them in

---

[8] Swan, pp. 90 f.
[9] Swan, p. 88.
[10] Swan, p. 87; Boas, *Chinook Texts,* p. 231.
[11] Cf. Piper, p. 333; Swan, p. 88.

water."[12]

Several other species of blueberries were used, presumably in the same manner.

14.   Red Huckleberry (*Vaccinium parvifolium*).   This berry was eaten raw; it is not adapted to drying.

15. Blackberry (*Rubus* sp. {now *Rubus ursinus* Trailing Blackberry}).

16. Gooseberry (*Ribes* sp. {now *Ribes lacustre* Black Gooseberry}).

17. Black Currant (*Ribes* sp. {now *Ribes laxiflorum* Trailing Black Currant}).[13]

18.   Salal (*Gaultheria shallon*).   The salal bush varies in height from three to five feet. The shrub is an evergreen with somewhat reclining branches bearing oval leaves of glossy deep green. Its fruit is a deep purple berry of ovate form quite small. The berries were either eaten raw when ripe, dried in the sun, or cooked by the fireless or earth oven method, similarly to camas. Frequently they were pounded and baked into loaves weighing ten to fifteen pounds. These loaves remained well preserved for a season, retaining the juices of the fruit very well. When used the loaf was broken and mixed with cold water to form a paste and then eaten with clam shell spoons.[14]

19. Oregon Crab-apple (*Pyrus rivularis* {now *Malus fusca* Pacific Crabapple}). The apples of this tree, which grows in abundance, are quite small but appear in clusters of three to twenty, averaging about eight. They were gathered in considerable quantity each fall and prepared for immediate use by boiling.[15]

20.   Cranberry (*Oxy'coccus oxycoccus intermedius* {now *Vaccinium oxycoccos* Small Cranberry}), The cranberry was very plentiful and extensively used.[16]

21.   Bearberry (*Arctostaphylos uva-ursi* {Kinnickinnick}).   The bearberry occurs in the prairies or on their borders in the more open woodlands. The fruit ripens in September and remains on the bushes all winter. They were eaten fresh or dried for winter use. When fresh they were sometimes mashed and eaten with oil. In order to dry them, they were merely packed in bags and hung inside the house. The leaves were used as tobacco or mixed with tobacco.[17] [123]

22. "Shotberry" (*Rubus* sp. ? {now *Vaccinium ovatum* Evergreen Huckleberry}). These ripen in the fall and remain until December. "The berries grow in clusters and resemble the prim. The leaf is small, of oval shape, with finely-serrated edges. It is an excellent berry, and, if kept

---

[12] Thwaites, vol. 4, pp. 13 f , 52. Cf. Coues, p. 753; Swan, p. 89.

[13] Swan, p. 89.

[14] Thwaites, vol. 4, pp. 52, 14. Cf. idem, vol. 3, p. 392; vol. 4, pp. 13 f.; Swan, p. 89.

[15] Thwaites, vol. 4, p. 19; Swan, p. 89.

[16] Swan, p. 89; Thwaites, vol. 3, pp. 220 f.; idem, vol. 4, pp. 12, 16 f. (called "solme"), 19; Coues, p. 753.

[17] Thwaites, vol. 4, pp. 21 f.; Swan, p. 88. Cf. Thwaites, vol. 4, p. 12.

dry and cool, can be preserved fresh for several months. It is, however, usually dried by the Indians and eaten early in the spring, before the other berries begin to ripen."[18]

23. Oregon Grape (*Berberis nervosa* {Dwarf Oregon Grape}). These berries were eaten fresh.

24. [Unidentified] {= *Abronia latifolia* Coastal Sand Verbena}. This plant has "a root like a yam, which, baked or boiled, is excellent ... found on the seaside, in sand near the beach."[19]

STEMS AND NUTS

25. Horsetail Rush (*Equisetum arvense)*. The young shoots of this plant were eaten raw.

26. Salmon Berry (*Rubus spectabilis)*. The sprouts of this plant, which shoot up very rapidly, were eagerly sought as food. "These sprouts are collected in bundles and brought into the lodge, where they are denuded of their tough outer skin, and the center is as crisp and tender as a cucumber, and being slightly acid, is delicious."[19]

27. Cow Parsnip (*Heracleum lanatum* {now *Heracleum maximum*}. This plant grows abundantly in moist soil. The young stems {shoots} were eaten raw after the outer skin was peeled off. Swan comments that this tender vegetable formed a grateful addition to the dried salmon eggs extensively used in earliest spring."

28. Wild Celery (?). Used similarly to the cow parsnip.[18]

29. Oak (*Querms garryana* {Oregon White ~ Garry Oak}). Acorns were fairly extensively used.

DOMESTIC LIFE

DWELLINGS

All permanent houses (Plates 2, 3, 4) were constructed of split cedar planks supported on a heavy framework of cedar timbers. The gable style was invariably used for these structures, the flat or slightly sloping shed roof being reserved for temporary summer dwellings. Details of construction varied considerably, as did gross size. The most common will be described first.

A site was selected which would receive as much sunshine as possible and be relatively protected from strong winds. The rectangular ground plan was laid out so that the long dimension would align with the prevailing winds. Depending upon the affluency of the builder and the number of families to be accommodated the dimensions varied between a minimum of

---

[18] Swan, p. 89.
[19] Swan, pp. 87, 88.

fourteen by twenty feet and a maximum of perhaps forty by one hundred feet. Except at the extremes a width to length ratio of about one to three was fairly consistently maintained. The ground was excavated over the whole area to a uniform depth; three and one-half feet was perhaps the average, with a range of eighteen inches either way. Holes were then dug for the posts which were to support the single ridge pole. These were placed along the median line about twenty feet apart. Thus the smallest house required but one at either gable end; the largest demanded five or six, spaced equidistant. These posts were not unworked logs, but heavy split timbers of rectangular cross-section, each with notched top to receive the ridge pole. The height varied between twelve and eighteen feet. The ridge pole was often allowed to project beyond the gable ends a short distance. Corresponding rows of uprights were placed along each edge of the excavation, forming supports for heavy rafters. These extended five to seven feet above the surface of the excavation. Roof plates were not used. The rafters were held in place laterally by longitudinal poles spaced about three feet apart, and secured with root lashings. Withes of spruce root were preferred; cedar root was second choice. This completed the structural framework.

Cedar planks, about two inches thick and averaging two feet in width (but sometimes reaching five and one-half feet[1]) were sunk into the ground around the four edges of the excavation. These vertical planks were secured at their upper ends to the gable rafters and to the longitudinal eave poles. This was accomplished by laying secondary poles on the outside of the planks parallel to the inner stationary members and lashing the two together with thongs passing through holes in the planks, or between the cracks. Sometimes a similar exterior lashing pole extended along the ends from eave to eave.

The roof consisted of similar but somewhat thinner planks laid parallel to the rafters in a double course, the second course covering the cracks of the first. These were secured similarly to the wall planks, with exterior poles tied through the planks to the rafters or longitudinal roof poles. A single course of roof planks provided with overlapping grooves sometimes substituted for the double thickness. An [125] opening over each proposed fireplace was obtained by short roof boards at that point, or loose ones which could be moved.

A doorway was provided in one end of a small house or each end of a large one. It was a small oval opening at ground level or slightly above, through an especially wide plank. It is uncertain whether or not the door was placed slightly off center, in order to avoid the end ridge post. The end post may have been set in a few feet from the wall; or, in some cases at least, the end post itself seems merely to have been a wide, especially thick plank forming part of the wall. In the latter case the doorway was carved through this plank. The door was a section of plank sufficient in size to cover the opening, suspended by a thong. It was opened by swinging to one side; when let fall it automatically closed. It was commonly hung on the outside; the inside of the wall plank containing the opening was painted so that the aperture formed part of the design. The figure might be that of a man with the passageway between his legs, or a human face with the doorway forming the mouth. A ladder consisting of a notched log reached from the doorway to the excavated floor level.

Secondary construction inside the building provided platforms for sleeping and for storage. Paralleling each side wall, but removed by about four feet, a row of vertical posts was

---

[1] Coues, p. 754.

erected with each post corresponding in position to the eaves posts. In small houses the row was sometimes carried around the end wall opposite the door. At the tops these posts were lashed to the rafters. Horizontal poles were now secured from these secondary posts to the structural posts at the eaves, about two feet above the floor. A second series was sometimes added at the level of the eaves or somewhat lower. Planks were laid upon these supporting poles, forming a sleeping platform at the lower level and a storage platform at the upper. The space under the beds was also used for storage.

If the house were a large one partitions were provided. These consisted of a single range of planks secured in the ground at their lower ends and fastened to a cross beam in the fashion of the wall planks. The upper edge of the partition was irregular but no plank extended far above the eave levels. Comer compartments for pubescent girls were constructed likewise. Partitioning was always across the building, never lengthwise. Seldom more than a single median partition was erected. An opening was left for passage from room to room; this was essential when two or more partitions were used in order to provide access to the exterior doorway.

A rectangular fireplace excavation was made at the center of each room. The dimensions averaged six feet wide, eight feet long and twelve inches deep. Around the edges were placed heavy squared timbers to retain the fire and ashes within the enclosure. The rest of the floor surface was covered with cedar planks, cattail mats, or both.[2]

Houses so constructed appeared to Broughton to be more comfortable than those of the Nutka.[3] [3] He especially cites the greater inclination of the roof. This not only provided better drainage, but together with the excavation resulted in a [126] minimum of side wall exposure where winds might penetrate. From the exterior the eaves of these houses were but two or three feet above the ground. From a distance the shape appeared to be that of an inverted V.

Broughton also mentions a "thatch of bark" over the plank roofing.[4] In some cases the entire roofing consisted of layers of bark, and in summer the walls of temporary structures were likewise of bark. Cedar bark was most commonly used.[5]

Town send describes a house, seen at a Chinook village on the north side of the Columbia near the mouth, which was provided with a cedar bark roof and lined inside with mats.[6] Surprisingly, the fireplace extended as a ditch, twelve inches deep and four feet wide, the entire length of the building. The large, rudely carved and painted figure on a board, which he states occupied a conspicuous place in the house, was doubtless one of the "power boards" used in spirit dances.[6]

Horizontal wall planking and longitudinal roof planking was not unknown but was relatively uncommon. Franchère, however, describes this type without qualification. He also states that a door was provided for each family, which would require openings in the side

---

[2] Luscier; Bertrand; Thwaites, vol. 3, pp. 208, 274, 356 f.; Franchère, pp. 247 f.; Ross, pp. 98 f.; Coues, p. 754; Dunn, pp. 135-37; Townsend, p. 257; Vancouver, vol. 2, p. 77.

[3] Vancouver, *loc. cit.*

[4] Cf. Ross, p. 98.

[5] Townsend, p. 257.

[6] See the spirit dance.

walls.[7] Doors in side walls and gable corners are noted by Lewis and Clark for the Kathlamet near Tenas Ilahee Island. These houses, however, were constructed entirely above the ground. The fireplaces were placed in the end opposite the comer doorway.[8]

The houses described and illustrated (Plates 3, 4) by Swan show a combination of features described above, but there is little doubt that white influence had already been felt. This is suggested especially by the great overhang of the roof and the height of the eaves above the ground. The wall planks are vertical but the roof planks run longitudinally. The doorway is the traditional oval opening with swinging door. No excavation is mentioned but a double level is created by a five or six inch high platform extending into the room from the raised sleeping quarters. The fire is on the ground surface, not confined in a pit.[9] Some of these features were doubtless regional variations.

These habitations were used only during the winter; in the spring they were dismantled and only the frames were left standing. The planks were stored or used for the erection of the large flat or shed-roofed summer structures.[10] The cattail mats were extensively used for temporary summer shelters for single families. These were of gable type, the mats being supported by a light framework tied together. When mats were carried on summer excursions a separate canoe was used for them to prevent possible damage. House planks were transported from one place to another on a lighter consisting of two canoes. The canoes were placed parallel to each other and the planks themselves were laid across. [127] Figure 1

SWEAT HOUSES

Two types of sweat houses were built, a plank structure and the typical Plains hemispherical hut. The plank house was built over an excavation about five feet square and two feet deep. Short planks were extended from two edges of the pit to form an inverted V with the ridge two and one-half feet above the ground surface. The treatment of the gable ends and doorway is uncertain. One to three persons were accommodated in such a hut. Stones were heated outside, brought in, and water poured on them to produce steam.[11]

The Plains type structure was comparable in size and likewise built over an excavation, which was round and only about twelve inches deep. The frame consisted of willow poles bent, crossed over each other, and secured in the ground at the pit edges. Old mats, grass or plank fragments covered the frame to support the earth with which the entire hut was covered. A small round entrance at ground level was covered with a hanging mat. A shallow round depression at the center of the pit served to hold the hot rocks. The rest of the floor surface was covered with bracken fern.

Bark of the Douglas fir was preferred fuel for heating the rocks since it permitted concentration of heat.

Sweat houses were owned by families; men and women used the same structure at

---

[7] Franchère, *loc. cit.*
[8] Thwaites, vol. 3, p. 208.
[9] Swan, pp. 110 f.
[10] Cf. Ross, pp. 98 f.
[11] Dunn, pp. 115 f.

different times. There was no prescribed hour for sweating; the houses were not extensively used. Sweating was thought to cure minor ailments and Mrs. Luscier made vague reference to the sweat house as a place for praying. Special songs accompanied sweating; their content is unknown. The sweat bath was always followed by a plunge in cold fresh water; the huts were so located as to make this possible.

The sweat house was in no sense a club house or gathering place. It played only a minor role in Chinook life.

In addition to steam baths, Swan mentions sweating by rolling up in blankets near the fire and drinking hot herb tea. He attributes sweat houses to the Columbia river groups but states that he never saw one on Willapa Bay.[12]

THE DOMESTIC GROUP

The average domestic group consisted of about four families, their slaves, and visitors.[13] Each family, consisting of man and wife, dependent children, and related elderly persons without other connections, together with their slaves occupied a distinct portion of the house, sometimes separated from other families by plank partitions or hanging mats. Certain areas of the house were doubtless preferred over others but these details are unknown. Slaves belonging to the various families may at times have been grouped in the less desirable parts of unpartitioned houses. With few exceptions the families making up a household were fairly closely related; according to Lewis and Clark, "the greatest harmony appears to exist among [128] them."[14] Newly married couples commonly established first residence in the house of the man's father. This introduces the matter of house ownership. Uncertainty prevails, but title to each house seems to have rested with the head of one of the occupant families. Other occupants may have felt a certain right to residence there as a result of labor or materials contributed in the construction of the building, but the formal ownership was doubtless recognized in the name of the highest ranking occupant and his family. This would necessarily have been the case for a Chinook would not long have remained in the house of a lower ranking person. Visitors were often present, but visiting was not as free and common as further up the Columbia.

Nearly all of the early writers remark upon the freedom from oppression and drudgery enjoyed by the Chinook woman in her household.[15] The possession of numerous slaves, upon whom devolved the more arduous and disagreeable tasks, accounted in part for this condition, but in part only. A distinct feature of the culture was the enviable decree of independence and the domestic and political freedom enjoyed by women.[16] Lewis and Clark comment that the

---

[12] Swan, p. 180.

[13] Cf. Thwaites, vol. 3, p. 274.

[14] *Idem*, p. 360.

[15] Cf. Thwaites, vol. 4, pp. 187 f.; Ross, 92.

[16] See p. 55. "Notwithstanding the survile {servile} manner in which they treat their women they pay much more respect to their judgment and opinions in many respects than most Indian nations; their women are permitted to speak freely before them, and sometimes appear to command with a tone of authority; they generally consult them in their traffic

men

collect and prepare all the fuel, make the fires, assist in cleansing and preparing the fish, and always cook for the strangers who visit them. They also build their houses, construct their canoes and make all their wooden utensils. The peculiar province of the woman seems to be to collect roots and manufacture various articles which are prepared of rushes, flags, cedar bark, 95s or waytape. The management of the canoe for various purposes seems to be a duty common to both sexes, as also many other occupations which with most Indian nations devolves exclusively on the women. Their feasts of which they are very fond are always prepared and served by the men.

Some of the men engaged in these tasks were perhaps slaves, though Lewis and Clark were quite aware of the badge of the slave, the unflattened forehead. But they were doubtless quite unaware that some of these "duties" would have been vigorously defended by the men as sex prerogatives, particularly the preparation of feasts and serving of guests.

The domestic relationships between masters and slaves seem to have been of a very healthy order. Intimate accounts are lacking but the indications are all in the direction of tranquil and unoppressive relations.[17]

Activities within the household centered largely around meals and their preparation, the fashioning of articles and tools, and amusements. The two former are described below. [129]

PREPARATION OF FOOD

Cooking methods included boiling, broiling, roasting, and steaming. Almost all foods were subject to boiling either individually or in combination. Vessels used consisted of dugout wooden containers, bark containers, and baskets. The use of baskets for this purpose may have been a recently introduced or a regional trait; cooking baskets are not mentioned by Lewis and Clark, while Swan speaks only of them.[18] Mrs. Luscier specifically denied the use of baskets.

In boiling food, water was first placed in the container, then the heated rocks, and lastly the food. Rocks were removed from the fire with tongs and dipped into a separate container of water to remove the ashes before being placed in the cooking water. While cooking the food was covered with a small mat.[19] It was stirred with a small wooden paddle.

Broiling was a favorite method of preparing salmon and some meat. The fish were split dorsally, opened out and held in this position by thin cedar skewers placed laterally. A cedar stick, to be used as a spit, was pointed on one end and split at the other. The extended fish was inserted in the split portion with tail end opposite the point. Beach grass served to tie the open extremity together, whereupon the pointed end was forced into the ground near the fire so that the top inclined toward it. Clamshells were placed on the ground below to catch the oil as

---

and act in conformity to their opinions." (Thwaites, vol. 3, p. 315.)

[17] See slavery.

[18] Thwaites, vol. 3, pp. 353 f.; Swan, p. 164.

[19] Cf. Boas, *Chinook Texts,* p. 233; Franchère, p. 248.

it dripped. The spit was turned from time to time. The head was cooked in similar fashion, but usually separately. Meat was broiled in the same way except that the spit was simply a stick pointed on both ends.[20]

Certain roots, for example lupine and wapato, were roasted on glowing embers. Fowl and porcupine were often roasted whole by covering with hot embers.[21]

Clams, oysters and crabs were steamed by being held above the water in a covered container of boiling water. The rocks for boiling, together with crossed sticks, supported the shell-fish. Steaming was also accomplished with a shallow earth oven. The oven was heated before the food was put in but no fire was built on top. The food was wrapped and covered with skunk cabbage leaves, bracken fern, or old mats. Steaming resulted from water being poured in limited quantity on the food. Elderberries were cooked in this way.

The liquid remaining in the cooking utensil after boiled food had been removed was highly relished. Soup was made from meat bones or from moss which had been used to absorb the blood when game was butchered, then dried and stored. Liquid foods were commonly drunk from clam shell spoons. Marrow was extracted from bones and eaten. Dried elk and deer meat was pulverized and mixed with seal grease but not with other products. Roots of the bracken fern were singed and eaten or roasted. When dried they were mixed with fish eggs. Shell-fish, in addition to being steamed, were roasted, boiled, or dried and boiled. Seeds and nuts, with the [130] exception of the acorn, were little used. Acorns were buried in the mud for leeching before being used. Eggs of all kinds were eaten except perhaps those of the sea gull. Tea was made from blackberry leaves. Blood of game was drunk but whether raw or cooked is uncertain. Insects were not eaten, nor were barnacles. Dog meat was inconceivable as food. Mrs. Bertrand remarked at the question, "Why, a dog is like a human being." Meat and fish were not eaten at the same meal. Salt was not used.

Meals ordinarily were served three times a day, early in the morning, at noon, and at sunset. Regardless of the hour, a meal was served soon after guests arrived. Also, when game or fish was brought in a meal was prepared immediately. Special cattail mats were spread on the floor at meal time. Upon these were placed smaller mats for dry foods, wooden platters and bowls for boiled fish and meats, ladles and spoons for service, and shredded cedar bark napkins.

In preparing salmon for drying the fish was split down the back so that the head, backbone, and tail were separated from the rest of the body. The head and tail were cut from the backbone and strung together for drying. The flesh of the backbone was eaten immediately. The ventral portion was laid open with cedar skewers and slashed evenly so that as great an area would be exposed as possible. Thus prepared the fish was hung from poles near the ceiling of the house or upon specially constructed scaffolding.[22][22] When dried, and incidentally smoked, the salmon was taken down and stored in baskets for later use or for

---

[20] Thwaites, vol. 3, pp. 353 f.; Swan, p. 108.

[21] Bailey comments that "the strong body odor of the animal [porcupine) is conveyed to the flesh in skinning, but the Indian method of roasting them whole, quills and all, in a camp fire until nicely done, and then breaking open the charred crust and eating out the juicy flesh may be far superior to the frying-pan method." (Bailey, p. 231.)

[22] See Plates 2, 3.

barter. Pulverized salmon was prepared for storage and trade by partially broiling, then drying. After this the flesh was pounded, mixed with a small amount of water, and squeezed in the hands, forcing it out between the fingers until it became a homogeneous mass. It was then dried in the sun and packed in small baskets. The product was called *sq'we•tsəm*. Salmon eggs were dried and stored in salmon skins.[23]

Swan describes the preparation of sturgeon: The fish "is opened, care being taken to save all the blood, which is put into a kettle with some choice cuts, and then boiled. The head, like that of the salmon, is esteemed the best part, and is either boiled, or cut in strips and broiled or roasted before the fire. The pith of the back bone is considered a great luxury.... The rest of the fish is then cut in thin strips and dried in the smoke."[24]

Meat was dried by cutting it into small pieces and suspending it on an open-work platform over a slow fire.

Oil was rendered and stored in wooden vessels.

BOXES, BOWLS AND SPOONS

The Chinook household was supplied with a variety of receptacles made of wood, horn and shell. Wood-working technique appears to have been limited to fashioning articles from a solid piece of material. Kerfing, bending and joining of boards, typical of wood-working among more northerly groups, apparently was unknown. Yet a wide range of forms was produced, mainly variants of three fundamental [131] mental shapes: the square box, the bowl, and the platter. Some were provided with well-fitted covers. All, according to Lewis and Clark, were "extremely well executed."

The square dugout box of cedar was used mainly for carrying and storing water and for cooking; the larger ones were provided with hand-holes. Bowls and bowl-shaped vessels were made less consistently of cedar than the boxes. Alder, maple, ash and yew (*Taxus brevifolia*) were favorite supplementary materials. In addition to bowl-shaped or round-bottomed vessels of various sizes, small, round, flat-bottomed cups were made to be used for oil. Platters were long and shallow, with almost straight sides but rounded ends. Those designed for feasting often were elaborately carved, painted, and inlaid along the edges with shells.[25][26] The ends of some were raised and ornamented with animal figures. Others were carved very much in the shape of a canoe. These elaborate dishes were often named. On the occasion of an especially large feast actual canoes were sometimes used for cooking food.[26]

Hemispherical horn bowls with raised, rectangular "ears" (Figure 14) were widespread in western Washington and the Columbia valley. Those possessed by the Chinook were quite certainly of their own manufacture. These were invariably decorated with geometric designs (Figure 15), the simplest being rectangular perforations in the raised portions with incised outlining

---

[23] Luscier; Swan, pp. 11 f., 165 f.

[24] Swan, p. 246.

[25] Cf. canoes.

[26] Cf. p. 94.

FIG. 14. Horn bowl.

The commonest spoon was merely the shell of the clam. More elaborate spoons and ladles were carved of alder, yew, or maple; or were molded from horn. These had large, wide bowls and were provided with short, perforated handles, sometimes ornamented. Elaborately carved spoons of musk-ox horns were received in trade from the north.[27])

Large ladles and food stirrers were made of wood.[28]

BASKETRY AND MATTING

Chinook basketry (Plate 5) was dominantly in the twined technique, with a considerable amount of twilling. Checker-work, particularly with cedar bark, was important but secondary. Checker-work mats were small; all large mats were made [132]

FIG. 15. Designs from horn bowls (compare Field Museum specimens 19692-19698).

of cattail rushes sewed together except at the edges, which were braided. Coiling was not

---

[27] Swan, p. 163.

[28] Luscier; Thwaites, vol. 3, pp. 274, 353 f.; Swan, p. 163; Dunn, p. 138.

known.

It is somewhat difficult at this date to establish the types around which variation occurred and to judge the importance of each. Lewis and Clark emphasize the water-tight twined basket of cedar bark which they state was found in capacities "from that of the smallest cup to five or six gallons."[29] They add that these were truncated cones in form, the small end being the bottom, and that dyed bear grass, (*Xerophyllum tenax*) (*q'wıla•lstip*), a product imported from up the Columbia near the Cascade Mountains, was used for ornamentation. Swan, on the other hand, describes only baskets of spruce root, willow bark and bear grass.[30] Mrs. Luscier placed spruce root foremost as a basketry material and among the baskets I obtained from her (now in the Washington State Museum; see Plate 5), those of spruce root were most prominent while none of water-proof construction in cedar bark [133] was represented.[31] This may be a matter of regional variation but it should be remembered that woven cedar bark hats, in the same construction, were formerly common not only in the Columbia river region but also on Willapa Bay. In both areas these disappeared long ago. Also, Douglas writes of baskets woven from the roots of bear grass (his *Helonias tenax)* and adds that cedar root was similarly used, but he does not mention the use of cedar bark.[32]

Openwork baskets both of spruce root and cedar bark were extensively used for carrying shell-fish and salmon and for storing dried salmon. The trapezoidal spruce root clam basket of the northern coast was well represented here (Plate 5, D).

A description of the baskets illustrated on Plate 5 may serve for typological description: (A) A finely twined basket of spruce root, water-tight. This is not twilled, though the arrangement of the design gives that impression. It was used for packing pulverized salmon for trade; when filled a cover was sewed over the top. This basket, called *maxu'i'*, served as a standard measure (depth, 12 inches; diameter, 8 inches) and was transferred along with the contents when traded, (B) Openwork basket of cedar bark (*o'p'qanx̲*). Used for storing and trading dried salmon and dried clams; standard measure (depth, 10 inches; diameter, 15 inches), (C) Twined storage basket of small rushes, *Juncus* sp. ? (*q'a•'qtsux*), called cmu•'x̓lnɫ, "small-mouthed basket." Used for storing salal berries, blackberries, and others. Depth, 9 inches; diameter, 14 inches. This basket was made by *putu•'lutc*. (D) Openwork basket of spruce roots (*qɫo'muɫ'ya'unəks ?*). This is the trapezoidal clam basket mentioned above. Hung on the back while gathering shell-fish. Sometimes used to carry salmon. Depth, 8 inches; width, 12 inches, (E) Trinket basket of twined rushes. Depth, 4 inches; diameter, 5 inches, (F) Twilled basket of flat spruce roots (*sa•'pənux*). This basket, used for dried salmon heads (*spɫia•lat*) and ordinary dried salmon (*x̲et'sa•'ius*), was another standard measure (depth, 7 inches; width, 8 inches). (G) This bag of cattail trimmed with bear grass is of the type used for carrying, storing, and trading dried meat. It is identical in construction with the cattail mats (described below) except that it is doubled and two edges are braided together. The ornamentation is of bear grass. Depth, 20 inches; width, 24 inches.

Baskets for water were similar to that described under (A) above. Basketry hats were

---

[29] Thwaites, lo*c .cit.*

[30] Swan, p. 162.

[31] The group is too small to be anything more than suggestive.

[32] Douglas, pp. 261 f.

made in a similar close-twined technique.[33] Checker-work baskets of rushes were known but were made less frequently than the twined type.

Spruce root (*t'aq'e'xan'*) was steamed and then split into strips of proper size for basket work. Immediately before use it was soaked over night in water. Rough cedar bark (*q'we•'ł*) was scraped, dried, and split in order to prepare it for use. Cedar bark of black color (*sxwɪ'iuxł*) was obtained by burying it in the mud.

Cattail (*suwi'tc*) mats served a wide variety of uses, including house covering, house lining, partioning, floor covering, bedding, eating mats, and flat bags. The cattail was cut during July and August, carefully dried, and stored in a dry place until fall or winter, when mats ordinarily were made. In the manufacture of a mat the separate pieces were cut the proper length, about three feet, and laid side by side. [134]

Large and small ends were alternated so that an even edge would be obtained. A single row of twining along each side served to hold the pieces in place until the desired length was obtained. Then stakes were driven in the ground at the ends of the row to which the twining cords were made fast. A mat needle was threaded and thrust at right angles through the stems, beginning at one end near the edge of the row. Several elements were pierced . at a time and the stitching was continued until the opposite end of the row was reached. Further stitching, in parallel lines about four inches apart, bound the cattails into a strong unit. The seams were flattened

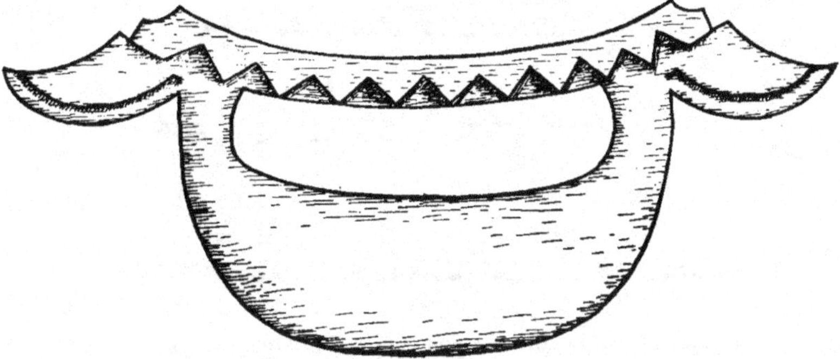

FIG. 16. Mat creaser (after Field Museum specimen 19640).

FIG. 17. Mat creaser (after Field Museum specimen 19636).

by means of a mat creaser with a grooved edge (Figures 16, 17). The mat edges were trimmed and bound by braiding with elements of contrasting colors, or colored grasses were introduced

---

[33] See clothing.

into the braiding.[34]

Mat needles were made of wood (Figure 18, c) or bone (Figure 18, B). The wooden needle (*ıla•'lcıt'*) was made of hard-wood and curved somewhat. Length varied greatly; the needle illustrated measures fourteen inches by three-eighths, while another one measured in the field was thirty-six inches long and curved much [135] more than the shorter one. Both of these were roughly triangular in cross-section but one of yew wood in the Washington State Museum is squarish and medium in length, seventeen inches long.

Bone needles were always relatively short, varying from eight to sixteen inches. They were also much straighter. Swan mentions the bone of the second joint of the wing of the heron (*Ardea herodias fannini;* Swan's "blue crane") as that utilized for the mat needle.[35] All needles were provided with distal eyes. Cord for sewing mats was made by twisting rushes very tightly, or of nettle or other fiber.

Mat creasers were likewise made of hard-wood or bone, more commonly of the former. They were quite carefully carved and decorated, varying around a fairly stable type as indicated by those illustrated. They averaged five inches in width.

Basketry dyes included alder, Oregon grape root, hemlock and mud.

Cordage was spun of nettle fibers, rushes, willow bark fiber[36] and other materials.

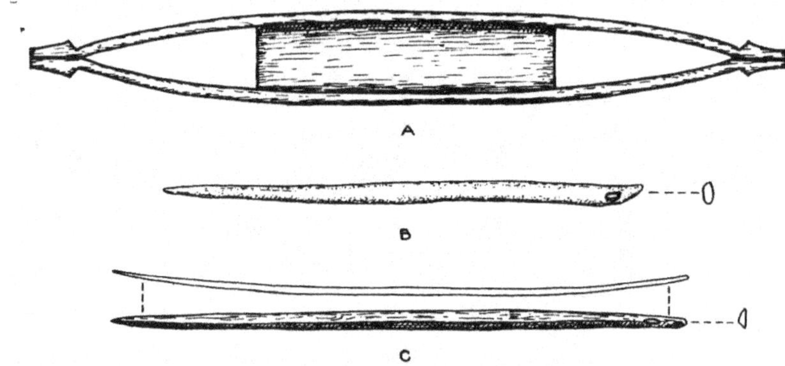

FIG. 18.   (A) Shuttle for weaving nets (after Field Museum specimen 19713);
(B) Bone mat needle: (C) Wooden mat needle.

FIG. 18.   (A) Shuttle for weaving nets (after Field Museum specimen 19713); (B) Bone mat needle: (C) Wooden mat needle.

MISCELLANEOUS IMPLEMENTS

Mussel shell knives were used for cutting food, fibers, skins and perhaps wood. Simple drills were tipped with points of horn or flint. Beaver teeth were used as engraving instruments. Awls were made of bear bone or raccoon bone, six or seven inches in length. They were used for basket making, skin work, and general utility.

Adzes were of the straight type. In Lewis' and Clark's time these already were provided with iron blades. The handle consisted of a large block of wood. In use they grasped "just below the block with the right hand holding the top of the block, and strike backward against

---

[34] Swan, p. 161 f.; Luscier.

[35] Swan, p. 162.

[36] Cf. Boas, *Chinook Texts,* p. 220.

the wood with the edge...."[37] It seems likely that the aboriginal blade was of shell or bone. Stone blades may have been known but stone never played a very important part in the culture of the Lower Chinook.[38] [136]

Wedges of wood or horn were used in splitting planks, fire wood, and for the rough work in canoe manufacture. The wood used was the Oregon crab-apple (*Pyrus diversifolia*), an extremely satisfactory material. The horn wedges were fashioned of elk antler.[39] Mallets of spruce knots, hardened with oil and heat, are mentioned by Dunn.[40] He also writes of oblong stone hammers.[41]

Mortars, which were made only of wood, were circular in shape and sometimes ornamented. With them were used pestles of wood, or less commonly, stone. The latter were plain and tapering; those of wood were somewhat broadened at the base and served largely for berries.

Fire making was accomplished with the simple fire drill and perhaps by concussion. Twisted cedar fibers carried in a hollow bone served as a slow match. Tongs for removing cooking stones from the fire were made of two sticks bound together at the handle end.

Wooden net shuttles (Figure 18, A) were used in weaving seines and other large nets. These may have been recent and of European origin in design.

---

[37] Thwaites, vol. 4, p. 36.

[38] Cf. Smith.

[39] Thwaites, vol. 4, p. 19 f.

[40] Dunn, p. 138.

[41] Cf. Smith., p 302.

DRESS AND ORNAMENT

CLOTHING

During mild weather, especially while working, men wore no clothing whatsoever. When protection from the cold was needed a fur robe was worn hung from the shoulders with a thong which passed around the neck. The side opening provided freedom for the arm on that side; it was shifted to the opposite side when there was a desire to use the other arm. When the free use of both arms was necessary the opening was moved to the front, allowing the back and shoulders to remain covered but exposing the front of the body. These robes, which hung to the middle of the thigh, depended for their outline shape upon the method of their fabrication. Four distinct modes of manufacture were used. Most commonly several small skins, or fewer large ones, were tanned with the fur adhering and sewed together to form a l roughly rectangular garment. The most frequently used small skin was that of the mountain beaver (often erroneously called the wood rat).[1] These pelts were quite small necessitating several to form a single robe. Perhaps second in frequency of use was the skin of the Oregon bobcat. Three or four of these sufficed for one robe. In similar manner were used many other furs, including the raccoon, beaver, musk-rat, and the most valuable of all furs, the sea otter. Two skins of this last animal were required for each robe. The second type of robe was that made from the skin of a single animal with the outline left irregular according to the natural shape of the pelt, but with the extremities cut off. Such skins as those of the deer, bear, cougar, and elk served this purpose. All were tanned without removing the hair. Perhaps even more frequently used were robes of the third type, skins cut in strips, twisted, and woven by twining with thin, strong cords. Thus a blanket was formed with fur exposed equally on both sides. Such a method was used for fragile skins and also when it was desired to produce an especially fine garment. Rabbit skins, with which this technique is best known elsewhere, were so used by the Chinook but not as extensively as those of the mountain beaver, raccoon, or sea otter. The fourth type of blanket was that made of the wool of the mountain goat spun into cord and woven on the loom. No details of this technique are known beyond the fact of its use. Whether dog wool or other fibers were intermixed is uncertain. Such robes or blankets seem to have been relatively uncommon and it is probable that most of them were imported from the north.[2] In any event it was necessary that the wool be imported for the goat was not found in Lower Chinook territory.[3]

For protection from the rain a poncho-like garment of small rushes was worn. This was merely a rectangular mat with a slit at the middle for the neck. Since it was open at both sides it permitted free arm action and was frequently used while paddling the canoe. [138]

No other garment was worn by men except the basketry hat (described below).

Moccasins and breech cloth were wholly unknown.

Women wore a cape or robe identical to that of the men except that it was shorter, never reaching below the waist. Consequently fewer skins were required but the same

---

[1] See physical environment.
[2] See Gunther, *Klallam Ethnography, p. 221;* Haeberlin and Gunther, pp. 30 f.
[3] See physical environment.

techniques were employed. In addition, women wore the shredded cedar bark skirt. This was the invariable garment. The robe was discarded except when exposure required it, but the skirt was worn at least whenever in company with men. The skirt was made by shredding the inner bark of the cedar into small strands by the use of a bluntly sharpened bone implement. These were arranged in skirt-like form by twining for several inches at the upper edge. This band did not form a circle. The skirt was wrapped around the waist and tied tightly at the side. The shredded pendants hung somewhat lower in back than front, reaching nearly to the knees. Sometimes the lower ends of the fibers were gathered into small bunches and knotted. Other materials than cedar bark were frequently used. Indian hemp or nettle fiber made finer and longer-lasting skirts, while small rushes were used in making rougher and poorer ones.

For maximum protection women made use of a small garment which covered the breasts and extended to the waist in front, passed under the armpits and was tied in back. This was a small rectangular piece made of twisted and woven strips of fur similar to some of the larger garments.

A rain garment of rushes identical to that worn by men was likewise utilized by women

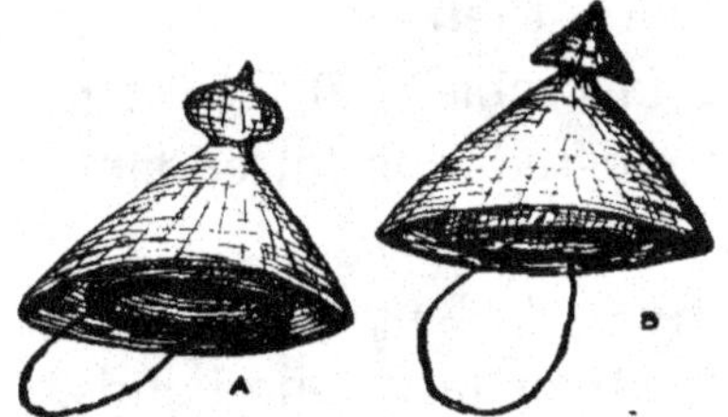

FIG. 19. Basketry hats. (A) With round knob;
(B) With conical knob. (After Lewis and Clark.)

Basketry hats were extensively used by both men and women. These were sub-conical in form with slightly flaring brims and superimposed at the crown with a small knob in round or conical shape. The knob was integrally woven with the body of the hat. A secondary brim was provided inside the hat so that the wide brim might be held up and away from the face. A string was fastened to this inside brim for fastening around the chin. Lewis and Clark illustrate one type[44] (see Figure 19). They were wholly waterproof, being twined of cedar bark, spruce root, and bear grass. Whether the bear grass was used only as overlay is uncertain. Designs and figures were woven into the hats, commonly using black and white (light) contrasts, but sometimes colors. Realistic designs such as whales and canoes are described by Lewis and Clark.[5] How long such designs had been in use and whether or not these were trade pieces, is unknown. [139]

That style of dress did not vary from the mouth of the river to at least as far up as Puget Island is indicated by Lewis and Clark's descriptions.[6] But Broughton, while near Puget Island, observed, "Their clothing was chiefly deer skins, though a few had garments made of sea otter skins."[7] At an indefinite but short distance upriver Cox observed the use by women of a skin

---

[4] Thwaites, vol. 4, pp. 23 f.

[5] *Idem,* p. 24.

[6] Cf. Thwaites, vol. 3, pp. 208 f.; vol. 4, pp. 23 f.

[7] Vancouver, vol. 2, p. 58.

apron or possibly breech cloth.[8] Ross writes specifically of the woman's breech cloth but does not state by what group it was worn.[9] Boit, in the earliest of all observations upon Chinook clothing, suggests that the women wore a small apron of woven fibers.[10]

Dance or ceremonial regalia consisted of the best of one's clothing together with a few additions. A cedar bark band about two inches wide was worn around the head with several eagle feathers projecting upward from it (see Frontispiece). The band was painted red and black with a simple geometric design such as a wavy line. Sometimes it was decorated with dentalia. Whether or not this was a recent custom is uncertain.

Sometimes a single eagle feather was worn in the hair. Down of the fish duck was sprinkled over the hair, whitening it. The band and down were used by both men and women.[11]

BODY CARE, PAINTING AND TATOOING

As one follows the comments on body care and cleanliness of the Chinook from the first writers through succeeding years, there is an almost uniform progression from favorable remarks to those less and less favorable.[12] Thus we have substantial documentation for the usually assumed progressive degradation attendant to greater and greater contact of northwest natives with whites.

These people, Clark observed, "Appeared much neater in their diet than Indians are commonly, and frequently wash their faces and hands."[13] Lewis comments in a similar vein, "They are fond of combs and use them when they can obtain them; and even without the aid of the comb keep their hair in better order than many nations who are in other respects much more civilized than themselves."[14]

From a somewhat different point of reference Franchère declares that "They possess, in an eminent degree, the qualities opposed to indolence, improvidence and stupidity: the chiefs, above all are distinguished for their good sense and intelligence. Generally speaking, they have a ready intellect and a tenacious memory".[15]

But in 1840 Wilkes writes, "Both sexes are equally filthy, and I am inclined to believe they will continue so; for their habits are inveterate, and from all the accounts [140] I could gather from different sources, there is reason to believe that they have not been improved or been benefited by their constant intercourse with the whites.... "[16] How true!

---

[8] Cox, p. 76.

[9] Ross ,pp. 91 f.

[10] Boit, p. 248.

[11] Luscier; Thwaites, vol. 3, pp. 208 f., 238, 359 f.; idem, vol. 4, pp. 86, 94, 185 f.; Coues, p. 749; Ross, pp. 89, 91; Franchère, pp. 242-44; Cox, p. 69; Swan, p. 155; Boas, *Chinook Texts*, p. 220.

[12] With notable exceptions among objective observers such as Swan.

[13] Thwaites, vol. 3, p. 274.

[14] Thwaites, vol, 4, p. 184.

[15] Franchère, p. 261.

[16] Wilkes, vol. 5, p. 116.

On the other hand, that excellent observer, Swan, at an even later date remarks:

While the Indians are engaged in curing salmon, or when they are boiling the blubber of a whale or seal, they are as necessarily dirty as the crew of a whale-ship or butchers in a slaughterhouse; and at such times, casual visitors form an opinion that they are a filthy, greasy set, and we find many writers willing to assert that they regularly anoint their bodies with fish-oil and red ochre. Such, however, is not the fact. As soon as their work is done, they wash themselves, and generally bathe two or three times a day. All the painting or oiling I have ever seen them do is rub a little grease and vermillion, or red ochre between their hands, and then smear it over their faces. The women will also paint the head, in the line of the parting of the hair, with dry vermillion, and give an extra touch to their eyebrows; but I have never seen either men or women put oil or grease of any kind on their bodies. The women tattoo their legs and arms with dotted lines, but without any particular figure or design; they are also fond, during the blackberry season, of dotting their limbs with blackberry juice. The tattooing is done with charcoal and water, and pricked into the skin with needles. I very seldom saw a man with tattoo-marks on him.[17]

Lewis and Clark make similar observations regarding painting and tattooing. They suggest that the tattoo designs consisted of parallel lines of dots arranged either around the limbs or linearly.[18] Figures are also mentioned but it is intimated that these were not aboriginal. They add that such decoration was a mark of upper class membership,[19] a point corroborated by Mrs. Luscier.

Facial painting was used for war,[20] ceremony, relief from illness, or mere decoration. Broughton observed that the Chinook "surpassed all other tribes with paints of different colors, feathers, and ornaments."[21] It seems certain, despite Swan, that the body was painted as well as the face, though not as extensively.[22] On the face solid coloring was most commonly used, varied with bands across the cheek bones and around the chin. Special designs were used, as directed by one's guardian spirit, when the painting was used as a therapeutic measure. Red, black, and white were the colors most frequently utilized. Red was made of mineral pigment scraped from the outcroppings, pulverized, and baked in a bark fire. Black was made of alder charcoal. White was obtained from an outcropping on a precipitous cliff near; Tillamook territory. The clay was reached only by lowering the gatherer down the cliff on a rope.[23] All pigments were mixed with either bear or elk oil.

The hair of both sexes was parted in the middle and allowed to fall loosely about the shoulders (see Figure 4, page 69). It was not allowed to grow much beyond the shoulders, and was kept back of the ears as much as possible.[24] The [141] part, as Swan mentions above, was

---

[17] Swan, p. 112. Cf. Boas, *op. tit.,* p. 236.

[18] Thwaites, vol. 4, p. 186.

[19] Thwaites, vol. 3, p. 241.

[20] See warfare.

[21] Vancouver, vol. 2, p. 77.

[22] Cf. Franchère, p. 244.

[23] Thwaites, vol. 3, p. 231.

[24] Cf. Thwaites, vol. 4, p. 184.

often painted with red ochre. Mrs. Luscier explained that in recent years it became the practice for women to plait the hair into two braids and gather it up with a thong at the back. Men, at the same time, came to use one braid occasionally.[25]

Men consistently plucked out the scanty beard growth except that a small tuft was sometimes allowed to grow on the chin.[26]

Ears of both sexes were pierced, both in the lobe and around the rim. Five holes was usual for the rim. From these ornaments were hung, usually of dentalia.[27]

Men had the nasal septum pierced, but not women. Through the opening a thread was passed from which hung dentalia or other ornaments.[28]

Women bound their ankles by encircling them with cordage, causing a swelling of the leg above the wrapping. This was the "deformity" so often referred to in the early literature.[29]

The favorite native bead, ornament, and medium of exchange was the imported dentalium.[3030] This was used for pendants, necklaces, arm bands, bracelets and ankle bands. It is interesting to note that when glass beads were received blue ones were preferred.[31]

---

[25] Cf. Swan, p. 154.

[26] Cf. Franchère, p. 240; Boas, op. cit., frontispiece; Dunn, p. 124; Kane, p. 181.

[27] Cf. Thwaites, vol. 4, p. 187; Scouler, p. 165.

[28] Cf. Thwaites, loc. cit.; Lee and Frost, p. 101; Cox, p. 69.

[29] Cf. Thwaites, loc. cit.; Dunn, p. 123.

[30] See trade.

[31] Cf. Thwaites, vol. 3, pp. 328, 352 f.; idem, vol. 4, p. 187; Franchère, pp. 245 f.

MYTHOLOGY[1]

BUNGLING HOST[2]

There was Bluejay (*te•'xanat*). His sister's name was *io•'i*. They were sitting down, brother and sister. Pretty soon the sister said, "Oh brother, you should go fishing."

He went out early in the morning. It was low tide. He saw someone fishing.

He went over to see him. It was an old fellow. When Bluejay reached him he said, "Oh, are you fishing?" "Yes, brother, I'm fishing. That's all the food I can get," the old man answered. Bluejay watched him. Soon he speared a flounder (*p'oma'i*). Bluejay watched a while longer. The old man speared another one, a bullhead (*sxotno'*). He got five flounders and five bullheads. The old fellow said, "I guess I'll go home now; the tide is coming in. Did you get anything?" "No, I didn't," Bluejay answered; "not even a thing." "Well," the old fellow said, "you can come to eat with me."

Bluejay went home and told his sister. She took a bag on her back. They went in a canoe. They reached the old fellow's house. He had many fish, all kinds. "What kind do you want me to cook for you?" he asked. "Oh, anything," Bluejay answered. The old man took a flounder and roasted it for them. They ate it and got ready to go home. "You had better go first," Bluejay's sister said to him. "No, you go first," he answered. "You won't say anything to him?" the sister asked. "No, I won't say anything," he promised. So she took all of the flounder that they hadn't eaten and put it in her basket and left. Bluejay said to Crane (*sqwa's*) [the old man], "You'd better come to our house tomorrow." "All right," Crane answered.

The next morning Bluejay went out early. Then he came in and said, "There is a little canoe coming." "Oh, you must have asked Crane to come," his sister said. "What can we feed him?" 'Oh, that's all right," Bluejay answered.

Crane came in. They put down a food mat and sat down. Then Bluejay unwrapped a mat and took out three pieces of flounder and three pieces of bullhead. They were small pieces. He gave them to Crane. Crane saw that they were his fish. He didn't eat much; he said that he was in a hurry and left. Bluejay was angry. "Why did he go?" he asked. His sister said, "Why, he couldn't eat that! It was his own fish!" "No, that was my fish," Bluejay said.

The next morning Bluejay said to his sister, "Let's visit Seal (*o•'lxa'iu*)." They went to Seal's house. They got there. Seal was lying down on her bed. They went in. Seal saw the old people; "Oh, you have come !" "Yes, my sister and I decided to come and see you." Seal was glad. Seal had two boys and three girls. She told her oldest daughter, "You had better go over and lie down on that snag." Then they talked. After a while Seal asked another daughter, "Is your sister lying on that snag?" The girl went out. She saw her sister on the snag. She went in and [143] told her mother. Seal went out and got a club. She went to the snag. Her daughter was lying there sound asleep. Seal went behind her and clubbed her. The girl floundered

---

[1] These myths were obtained incidentally during the recording of ethnographic data from Emma Luscier. All were recorded during the summer of 1931. They are presented here to give something of the flavor of Chinook mythology and to provide a bit of comparative material.

[2] Cf. Boas, *Chinook Texts,* pp. 167-71, 178-82.

around, dead. Seal carried her home. She put her on the fire and singed the hair off. Pretty soon she got brown. The hair was all burned off. Seal scraped her with a stick. Then she skinned her and took all of the fat off. It was her little daughter. After all the fat was taken out she got a vessel and heated rocks until they were red. She put sticks under the pot. Then she put in five pieces of fat and five pieces of meat. Then she put in the rocks and poured water in until everything was covered. She waited. Now everything was cooked good. She took it out. She got plates and put the meat on them. She gave it to the visitors. She gave them soup, too. She gave them shell spoons. They ate the soup, the meat, and the fat. They finished. Bluejay's sister put what was left on a bone stick, the meat and the fat, to take home. They got ready to go home. Bluejay's sister said, "You go first." "No, you go first," Bluejay answered; "you might say something to her." His sister became angry. As soon as she had gone Bluejay asked Seal to visit them.

It was morning. Bluejay made the fire. He saw a canoe and told his sister. "What will we give them to eat?" she asked. "Oh, I'll give them something," Bluejay answered. Seal came in. Bluejay's sister put down good mats for Seal to sit on. She sat down. Bluejay had children but he had no wife. He called his children. They came. He spoke to the youngest one, "Now you go and lie down over there." She lay down. Bluejay talked. Then he went out. His daughter was lying down. He clubbed the girl. She kicked, kicked and died. Then he wondered, "What shall I do? Should I pluck her feathers or cook her whole? I'd better pluck her feathers." He heated rocks. He put his daughter in the vessel. Then he put in the hot rocks and covered them with water. He tried to do everything just as Seal did. Now she was cooked. He took the cover off the vessel. The little girl was all dried up. She was burned because she had no fat. Bluejay fainted. Seal looked in the vessel. "It's too bad what you have done," she said.

Seal called her children. All five of them came. The one she had killed came. Seal had brought her to life again. Her forehead hadn't been cooked. Seal had blown on her at that spot and brought her back to life.

All the children were there. Bluejay was lying dead [unconscious]. Seal spoke to her daughter, "Lie down there, quickly! I'm in a hurry!" Her daughter lay down. Seal clubbed her. She floundered and died. Seal singed her, scraped her, skinned her, and took off the fat. She told *io•'i* to take Bluejay away. Then she heated the rocks and put the meat and the rocks in the vessel and covered them with water. She waited. Now the meat was cooked. She took it out. It was well cooked. She asked *io•'i* if she had a wooden platter. She answered, "Yes." She brought the platter to Seal. Bluejay was still dead. Seal went out. She found Bluejay's daughter's head. Her forehead hadn't been burned. Seal blew on it five times and put it in the water. The girl came to life. Pretty soon she went into the house, shaking off the water.

Seal went home. She felt badly because of what Bluejay had done. [144]

Bluejay came to life. Then he saw the meat. "Why didn't Seal eat any meat? Why didn't she eat my meat?" he asked. "That's not your meat; that's Seal's meat. There's your daughter, over there," his sister answered. "No!" Bluejay exclaimed, "that's my meat." "Be quiet!" *io•'i* said, "you can't do those things!" Then they ate. They drank soup and ate meat.

Then they visited *xwa'saqwax.*[3]

---

[3] A small gray bird, fond of salmon eggs.

Early in the morning Bluejay said to his sister, "We'll go to visit *xwa'saqwax."* "No," she answered, "we shouldn't go." "Come on, let's go," Bluejay insisted. "Oh, you always want to do what everyone else does, and you can't," she objected. They argued. Then they went. They went up the river.

"A canoe is coming," the children of xwa'saqwax called. "It's a little canoe with two people." "Oh, that's Bluejay," their father thought. He had already heard what Bluejay was doing. Bluejay and his sister landed. They went in. "Put down the good mats," xwa'saqwax told his children. They put them down. "Oh, you decided to come up and see me?" "Yes," Bluejay answered, "we made up our minds all at once to come and visit you." xwa'saqwax was glad. "We won't stay long," *io•'i* said; "we'll go home soon." "Oh, no ! You must stay and eat," xwa/'saqwax answered. Bluejay's sister was afraid. She was afraid Bluejay would try to do something that he couldn't. xwa'saqwax picked up a vessel. Bluejay looked around; he couldn't see any fish, or anything. He wondered what they would eat. He could see nothing. xwa"saqwax had lots of hair. It was thick and long. After the rocks were all heated, he was walking around. He took one salmon egg out of his hair. He put it in the vessel. Then he put in the rocks and poured on the water. In a little while he took off the cover. The vessel was full of salmon eggs. He gave spoons to Bluejay and *io•'i*, and food. They ate soup. After they had finished they got ready to go home. "You had better go first," *io•'i* said to Bluejay. "No, you go first," Bluejay answered. "No, you'll invite him to visit us," said *io•'i*. "No, you go !" They argued. They were angry. Bluejay's sister went out. Bluejay said to the old man, "You had better come and visit us tomorrow." "All right," the old man answered. They went home.

It was early in the morning. Bluejay had the fire going. He looked up. He saw a canoe coming. It was a little canoe. "Here comes the old man," he told his sister. "What are you going to feed him?" she asked. "Oh, I'll get something." "Yes, you'll try to do what he did and you can't." They argued. The old fellow got there. He landed his canoe and went ashore. "Put down the good mats," Bluejay told his sister. She put them down. The old man sat down. He looked around. He saw nothing. "What will they give me to eat?" he wondered. He saw nothing. Now Bluejay got a vessel ready. He did the same as the old fellow. When he was eating at the old man's house he had put away one salmon egg. Soon everything was ready. Bluejay took the egg. He put it into the vessel. Then he sat down. He talked. Then he opened the pot. Only one egg was there; it was all dried up. Bluejay died [fainted]. "That's too bad," xwa"saqwax said. He told *io•'i* to clean the vessel. She cleaned it. He heated rocks. Soon all was ready. He put one egg in the [145] vessel. "Don't keep it there long," he said; "I am going home. I have lots of work to do." He went out. He started away.

Bluejaywokeup. He uncovered the vessel. It was full of salmon eggs. "What's the matter with that fellow?" he asked, "Why didn't he eat any of my food?" His sister exclaimed, "Aren't you ashamed? You try to do everything that you can't do. There's your egg, all dried up. The old fellow felt sorry for you." They ate the salmon eggs.

The next morning Bluejay said, "Let's visit Beaver (i•'na')." "No," *io•'i* answered. They argued. They went up, far up. They went to visit Beaver. "How are we going to get in" *io•'i* asked. "His door is under water; we'll have to dive." Beaver had five doors, like steps, under the water. Bluejay tried to dive to the first door. He put his nose in the water. He pulled it out. But he wanted to go in. "You go first," he said to his sister; "then call me and tell me how you get along." "It's easy," she answered. She held her breath and shut her eyes. She dived in quickly and got to the second door. It was nice and dry. She sat down and looked out. She called to Bluejay and told him to shut his eyes and hold his breath. He tried four times. The fifth time he made it. He got to Beaver's house. Beaver was lying down, tired. He was fat, so fat he could hardly move. "Oh, you decided to come," he said. "Yes, I decided to come," Bluejay answered. Bluejay looked around. He saw nothing but green sticks; willow, alder, salmon-berry, and two other kinds. They were piled thickly, all over the house. There was one pile there, and one there —five piles in all. Soon Beaver said, "I just came in; I was out fishing. I'm tired, I fished all night. I'll give you fresh trout to eat that I caught just last night." "I was just wishing for trout," Bluejay answered. Beaver took one bunch of sticks and put it on the mat. "What is he doing?" Bluejay asked his sister; "we can't eat those sticks." "Shut your eyes and eat," she said. "That's his food. It will be trout." "What can we do?" Bluejay asked again. His sister shut her eyes. She ate trout. Then Bluejay did the same. He ate trout. Then he opened his eyes. He saw nothing but sticks. "Oh, *io•'i*," he asked, "what did you do with the fish?" "That's it," she answered; "shut your eyes and eat." Bluejay shut his eyes and ate; it was good. Then Beaver gave them salmon-berry sprouts. They were just sticks. Bluejay and his sister shut their eyes and ate fish. The old fellow didn't move. What they couldn't eat *io•'i* put in her basket. They stayed awhile. "We'd better go home now. It's late," *io•'i* said. "You go first," she told her brother. "No, you go," he answered. They argued. She put her basket on her back and dived out. Bluejay asked Beaver to visit them. "All right," Beaver answered. Bluejay had a hard time getting out. He tried four times. He had a hard time. The next time that he tried, he got out. They started home. They went home.

The next morning Bluejay saw Beaver coming. He told his sister to put down the good mats. Bluejay got his knife and rushed out. He looked around. He saw some willow; he cut five sprouts. He found some salmon-berry; he cut five sprouts. He ran to some alder; he cut five alder sprouts. He found the other two bushes and cut five sprouts from each. Then he went in. He had all that he could pack. He got a dish. "I just got back," he said; "I've been fishing." Beaver shut his eyes and ate. It was good. He ate until the first bunch was gone. Then he ate another [146] bunch. He ate and ate. He ate all five bunches. He was glad for the good meal. Bluejay did well that time. Beaver got ready to go. "I'll go home now," he said.

Talapas[44] spoke to Bluejay: "People in the future will try to do things that they can't. If they have power, they will be able to; otherwise, they won't. You will be bluejay after this. You won't try to do those things. You will tell hunters whether to go hunting or not."

WREN KILLS ELK

There was Wren (qaqo'p) and his grandmother. Soon his grandmother said, "Oh, my grandson, I wish you would go out and hunt. I'm hungry. I want some meat." Wren asked, "What is it that you wish?" "Well," his grandmother answered, "if you go out, go to one certain spot, then sit down and call for Elk."

Wren went out. He sat down upon a stump. He began to sing. He called for Elk to come. Soon Raccoon came along. Wren looked at him; he watched him. "Oh, this isn't any Elk !" Then he spoke to Raccoon, "I don't want you. I want Elk."

---

[4] Chinook jargon for Coyote.

Wren called again. Another animal came. This time, it was Mink. Wren saw that it was Mink. He said, "I don't want you. I want Elk." "I'm Elk," answered Mink. "No, you aren't," answered Wren. "Grandmother said that Elk was large."

Wren called again. Then Otter came. Otter said that he was Elk. But Wren answered, "I know that you are Otter. I don't want you." Now it was three that had come.

Wren called once more. He wanted Elk to come. He heard something coming. Pretty soon Deer came. "Maybe this is Elk," thought Wren. But it wasn't Elk. Wren found out who it was. It was Deer.

Then Wren called loudly, and sang. He called Elk. Soon he heard a loud cracking in the woods. Then Elk came. Wren wondered what he could do. "You called me," said Elk; "here I am." Wren wondered what he could do. "How could you ever kill me?" asked Elk; "you are too small." "Oh, I'll jump on your neck, then crawl into your heart and cut it out," answered Wren. "No, you won't," said Elk. "I'll sneeze and blow you out." "Then I'll crawl into your eye," Wren said. "I'll close my eye and smash you," answered Elk. "Well, I'll crawl into your ear then," Wren said. "But I'll shake my head and throw you out," Elk answered. "Then I'll watch until you open your mouth and get in that way," Wren said. "I'll spit you out," Elk answered.

Wren watched Elk. He turned around. Pretty soon he raised his tail. Wren jumped in. Elk shook and shook but he couldn't get him out. Wren crawled in a long way. He reached Elk's heart and cut it out. It took a long time. Elk jumped and ran, trying to get Wren out, but he couldn't. After a while he fell down. Then Wren crawled out. It was very hard to do. He was all greasy and bloody. He brought out some fat with him. He wondered what he could do with it to keep from getting it dirty. He was all greasy and bloody. Then he thought of skunk cabbage leaf. He went to a swamp and wrapped the fat up in a skunk cabbage leaf that he found there. Then he went home. [147]

Wren's grandmother was making tamanawas.[5] She was pounding the floor with a stick. She was saying, "I hope my grandson will come home soon." Then Wren came in. "Oh, I'm glad!" she said. "Yes, I'm home," Wren answered. He opened his package of grease. The woman was glad when she saw it. "We can't go after Elk this evening. We'll go in the morning," she decided. Wren was very tired. "You must lie down," his grandmother said. But she stayed awake all night, so they could be ready to leave early the next morning. She really didn't sleep at all.

Early in the morning she awakened Wren. She told him to wash himself. He was covered with blood. Wren washed. Then they started out. After a while they reached Elk. He was really there. Wren's grandmother was overjoyed. She started to sing, "Grandson killed Elk, grandson killed Elk.' Wren asked her how to skin Elk. "What?" she asked. "You — you, a hunter, and you don't know how to skin Elk?" Then she showed him. "Cut here and here, and here," she said. Then Wren skinned Elk. After he was skinned the old woman said, "You will have to dry the meat right here." "But how do you dry it?" asked Wren. She showed him how to dry the meat. She put four sticks in the ground. Then she put two poles on the sticks. Then she put brush across the poles. After that she cut up all the meat and made it ready to dry. She put it all on top of the brush. Then she was finished.

She sent Wren to bring wood. She told him to get wood without any pitch; elder and

---

[5] Chinook jargon for guardian spirit ~ taa<u>x</u> ~ tah.

bark. Wren brought the wood and made a fire under the meat to cook it. "Now, my grandson," the old woman said, "I want you to get some good hemlock; some small round sticks. Then we can turn the meat over so that it will dry quickly." The old woman was very glad. She took a bite of the meat over there, here, and over there. She was eating meat and grease once more.

The next day they started home. Wren wondered how they could take the meat. "We can't pack it all back, grandmother," he said. "Now, my grandson," she asked, "why do you say that you want to be a hunter? Go and find cedar bark and cedar poles; poles that are easy to bend." Wren brought the bark and poles. The old woman put them together. She made a basket to carry the meat. Then she made a carrying strap. "It will be like that," she said; "that's how they will pack meat home. They will clean it all, saving every thing. That's the way they will do it."

After the meat was taken care of, the old woman asked what should be done with the hide. "Oh, I'll take that along," Wren answered. "All right, grandson, we'll fix it up for a blanket." "Oh, my grandmother, really?" Wren exclaimed. They rolled the hide up tight. Then they carried everything home. They packed it out.

When they reached home they made frames for curing the hide. They got bone scrapers. Every day, every day, they worked, scraping the hide. Then it was finished. It was nice and soft. The old woman said, "It will be like that a long time from now. Somebody will have good luck at hunting. He will use the hide that way. He will waste nothing. He will save all the meat, and even the bones. The head will be saved. It will be put in the fire to burn the hair *off*. Then it will be scraped clean." "But what will be done with it?" asked Wren. "It will be saved for winter food. It won't spoil," the old woman answered. "The same will be done [148] with the feet. They will be dried and saved. The grease will be stored too. It will be kept in bags made from intestines."

After a while Wolf came. He begged for some meat. "Oh, grandson," the old woman said, "we had a hard time to get this meat. We don't want to give it away." Wolf went away.

Wren and his grandmother went out. They got in a canoe and went down the river. Wolf went back to the house to ask for meat again. He wanted dried meat and grease. When he got there he found no one, so he went in and ate. He ate grease and dried meat. The old woman had put some wood on the fire before she left. Wolf put some fat on a stick and held it over the fire to melt it. The fat dropped on the fire. Wolf went out. He took some meat. Wren and his grandmother were in the canoe. Wren said, "Grandmother, someone is in our house. Let's go home." Wolf was afraid that someone would come. He took a lot of meat and left. Wren and the old woman returned. She saw what had happened. She saw drops of fat on the fireplace. She called Wren, "Come and see! The meat is nearly all gone." The fat was over half gone; the best meat was gone. Wren came in and looked around. Then he went outside. He saw tracks. "Come grandmother," he called;

"Wolf's tracks are here. He was the one that took the meat."

The old woman came and saw that what he said was true.

PHEASANT, COON AND THE ACORNS;
COYOTE TURNS COTTONWOOD INTO SALMON

Pheasant always dried lots of blackberries. Every day she went out and gathered berries, then dried them for winter. She gathered acorns and dried them and put them away for winter. She got salmon eggs and dried them. Also she dried lots of salmon. She gathered salal berries and hazelnuts and stored them.

In winter Coon got hungry. Pheasant had stored many acorns. She cooked the acoms, then put them in five piles, out in a swamp, so that they would stay damp. Coon was hungry. He said, "Grandma, I'm hungry." Grandma had worked hard all summer and stored food. She said, "What do you want, what do you want?" But Coon just cried. "Do you want acorns?" she asked. "Yes ! that's what I want," Coon answered. "All right," Pheasant said, "get your little canoe and paddle out to my first pile of acorns. Take acorns from the first pile only. You know where they **are;** you helped me put them away. But only fill your canoe half full."

Coon paddled out to the acorns. He filled his canoe full at the first pile, then went back. He ate them all, but he didn't have enough, so he went back. He filled his canoe more than half full again, and ate all of it, but still he didn't have enough, so he stayed at the acorn pile. He ate all of the acoms. But still he was hungry. So he went to the next pile and did the same thing. **He** ate four piles of the acorns. Then he ate half of the last pile.

Crow came along. She saw Coon. She said, "You ate all the acorns!" "No, don't say that," Coon answered. "Come here and I'll give you some." He threw four or five acorns to her. Soon she began to call out again, "Oh! Coon ate all the oak berries." Coon called her down again and gave her some more acorns. Finally, [149] she ate them all. Then Coon wondered what he could do. He thought, "If I go home, I'll get whipped." Then he thought, "Well, I'll have to go home."

Pheasant wondered why Coon was gone so long. "He must have eaten all the acorns," she thought. The old woman got up, got her cane, and went to the place she had stored the acorns. "This is all gone," she thought, as she looked where the first pile had been. "And this is all gone, the second pile, and the third, and the fourth. All five are all gone." She became angry. "When I find Coon I'll give him a good whipping," she thought.

Coon didn't know where to hide. He ran into the house. "I'll hide in the corner," he thought. "No, grandma will see me there. — I'll hide under the bed. — No, I'll hide under the ashes." So he dug a hole in the ashes and lay down next to a charred limb.

Pheasant called and called, but didn't get any answer so she went home. "I'd better make a fire now," she thought. She pulled the coals together. There was a little fire left, live coals. She blew and blew on the coals. But they were Coon's eyes, not coals. Coon finally said, "Don't do that." "Oh, it's you," Pheasant said. Then she grabbed Coon by the hair and took the limb, spruce, and whipped him. Coon was all black. She nearly killed him. Coon cried, "Grandma, I've had enough !" "Why did you eat all the berries?" she asked, and started to whip him again. His face was all black and blue. Then she left him. He jumped out of the ashes, crying. Coon made up his mind to leave home.

His body was all blue, all hurt, when he started on the trail. He came to a creek. There were lots of crab-apples by the creek. Some of them were ripe. He thought, "I'm getting hungry. I'd better climb a tree and get some apples." He was still crying, but he stopped. He climbed the tree and wiped his eyes. He was all hurt and sore. He thought about his grandma. "I like her," he thought, "but she whipped me so hard I left her." He started eating. The crab-apple tasted very good. "I'd better quit crying," he thought. "I'll leave grandma for good, but I'd better quit crying. I like her, hut I'll leave her anyway." Then he heard someone coming down the trail. He listened. "It's grandma," he thought. "She's looking for me now." She was tracking him. "Where has my grandson gone? I'll follow him and be there too." Coon was eating berries; he was glad. He was singing, "Oh my grandma, she whipped me. My body is all blue." He was singing, real Chinook. Soon the old woman heard. She listened. "Oh, that's my grandson," she thought. "I'll talk to him soon, so he will be good to me again." She looked up. She saw her grandson far up in the tree. "Is that you, my grandson?" she called. He didn't answer. She asked again. "Oh, shut up; you bother me. I might fall down." She asked then, "Oh, my grandson, what are you eating?" "I'm eating crab-apples," he answered. "Don't bother me. I might fall down." "Oh, grandson, if you'll pick lots of apples for me, I'll sit down here and open my mouth and you can drop them in." Coon said, "All right, sit down where I tell you. Wait a while; not many are ripe." "All right," she answered.

Coon picked apples; he picked thorns. He stuck the thorns in the apples. "Now," he thought, "I'll get even with grandma. I'm all sore. I'll get even with her." He called to Pheasant, "Now sit down good. Open your mouth good. Shut [150] your eyes and don't look." She did so and Coon climbed down. "Now open your mouth wide," he said. He dropped in an apple. It stuck far down in her throat. She couldn't spit it out, or swallow it. She tried, but she couldn't. She called to Coon, "Take my basket, my hat, and get water. I'm choking." "Oh, don't bother me," Coon answered. "I'm coming down, but I'm all sore. I can hardly move." Finally he got down and took her hat. He took his time. There was fresh water nearby. Coon sang about his whipping. Grandma told him to hurry. He answered, "I can't hurry; you whipped me." He washed his face, then filled the hat with water. He started back. Pheasant tried to cry out but couldn't. Coon came close, then grandma flew to him. Coon said, "You fly now; you'll be pheasant." He went on, "If it were not for you, I wouldn't be all blue like this. You'll be pheasant." He thought, "Now, where am I to go? — Myself, I'll be going."

He went up the creek. Soon he got hungry. "I'd better look around on these rocks," he thought. He went into the water and waded around. He turned over all the big rocks. Pretty soon he found some crawfish. "Oh, I'm all right now," he thought. "I can eat again." He found some more, two or three under one big rock. It was evening then. "What can I do?" he wondered. He looked around for a good, nice, dry place to stay overnight. "I'd better go to the other side of this point," he thought. Then he saw a fire, smoke, and people. "I'll go over there," he thought. "I can make friends with everybody." Soon he met an old fellow. The old fellow asked, "Brother, where are you going?" "I don't know, brother," Coon answered. "I'm looking for a place to stay." "I have a little place. You can stay with me tonight," the other said. So they went home together. They reached home. Coon stayed there that night. The next morning the old fellow said to Coon, "You go up the river; I'll go downriver. We'll fish for crawfish." Coon answered, "You won't find many downstream. I came up and found two or three."

Coon stayed with the old fellow. Every day they fished; Coon went upstream, the other went downstream. Then the old fellow asked Coon what to do to get something else to eat. He said he was tired of crawfish. "What do you think if we wish for big, fat spring salmon?"

Coon asked. The old fellow said, "All right, I'll wish too. We'll go out early in the morning and look around. We'll find cottonwood. You get five pieces; I'll get five pieces." In the morning they started out. The old man said, "If we store the cottonwood, in the morning it will be nice, fat spring salmon." That evening each of them put five pieces of cottonwood under his pillow and went to bed. They wished that in the morning it would be spring salmon. Coon didn't rest all night. "What can I do?" he wondered. "Maybe the old fellow is good. I don't know." Daylight came and the old fellow got up and made the fire. Coon was still in bed. The old fellow said to him, "You'd better get up. Look and see." Coon said, "All right, brother." The old fellow said, "You look first." "No, you look first. You asked me to go for cottonwood." "Don't say that!" the old fellow answered. "Say salmon. Wish for fish." The old fellow raised his pillow, then said, "Now you raise yours." Coon was afraid to. There was a nice fish under the old fellow's pillow. "How about you?" Coon asked. "Let me see if we really got our wish." The old man put a nice, fat, dried spring salmon over for him to see. [151]

Then the old man said, "Now you put your salmon over there, then I'll put mine." "You put yours down first; you asked me," Coon said. The old man counted them out and put them down, five dried salmon.

Coon looked. "Well, brother, I'm in bad luck," he said. "I have five pieces of wood." The old man got his wish. "Well, brother," he said; "don't feel badly. We'll eat. I'll give you two salmon. We'll cut this one in half. I'll give you two and a half, I'll keep two and a half." So they had the nice fish. The old fellow said, "Now every morning we'll have to fish for crawfish again." Coon was getting so fat he could hardly move. One morning the old man said, "Go before daylight upstream;

I'll go downstream. This is the last day we'll be here. We'll have to move." "All right," Coon answered. They got up early. Coon went just a little way. He caught one or two crawfish, not many. He heard something crack in the woods. He started to turn over a rock. He heard a noise in the woods. People came with spears. They speared Coon. "Oh, why did you do that? We have been together for a long time," Coon cried. It was the old fellow with his face all painted. He went away, hurried back to the house, washed his face and lay down.

Then Coon tried to pull out the spear, but he couldn't. He went home but he could hardly walk. The old fellow said, "Oh, brother, I told you to watch out. There are lots of wild people around here." "Oh, I know you did it. You'd better change your mind and help me. Cut out the spear." The old fellow could hardly move, he was so old. He got his knife and cut out the spear, but some fat came out, too. Coon was very fat. "Well, if you're willing, I'll doctor you so that you'll get well," he said to Coon. "All right, go ahead if you think you can help me," Coon answered. The old fellow went out to find a hard limb to beat with. He said, "Shut your eyes, I'll help you." Coon shut his eyes. The old fellow sat close to him. He thought, "Well, he's fat now. I'll hit him on the head and kill him now, and eat him." He told Coon to turn over. Then he hit him on the head and killed him. He said, "You'll be coon. After this people will kill you and eat you when you are fat. That's what I'm going to do with you now." The old fellow was Talapas. Now today lots of people eat coon.

WILDCAT RESCUES HIS SISTER FROM BEAR

Some Chinook came from the Columbia river to camp on Willapa Harbor. There were five of them, four brothers and one sister. The sister was the youngest. Every morning the four brothers went out to hunt elk. They told their sister not to leave. They told her to go and swim in the big pool they had made for her. They told her to stay there all the time. She was at puberty. Every morning the brothers wakened their sister and sent her down to swim. When they came home at night they called, "Are you there?" "Yes, I'm here," their sister would answer. Every day they did that. Every day they went hunting.

One day the sister was walking along her trail. She looked toward the place her brothers had told her not to go. "I wonder why my brothers do not want me to go there?" she thought. She looked again. "I guess I'll go and see." She went a little way and came to a deep, clear pool. "Well," she thought, "I'll stay here and bathe. This is a much better place." She took oft her clothes and went in. She was washing [152] her arms and legs when suddenly she heard a noise behind her back. She looked around and saw a black Bear standing beside her clothes. "Oh, what can I do?" she wondered. She waited a little while. Then she began to get cold. She said to the Bear, "Won't you go away from my clothes? I want to put them on." Bear answered, "If you will say, 'Husband, let me have my clothes,' I'll give them to you." "No, no! I won't do that!" she cried. She made up her mind not to say that. She was just a girl yet. She said, "Oh, uncle, give me my clothes." Bear answered, "Call me husband and you can have your clothes." The girl said, "Please go away from my clothes. I'm getting cold now, cousin." "Call me husband," Bear answered, "and I'll give you your clothes." But she wouldn't do that. She was just a girl yet. She had a very hard time. She called Bear brother and everything she could think of, but he would not give in. It was getting late, the sun was setting. She was getting very cold. Then she offered to pay Bear for her clothes but he said, "No, you must call me husband." After a while she gave up. She called him husband. Old Bear moved. She got her clothes. When she had put them on, old Bear grabbed her, picked her up and took her with him. He went along his trail. "Well, I'll take you home, to my house, now," he said. They went along, across mountains and mountains, all that evening and until morning. Then they reached a prairie, Chehalis prairie. There was a big smoke house.[1] Bear took her inside. He showed her the food for her to eat, camas, and all kinds of roots. Then it was morning. He showed her where to wash her face. She stayed there.

Her brothers came home the same evening. The oldest brother was Cougar. He was a great hunter. The youngest brother was Wildcat. Cougar called, "Are you home?" There was no answer. He called five times. Each time he got no answer. Then he said to the other brothers, "Our sister is gone now. I told her not to go over there but I think she is gone now." The next morning Cougar got up; he hadn't rested any that night. He got his bow and arrows and went to the place he had told his sister not to go. He went and found the trail. He found Bear's tracks. He thought, "Oh, well, she's gone now." He found Bear's tracks. He tracked him for a while, until it was getting late. He made up his mind to go home and tell his brothers that their sister was gone. It was late. He turned around and started home.

As he was going along the trail he saw a pheasant, rolling over and over. He thought,

---

[1] That is, native dwelling.

"I'll kill it and take it home for supper." He shot it with an arrow and tied it to a limb above. Then he went on home. He reached home. He told his brothers, "Our sister is gone. She went where I told her not to go. I found her trail." He said, "I went to the place she washed. I found where Bear had sat and where she put on her clothes. I saw old Bear's tracks and saw the way they led. I tracked him for a while but then I made up my mind to come home and let you know what had happened." Cougar went on, "Early tomorrow morning I'll be going." He told his brothers, "If I don't come back you will know what has happened."

Early the next morning Cougar woke up, took his bow and arrows, and went to the place where old Bear had been sitting. Then he tracked him. He went across mountains and mountains. When night came, he made camp. He travelled five [153] days, then he reached the prairie. He saw a huge house. When he got there he stopped and thought, "I'd better look inside." He opened the door and saw two little Bears playing and old Bear lying down asleep. The smaller Bear said, "Oh, that's uncle. Come on in, uncle." Cougar went in and sat down. The little Bears went over and talked to him and hugged him. The older Bear said, "Mama, she is getting camas. She'll be in pretty soon. Oh ! what a lot of lice there are on your head, uncle! I'd better kill them." Their uncle had very long hair. One Bear picked lice on one side and the other on the other. Then both at once bit him on the throat. Cougar could do nothing about it; there were two of them. They killed him. Then old Bear woke up and took the fellow out. There was a big log behind the house. He packed[2] him there and hid his bow and arrows. Then he went in and told the two young bears to pack water and wash away the blood or their mother would come home and know that it was her brother. They packed the water and washed away the blood.

The mother came home and saw that the floor was all wet. "What has been going on here?" she asked. Old Bear answered, "The two children were playing and spilled water. That's how it happened." Later she thought, "Something must be wrong."

The next morning another brother (there were four then) said, "It's queer, our brother didn't come home. I'll go to look for him." Early the next morning he took his bow and arrows and left. He went to the pool where his sister had bathed. He found his brother's tracks, leading from there toward the mountains. After a while he found the pheasant tied to the tree. He thought, "That's my brother's pheasant. He killed it and tied it there so that he could come back and pick it up." He went a little way. A pheasant began to bother him. It flew around and around him. He thought, "I'd better kill it. Then when I find my brother we'll have two pheasants for supper." So he killed it and hung it up in a tree, the same way. Then he went on. After five days he reached the prairie. He saw a big house with smoke coming out. "That's where brother is," he thought. He went up to the house. "I'll ask to see my sister or brother." He looked inside and saw two little Bears, and the old Bear asleep. The biggest cub saw him and called him in. "Uncle," he said, "sit down." The Bear hugged him. "Mama is out gathering camas," he said. "She'll be back pretty soon." The older one said, "Look at all the lice you have !" He started to pick them but pretty soon he bit him in the neck and killed him. Then old Bear woke up and packed him out. He put him the same place he had put the other brother. Then he told the young Bears to pack water and clean up the floor. They packed the water and cleaned the floor.

---

[2] That is, carried.

After a while the Bears' mother came home and saw the same thing as before. "What has happened here?" she asked. "Oh, the children were just wrestling and spilled a little water," old Bear said. Early the next morning the mother went out to dig camas.

Two brothers were gone now. "I wonder what's going on," the third brother thought. "I'll have to go and find out." He tracked his sister and brothers in the [154] same way. He thought, "Maybe I'll find them and stay there." After a while he found the pheasant his oldest brother had killed and hung up. "Well," he thought, "my oldest brother must have done that." A little later he saw the other pheasant. "Here's another one; my next brother must have killed that one." He went on for a while and a pheasant started to fly around in his path. "Well, my brothers have killed two. This makes three. I'd better kill it." So he shot the pheasant with an arrow and hung it in a tree the same way. Then he went on and crossed mountains and mountains. After five days he came to the prairie and saw the big house with the smoke coming out. "I'll go and ask to see my sister and brothers," he thought. He got to the house and looked inside. He saw two little Bears, one a little bigger, one a little smaller. The oldest one saw him. He called him in and said the same thing as to the oldest brother and the next brother. "You have lots of lice, uncle. We'll pick them out." But pretty soon they bit him in the neck and killed him. Old Bear woke up and packed him out where he had put the others, and hid his bow and arrows.

The woman came home. She saw the ashes all wet, everything all wet. "That would be three," she thought. "Something is going on. Maybe my brothers have been around." Then the woman went out.

The youngest brother, Wildcat, wondered, "What's the matter with my brothers?" He hadn't slept at all since his three brothers had been gone. "I'm alone now," he thought. "Maybe my brothers have found our sister and are having a good time. I'll go too." The next morning he got up early and took his bow and arrows. Then he left. He went to the place his sister had been told not to go. He saw where Bear had been sitting on the girl's clothes. Then he tracked Bear and his brothers. That night he slept just a little bit. He dreamed. He dreamed that he wood find pheasants tied in the trees — one, two, three of them. His dream told him that.

He went on. He followed the trail. Then he found a pheasant tied in a tree. It was a little hit spoiled. "Oh, yes, my oldest brother left this pheasant here," he thought. He found the second pheasant. "This one my next brother left," he thought. He went on. Then he came to the last pheasant. "Oh, yes, my other brother left this one." After a while a pheasant came to him. But he didn't bother the pheasant. He remembered his dream. He didn't kick it or touch it. He remembered his dream. The pheasant rolled over and jumped in front of him. But he remembered his dream. The pheasant left the woods. Wildcat kept on going, thinking about his brothers and sister. He kept on going, past mountains and mountains. Pretty soon he reached the prairie. He saw all his brothers' tracks. He saw the big house and the smoke. "Oh, that's where my brothers are," he thought. He reached the house and looked in. He saw two young Bears and the old Bear asleep. The young Bears saw him and called him in. "Sit down, uncle." Then they asked to delouse him. "No, don't delouse me." (They bite the lice, just like dogs.) "But you have lots of lice," the young Bears said. "No, I have no lice," Wildcat answered. Wildcat dreamed and saw all his brothers behind the log. He sat there for a long time. The Bears kept bothering him but he wouldn't let them touch him. After a while the door opened and his sister came in. "Oh! I'm so glad to see you," she said. After a while she was crying. Her brother asked her what was the matter. [155]

"Where are my other brothers?" she asked. "Why, they came; they're around somewhere," he answered. Wildcat's sister fed him camas and other food. Later the two of them went out together. The little Bears wanted to go too but their mother wouldn't let them. When they were outside she asked, "Did my brothers really come?" "Yes, one, two, three of them came. Oh, they're home by now." "No," she said, "that's how they got killed. They had lots of lice. The Bears killed them, I know. Every time I came home I saw dirt and water. Old Bear said the children spilled the water. But they killed them, I know." Then she asked, "Did you find pheasants along the trail, dead?" "Yes," Wildcat answered. "That's why, then," his sister said. (Pheasant was the guardian spirit of all the brothers.)

Wildcat's sister told him to stay near her but not to let the little Bears come near him. "They are my children, I had twins, both boys, those little Bears," she said. "Every day I'll go out. I'll tell the others I'm going for camas but I'll go to work. I'll work for five days. You do what I tell you to." "Yes, that's why I'm here," her brother answered. "You go out every day and I'll gather pitch wood in the forest. I'll split it." So Wildcat's sister went out early, to pick camas, she said. She went out to work. She twisted cedar limbs, split them and scraped them, and made rope. She worked. Her brother looked for pitch. He found good fir pitch. He split it and took it in. He started at the door and put it all around the house. Every day he went out and got pitch wood. He went out for five days. In five days he got enough pitch wood to stand pieces on end from the door all around the house and back to the door again. "Pretty soon old Bear will be asleep[3] and won't be able to move," the sister said. "The children will be asleep, too." They worked. They went out every morning. The brother got pitch. The old Bear saw the pitch. "What are you doing?" he asked. His wife said, "Oh, we need that for winter time. In the morning it is hard to make a fire." She said to her brother, "I have all my work done. How much have you got done?" Wildcat answered, "I've got all I want."

"All right, now we'll watch him," the girl said. "Every once in a while I'll move him. If he moves we can't do anything." Then one evening she told her brother, "I think it's time now; we'll start. The children can't move now." She made a pin of yew wood and tickled their feet. She said to her brother, "Wake up early in the morning. I pulled their hair and pinched them but they didn't move. Let's go out now to get the rope I made." Her brother carried all the rope to the house. The Bears were asleep. The girl said, "Put strong pieces of yew wood on each side of old Bear's feet, tie him up tight. Put yew wood stakes in the ground and rope around his neck. Do the same to the children. It's easy to handle them when they're asleep." She showed her brother what to do. He finished with old Bear and the two little ones. "Get up early tomorrow morning," she said. "Now when you start to bum the pitch, make a fire here, and here, and here." They had a little dog, Wolf. It was the girl's dog. They put Wolf near the door. They told him that if anyone asked where they had gone to just look up and holler. "Don't forget," they said, "don't look down. We're going to burn up the house." [156]

Early in the morning they started in. They put the dog at the door. They put the pitch around. Wildcat said, "I'll try to wake up our brothers. I know where they are sleeping." His sister answered, "All right, you can try, but I don't know whether you can do it or not." They

---

[3] That is, hibernating.

burned the house. They went around and found their brothers. Wildcat told his sister to help. "Hold their bodies up," he said. Then he blew five times on the face of his oldest brother, and he woke up. "When did you come?" he asked. "Oh, I just came. I came to find you. Now you can go. You will always be in the woods, cougar." The girl looked at the house. It was burning well. She said, "I'll go toward where the sun rises." "All right," Wildcat answered, "I'll come later, when all my work is done." "Be careful," his sister said, "if you see a large black cloud, then another smaller one."

Wildcat watched the fire. After a while he saw a large black cloud, then he saw another. "That's the boy," he thought. Then he saw another. "That's the younger,"[4] he thought. Pretty soon it got smaller, and then smaller. Then it was gone. It fell down, as ashes, next to the dog. "Which way did your owner go?" it asked. The dog just looked up and howled. It asked the dog five times. Five times the dog looked up and howled. Then Bear was all right again. He slapped the dog and said, "So you won't tell me. From now on you'll be wolf." Bear looked around and found Wildcat's tracks.

Wildcat's sister went high in the mountains and waited for her brother. He came. "What did you tell my dog?" she asked. "I told him to look up," he answered. "But Bear — here he comes now," she said. "I told the dog to look up, though," Wildcat answered. Talapas[5] was coming. Wildcat and his sister met him. He asked what they were doing. "We're running away from Bear," they answered. "He ran away with me," the girl said. "He took me from Naselle (i'tsqwił Bear river)." Talapas said, "You don't need to worry. Bear won't do that."

Talapas met Bear, tracking Wildcat and his sister. "Where are you going?" he asked. "Oh, my wife ran away and left me," Bear said. "Oh! Your wife ran away and left you? How is it that you do that with people? Bears never do that, or eat people. People, if they get hungry, and if they can kill a bear, will smoke and dry and bake the meat and eat it. But bears will not kill people." Then he blew on Bear's eyes. That is why bears have small eyes.

Pretty soon the girl and her brother, far up the mountain, met their oldest brother. He said, "Oh, brother, you have helped me a lot. I wouldn't have been like that if she had minded, but you helped me a lot. I'll never forget you; I'll remember you always. When I kill something, I'll eat what I can eat, then I'll. put the rest away for you. If you smell meat, look around, and you can get meat."[6] That is the way it is now. Whenever cougar kills a deer, he saves some for wildcat, and caches it. Wildcat smells it and finds it.

Then Cougar blew on his sister. He told her what she would be." He blew on his youngest brother and said that he would be wildcat. "Myself," he said, "I'll be a traveller; I'll travel all over." He went.

---

[4] Smaller ?

[5] Coyote.

[6] Mrs. Luscier had forgotten.

BIBLIOGRAPHY

ALLEN, A. J. [Elijah White's] Ten Years in Oregon. Ithaca, 1848.

BAILEY, VERNON. The Mammals and Life Zones of Oregon. North American Fauna, 55, Washington, 1936.

BANCROFT, HUBERT HOWE. The Native Races of the Pacific States of North America. New York, 1875. 5 vols.

BOAS, FRANZ. Chinook Texts. Bulletin, Bureau of American Ethnology, #20, 1894.

The Doctrine of Souls and of Disease among the Chinook Indians. Journal of American Folk-lore, 6, 1893, 39-43.

Handbook of American Indian Languages, Bulletin, Bureau of American Ethnology, 40, 1911. Part 1.

Kathlamet Texts. Bulletin, Bureau of American Ethnology, 26,1901.

Zur Mythologie der Indianer von Washington und Oregon. Globus, 63, 1893, 154-57, 172-75, 190-93.

BOIT, JOHN. Boit's Log of the Columbia, 1790-1792. Proceedings, Massachusetts Historical Society, 53, 1920, 217-75. (Reprinted in the Washington Historical Quarterly, 12, 1921, 3-50; and in the Oregon Historical Quarterly, 22, 1921, 257-352.)

CLIMATOLOGICAL Data, Washington Section, 24-39, Weather Bureau, Seattle, 1921-1935.

COBB, JOHN N. Pacific Salmon Fisheries. Report, U.S. Commissioner of Fisheries, 1921, Appendix 1 (Bureau of Fisheries Document 902), 1921.

COUES, ELLIOTT. New Light on the Early History of the Greater Northwest. The Manuscript Journals of Alexander Henry ... and of David Thompson ... , 1799-1814, etc. New York, 1897. 3 vols.

Cox, Ross. Adventures on the Columbia River, etc. New York, 1832.

CURTIS, EDWARD S. The North American Indian. Cambridge, Mass., 1907-1930. 20 vols.

DAY, P.C. The Daily, Monthly, and Annual Normals of Precipitation in the United States, etc. Monthly Weather Review, Supplement 34, Washington, 1930.

DOUGLAS, DAVID. Sketch of a Journey to the Northwestern Part of the Continent during the years 1824-27. Oregon Historical Quarterly, 5-6, 1904-1905. (Reprinted from: The Companion to the Botanical Magazine, 2, London, 1836.)

DUNN, JOHN. History of the Oregon Territory. London, 1844.

FRANCHÈRE, GABRIEL. Narrative of a Voyage to the Northwest Coast of America in the years 1811, 1812, 1813, and 1814, etc. New York, 1854.

GAIRDNER, Dr. Notes on the Geography of the Columbia River. Journal, Royal Geographical Society of London, 11, 1841, 250-57.

GIBBS, GEORGE. Alphabetical Vocabulary of the Chinook Language. Shea's Library of American Linguistics, 8, New York, 1863.

Report on the Indian Tribes of the Territory of Washington. Pacific Railroad Report, 1, Washington, 1890, 419-65.

Tribes of Western Washington and Northwestern Oregon. Contributions to North American Ethnology, 1, Washington, 1877, 157-241.

GRAY, ROBERT. Log-Book of the Ship Columbia. In: Greenhow, Memoir, 125-27; History, 434-36.

GREENHOW, ROBERT. The History of Oregon and California, etc. Boston, 1844.

Memoir, Historical and Political, on the Northwest Coast of America, and the Adjacent Territories. New York, 1840. [158]

GUNTHER, ERNA. An Analysis of the First Salmon Ceremony. American Anthropologist, 28, 1926, 605-17.

A Further Analysis of the First Salmon Ceremony. University of Washington Publications in Anthropology, 2, 1928, 129-73.

Klallam Ethnography. University of Washington Publications in Anthropology, 1, 1927, 171-314.

HAEBERLIN, HERMAN K. SbEtrda'q, a Shamanistic Performance of the Coast Salish. American Anthropologist, 20, 1918, 249-57.

HAEBERLIN, HERMAN, and ERNA GUNTHER. The Indians of Puget Sound. University of Washington Publications in Anthropology, 4, 1930, 1-84.

HALE, HORATIO. Ethnography and Philology. United States Exploring Expedition, during the years 1838-1842. Under the Command of Charles Wilkes, 6, Philadelphia, 1846.

An International Idiom. A Manual of the Oregon Trade Language, or "Chinook Jargon." London, 1890.

HODGE, FREDERICK WEBB, editor. Handbook of American Indians North of Mexico. Bulletin, Bureau of American Ethnology, 30, 1907-1910. 2 parts.

IRVING, WASHINGTON. Astoria. New York, 1868.

JACOBS, MELVILLE. Notes on the Structure of Chinook Jargon. Language, 8, 1932, 27-50.

Review of: E.H. Thomas, Chinook. Pacific Northwest Quarterly, 27, 1936, 180-81.

JOBDON, DAVID STARR, el al. Check List of the Fishes and Fishlike Vertebrates of North and Middle America, etc. Report, U.S. Commissioner of Fisheries for 1928, part 2, Washington, 1930.

KANE, PAUL. Wanderings of an Artist among the Indians of North America. London, 1859.

LANDES, HENRY. A Geographic Dictionary of Washington. Washington Geological Survey, 17, Olympia, 1917.

LEE, D., and J.H. FROST. Ten Years in Oregon. New York, 1844.

LEWIS, ALBERT BUELL. Tribes of the Columbia Valley and the Coast of Washington and Oregon. Memoir, American Anthropological Association, 1, 1906, 147-209.

MARVIN, CHARLES F., and P.C. DAY. Normals of Daily Temperature for the U.S. Monthly Weather Review, Supplement 25, Washington, 1925.

MOONEY, JAMES. The Aboriginal Population of America North of Mexico. Smithsonian Miscellaneous Collections, 80, 1928, no. 7.

The Ghost Dance Religion and the Sioux Outbreak of 1890. Report, Bureau of American Ethnology, 14, 1896, 641-1110.

OLSON, RONALD L. Adze, Canoe and House Types of the Northwest Coast. University of Washington Publications in Anthropology, 2, 1927, 1-38.

The Quinault Indians. University of Washington Publications in Anthropology, 6, 1937.

PARKER, SAMUEL. Journal of an Exploring Tour beyond the Rocky Mountains ... in the Years 1835, '36, and '37, etc. Ithaca, N.Y., 1838.

PHONETIC Transcription of American Indian Languages. Smithsonian Miscellaneous Collections, 66, 1916, # 6.

PILLING, JAMES CONSTANTINE. Bibliography of the Chinookan Languages (Including the Chinook Jargon). Bulletin, Bureau of American Ethnology, #15, 1893.

PIPER, CHARLES V. Flora of the State of Washington. Contributions, U.S. Herbarium, 11, 1906.

PIPER, CHARLES V., and R. KENT BEATTIE. Flora of the Northwest Coast ... Lancaster, Penn., 1915. [159]

RAY, VERNE F. Native Villages and Groupings of the Columbia Basin. Pacific Northwest Quarterly, 27, 1936, 99-152.

The Historical Position of the Lower Chinook in the Native Culture of the Northwest. Pacific Northwest Quarterly, 28, 1937, 363-72.

The Sanpoil and Nespelem: Salishan Peoples of Northeastern Washington. University of Washington Publications in Anthropology, 5, 1932.

ROSS, ALEXANDER. Adventures of the First Settlers on the Oregon or Columbia River, etc. London, 1849.

SCHOOLCRAFT, HENRY R. Information Respecting the History, Condition, and Prospects of the Indian Tribes of the United States, etc. Philadelphia, 1860. 6 vols.

SCOULER, JOHN. Journal of a Voyage to N.W. America (1824-1826). Quarterly, Oregon Historical Society, 6, 1905.

SHAW, GEORGE C. The Chinook Jargon and How to Use It. Seattle, 1909.

SMITH, HARLAN I. Noteworthy Archaeological Specimens from the Lower Columbia Valley. American Anthropologist, 8, 1906, 298-307.

SPIER, LESLIE. Klamath Ethnography. University of California Publications in American Archaeology and Ethnology, 30, 1930.

The Prophet Dance of the Northwest and its Derivatives, etc. General Series in Anthropology, 1, Menasha, Wis., 1935.

Tribal Distribution in Washington. General Series in Anthropology, 3, Menasha, Wis., 1936.

SPIER, LESLIE, and EDWARD SAPIR. Wishram Ethnography. University of Washington Publications in Anthropology, 3, 1930, 151-300.

STRONG, THOMAS NELSON. Cathlamet on the Columbia. Portland, Ore., 1930.

SWAN, JAMES G. The Northwest Coast; or, Three Years' Residence in Washington Territory. New York, 1857.

THOMAS, EDWARD HARPER. Chinook, a History and Dictionary of the Northwest Coast Trade Jargon. Portland, Ore., 1935.

THORNTON, J. QUINN. Oregon and California in 1848. New York, 1849. 2 vols.

THWAITES, REUBEN GOLD, editor. Original Journals of the Lewis and Clark Expedition, 1804-1806, etc. New York, 1904-1905. 8 vols.

TOWNSEND, JOHN K. Narrative of a Journey across the Rocky Mountains to the Columbia River. Philadelphia, 1839.

TYRRELL, J.B., editor. David Thompson's Narrative of his Explorations in Western America, 1784-1812. Publications, Champlain Society, 12, Toronto, 1916.

VANCOUVER, GEORGE. A Voyage of Discovery to the North Pacific Ocean ... in the years 1790-1795. London, 1798. 3 vols.

WATERMAN, T.T., and GERALDINE COFFIN. Types of Canoes on Puget Sound. Indian Notes and Monographs, 1920.

WATERMAN, T.T., and collaborators. Native Houses of Western North America. Indian Notes and Monographs, 1921.

WILKES, CHARLES. Narrative of the United States Exploring Expedition during the Years 1838, 1839, 1840, 1841, 1842. Philadelphia, 1845. 5 vols., atlas.

PLATE 1. Portrait by Paul Kane (*Wanderings of an Artist.*) This is presumably a Cowlitz woman but the type of head flattening and the cradle are identical with the Chinook.

PLATE 2. Interior of a Clatsop house. From Wilkes (*Narrative*).

PLATE 3. Upper: House interior, From Swan (*Northwest Coast*). Lower: Canoe interment

PLATE 4. Upper: House exterior. Lower: Salmon fishing. From Swan.

PLATE 5. (A) Finely twined basket of spruce root. Depth, 12 inches; diameter, 8 inches. (B) Openwork basket of cedar bark; used for storing clams and dried salmon. Depth, 10 inches; diameter, 15 inches. (C) Twined storage basket of rushes, with cover. Used for storing dried berries. Depth, 9 inches; diameter, 14 inches. (D) Openwork basket of spruce roots, with carrying strap of twilled rushes. Used principally for carrying shell-fish. Depth, 8 inches; width, 12 inches. (E) Trinket basket of twined rushes. Depth, 4 inches; diameter, 5 inches. (F) Twilled basket of flat spruce roots. Depth, 7 inches; width, 8 inches. (G) Flat bag of cattail, trimmed with bear grass. Depth, 20 inches; width, 24 inches. (Washington State Museum: A, Acc. 1606, loaned by Abigail Robb; B, 1-11183; C, 1-11187; D, 1-11184 [basket], 1-11185 [strap]; E, 1-11181; F, 1-11186.)

Appendices A > E

Verne F. Ray (1905-2003)

Verne Frederick Ray was born on 13 March 1905 in Enfield, Illinois, to Della (Duncan) Ray and Arden Humphrey Ray, a farmer. In 1906 the family moved to Spokane, Washington. His siblings Hersal, Everett, and Irene were all born in Washington State. In 1919 the family moved to Seattle, where Verne attended Franklin High School, graduating in 1924. Verne enrolled at the University of Washington as an undergraduate from 1924 to 1928, first studying law for a year, then switching to anthropology, where he studied with Professor Leslie Spier — the department's only instructor at the time. After one term of anthropology course work Ray reports: "... I never gave any thought to following any other course over a lifetime of study and teaching. At this time I had unequivocally decided that university teaching was to be my career" (1990: 9). Spier must have been pleased with Ray's academic progress for he appointed him Assistant in Anthropology as well as Curator of Anthropology at the Washington State Museum, housed on campus. In addition, Verne began teaching anthropology courses for the University's extension division.

After Spier's departure to Oklahoma in 1927, Verne left the University of Washington for the University of California, Berkeley, where he studied with Professors Kroeber, Lowie, Gifford, and Radin between 1929-1930, obtaining a Junior Certificate in 1929. Melville Jacobs's arrival at Washington in 1928 resuscitated anthropology there, and Ray chose to return to Washington in 1930 where he completed his BA in 1931 with double majors in anthropology and psychology. Verne married Julia C Wright in 1927 and they had one child, LaVerne Charlotte Ray in 1930. Verne and Julia were divorced in 1953.

Ray began his Plateau fieldwork with the Sanpoil and Nespelem, conducting several fieldtrips between 1928 and 1930. The write-up of his ethnographic fieldnotes was published in 1932 and served as the thesis for his MA in Anthropology, awarded in 1933. Ray's Sanpoil-Nespelem ethnography is still considered by some to be the best ethnography of any Plateau culture group. His subsequent extensive fieldwork in the Plateau culture area during his long career eventually included work with the Klikitat, Tenino (Wayampam), Umatilla, Kittitas, Wenatchee, Columbia, Chelan, Entiat, Confederated Tribes of Colville, Spokane, Wasco, Tygh, Palus, Yakima, Confederated Tribes of Warm Springs, Confederated Tribes of Umatilla, Kalispel, Shuswap, Lillooet, Lower Thompson, Chilcotin, Lower Carrier, Kutenai, Flathead, Coeur d'Alene, Nez Perce, Klamath, and Modoc.

A recurring motif in salvage ethnography is the premature report of the death of the last knowledgeable culture bearers. Such was the case with the Lower Chinookan peoples in the 1930s. It was Ray's good fortune to locate and work intermittently with two Lower Chinookan consultants between 1931 and 1936, culminating in publication of his valuable gleanings, entitled *Lower Chinook Ethnographic Notes* (1938). Ray's careful use of the earliest records on the Lower Chinook in this volume anticipates the considerable ethnohistorical research of his later Indian Claims Commission research.

Ray was a Teaching Fellow in Anthropology from 1930-1932. In 1933 he was the Director, Emergency Conservation Program, Colville and Spokane Indian Reservations, U.S. Department of the Interior. He continued teaching in the anthropology department as an Associate from 1933-1936.

Verne was bright, talented, and resourceful. As a fitting example, to finance his PhD at some yet to be determined eastern university, he decided to build houses to sell. Never mind that his carpentry skills were minimal, that he had never built or helped to build a house before. But due to an interest in architecture, for several years he'd had a habit of closely inspecting construction sites in some detail. He bought two small lots in the Green Lake district of Seattle, books on house construction, the necessary tools and lumber, and went to work. He describes the process:

Using only after-class hours — evenings until very late — and weekends, I built a small house from the ground up, including carpentry, masonry, plumbing, electrical work, and landscaping. I never hired any help nor commissioned any component of the construction. When the house was completed I made it my living quarters, and then built a second house on the lot next door. [Ray 1990:11]

Some seventy years later the original house, looking modest and very much as it must have in the 1930s, is still in use as a residence — a testament to the quality of Ray's craftsmanship.

Verne was accepted into the Ph.D. program at Yale University but without funding. So, he sold his two houses and moved to New Haven, where he attended classes for one academic year, 1936-1937. During his year at Yale he worked as Assistant to the Editor of the *American Anthropologist,* Leslie Spier. He submitted as his dissertation a manuscript already accepted for publication: *Cultural Relations in the Plateau of Northwestern America.* The degree was officially awarded in 1939, the year of the dissertation's publication.

Under AL Kroeber's direction Ray prepared a culture element distribution list for the Plateau, submitted in late 1940 and published in 1942. As a non-resident Research Associate at the University of California, Berkeley from 1936-1938, funded by the Works Progress Administration, and under auspices of the University of Washington, Ray assembled an impressive list of 7,633 culture elements or traits from sixteen Plateau culture groups. In effect, Ray *defined* the distinct Plateau culture area, as he created most of the culture elements on the Plateau list himself — previous lists being of little value as templates for the Plateau cultures. As Ray's former student Robert J Theodoratus has remarked (pc, 2004), "Ray is to the Plateau as Kroeber was to California." Ray had no interest in a "statistical interpretation of the lists" and none is appended. For Ray the lists were "merely ethnological records," representing Plateau culture but at the same time "a tool for adding to the record" (1942: 100). Clearly Ray's strengths as an anthropologist included his traditional ethnographic fieldwork and his extensive knowledge of all aspects of Plateau Indian cultures from material culture and technology to religion. Virtually every tribal entry in the Smithsonian's Plateau volume of the *Handbook of North American Indians* (Walker 1998) cites Verne Ray's work, an apt index of the continuing importance of his pioneering research. Yet he himself was excluded from the volume, expecially from the Middle Columbia Salishan entry.

The conclusions of *Cultural Relations in the Plateau of Northwestern America* that are most widely contested in recent literature on the Plateau center around "such features as pacifism, egalitarianism, and communal land ownership as defining characteristics" (Furniss 2004: 138). Furniss, for example, proposes a new model of Secwepemc (Shuswap) sociopolitical organization that highlights "enduring tensions ...

between the autonomy of extended family groups and the solidarity of the band collective" (2004:138). Cannon (1992) focuses on conflict and salmon among the Lillooet, Shuswap, and Thompson Indians of the Fraser Plateau, British Columbia, citing clear evidence of patterns of regional conflict — *contra* Ray's (and others') emphasis on regional pacifism and communitarian sharing. Hayden stresses that the prehistoric and traditional historic Indian cultures of the Lillooet region represented *complex* hunter/gatherers and that "ownership, inequality, and corporate groups" were not recent overlays in the area as argued by Ray (1939) and others (1992: 558). See also work by Carstens (1991) and Kent (1980). I believe that Ray, who had a keen interest in historical process and culture change (e.g., 1937, 1941), would have welcomed renewed scholarly interest in the Plateau and the current ethnohistorical debates on these important issues for the region.

In 1963 Ray published the only monograph-length ethnography of the Modoc Indians of north-central California. It was based on his own fieldwork — 1934-1940 — and incorporated fieldnotes generated by six students from Leslie Spier's 1934 Laboratory of Anthropology field school: Ethel Alpenfels, Earl Count, Irving Goldman, Alice Marriott, Philleo Nash, and David Rodnick.

During World War II Ray performed intermittent service, temporary reserve, for the Coast Guard Reserve from 1942-1945 and was discharged at the rank of Seaman 1st class. It was during this time that he came to know the waterways of Puget Sound and the Strait of Juan de Fuca and became interested in a new hobby — boats and sailing. He built by hand a sailboat, the *Dulci Bella*, and he was a life member of the Seattle Yacht Club.

Ray was appointed Instructor at the University of Washington in 1939, Assistant Professor in 1940, Associate Professor in 1945, and Full Professor in 1947. From 1948-1954 he was Associate Dean of the Graduate School. From 1951-1954, on leave of absence from Washington, he was Professor of Anthropology and Research Director of the Human Relations Area Files at Yale University. With the help of large federal grants from the armed services and the State Department, during Ray's tenure at HRAF his administration added "tens of thousands of pages of compilation" to the files (Ray 1990:16). He also oversaw the translations of valuable ethnographic monographs and the reprinting of long out-of-print anthropological classics.

Upon his return to Washington in 1954 he met and fell in love with Dorothy Jean (Tostlebe) Thompson, an anthropology graduate student at the time whose field of interest was Eskimo ethnohistory and art, and they were married early in 1955. Ray described the synergy of their interests and relationship as an "ideal partnership" (Ray 1990:18).

According to Dorothy Jean Ray, Verne loved teaching. In the classes she attended he never taught with notes or even a sheet of paper at hand and he always used different illustrative examples each time he taught the same course. One former student remembers Ray as a devoted teacher, especially effective at the upper division and seminar level, who had a wide ranging interest in theories beyond the discipline of Anthropology. Another former student recalls Verne as an excellent teacher, one of the most stimulating in the department.

Among other positions held, Ray was a member of the editorial board of *Pacific Northwest Quarterly* (1935-1952), a council member for the American Folklore Society

(1941-1949), a member of the board of directors of the Human Relations Area Files (1947-1965), and a member of the editorial board of the *American Anthropologist* (1956-1962). He also performed valuable service as President of the American Ethnological Society (1953-1955) and more importantly as Editor of eleven books in the Publications of the American Ethnological Society series and four books in the Proceedings of the American Ethnological Society series between 1956-1962. Besides his membership and service in professional societies, Ray was a member of Sigma Xi (science honorary), Psi Chi (psychology honorary), and Phi Sigma (biology honorary). His interest in psychology and biology are evidenced by his publications on color perception and behavioral response (1952, 1953), with much field data on color perception remaining unpublished.

Ray served as Acting Executive Officer in Anthropology at the University of Washington from 1960-61. In 1966 he resigned his position at the University to pursue full-time ethnohistorical contract research, working out of Washington, D.C.

Besides teaching and service to the University, a good portion of Ray's professional activities from the late 1940s through the 1980s involved ethnohistorical research connected with the Indian Claims Act of 1946. Acting as expert witness and consultant in thirty-some cases Ray "represented thirty-five or forty tribes ranging in homelands from Alaska to Maine and from California to Florida." None of the cases for which Ray was an expert witness was lost by the Indians, although "many of the judgments were less, sometimes far less, than what was sought" (Ray 1990:16-17). Ray also inspired others in their ethnohistorical research and was remembered as being helpful and generous in sharing research materials. He was an honest and reliable scholar whose reports were well researched. As a token of their appreciation for his efforts in helping them gain federal recognition, Ray was made an honorary member of the Cowlitz Tribe in 2000.

Verne Ray died on 28 September 2003 in Port Townsend, Washington at the age of 98. He is survived by his wife of 48 years, Dorothy Jean, stepson Eric S. Thompson of Anchorage, Alaska, grandsons Paul Fromberg of Evanston, Illinois and Robert Fromberg of Oak Park, Illinois, and Steven Fromberg of Chapel Hill, North Carolina. He was preceded in death by his daughter LaVerne Ray Fromberg and son-in-law Gerald Fromberg, both well-known mid-western artists.

Ray's personal and professional papers and his library have been deposited in The Foley Center Library at Gonzaga University, Spokane, Washington.

Acknowledgements. For supplying materials and personal reminiscences I wish to thank Dorothy Jean Ray, Robert J. Theodoratus, Jay Miller, Barbara Lane, and Pamela T. Amoss.

References Cited

Cannon, Aubrey
1992 Conflict and Salmon on the Interior Plateau of British Columbia. *In* A Complex Culture of the British Columbia Plateau: Traditional Stl'atl'imx Resource Use. Brian Hayden, ed. pp. 506-524. Vancouver: University of British Columbia Press.
Carstens, Peter
1991 The Queen's People: A Study of Hegemony, Coercion, and Accommodation among the Okanagan of Canada. Toronto: University of Toronto Press.
Furniss, Elizabeth

2004. Cycles of History in Plateau Sociopolitical Organization: Reflections on the Nature of Indigenous Band Societies. Ethnohistory 51.1:137-170.

Hayden, Brian
1992 Conclusions: Ecology and Complex Hunter/Gatherers. *In* A Complex Culture of the British Columbia Plateau: Traditional Stl'atl'imx Resource Use. Brian Hayden, ed. Pp. 525-563. Vancouver: University of British Columbia Press.

Kent, Susan
1980 Pacifism: A Myth of the Plateau. Northwest Anthropological Research Notes 14:125-134.

Ray, Verne F.
1932 The Sanpoil and Nespelem: Salishan Peoples of Northeastern Washington. University of Washington Publications in Anthropology 5.

1937 The Historical Position of the Lower Chinook in the Native Culture of the Northwest. Pacific Northwest Quarterly 28.4:363-372.

1938 Lower Chinook Ethnographic Notes. University of Washington Publications in Anthropology 5. Seattle: University of Washington Press.

1939 Cultural Relations in the Plateau of Northwestern America. Publications of the Frederick Webb Hodge Anniversary Publications Fund, 3. Los Angeles: The Southwest Museum.

1941 Historic Backgrounds of the Conjuring Complex in the Plateau and the Plains. *In* Language, Culture, and Personality: Essays in Memory of Edward Sapir. L. Spier, A. I. Hallowell, and S. S. Newman, eds. Pp. 204-216. Menasha, WI: Banta Publishing Company.

1942 Culture Element Distributions: XXII Plateau. Anthropological Records 8.2. Berkeley University of California Press.

1952 Techniques and Problems in the Study of Human Color Perception. Southwestern Journal of Anthropology 8.3:251-259.

1953 Human Color Perception and Behavioral Response. Transactions of the New York Academy of Sciences 16.2:98-104.

1963 Primitive Pragmatists: The Modoc Indians of Northern California. Seattle: University of Washington Press.

1990 Looking Backward. Unpublished autobiographical sketch.

Walker, Deward, Jr., ed.
1998 Handbook of North American Indians, vol. 12: Plateau. Washington, D.C.: Smithsonian Institution.

William R. Seaburg

2016 Aboriginal Economy and Polity of the Lakes (Senijextee) Indians, With an Explanatory Endnote by Madilane Perry. Journal of Northwest Anthropology 50 (2): 145-166. Fall.

Of particular note, 33 years after Ray gave his 1947 Lakes ethnography and culture element distribution lists to Madilane Perry, she published the ethnography, finally naming Gregory's mother as their greatest chief. It immediately became vital to the legal reestablishment of Lakes resource rights in their Arrow Lakes British Columbia homeland. Ray insisted that his text and native word transcriptions be left untouched, though they are indeed awful.

Appendix B

Mountain Beavers

Misnamed and wrongly ignored, mountain beavers play strong roles in important stories and traditions. In the Northwest, mountain beaver (now *Aplodontia rufa* (Rafinesque)) has two subspecies of *A. rufa rufa* around Mt Hood and the Puget lowlands, which is smaller, and of *A. rufa rainieri* (Merriam), found in the higher Cascades. Distinguished by long whiskers and claws, it eats any and all vegetation, including fir and hemlock twigs in winter. It sometimes diverts streams into tunnels, and occasionally gnaws bark and trims trees.[1] It is a most curious animal.

The mountain beaver is not a beaver, nor does it live in the mountains. It inhabits the damp, forested foothills of the Cascade Range of Washington, Oregon, and California. Commonly known in Oregon as a boomer, it does not boom; in some sections called a whistler, it does not whistle. This much misnamed rodent and its eight subspecies have been set apart in a family of their own. They are found nowhere outside of North America.[2]

It often plays the role of heroine in epics, such as the War of the Winds set in the Duwamish Valley. Industry, year around activity, tunnel engineering, and plant care are hallmarks of this chubby, bobtailed rodent, which is usually about a foot long and weighs a few pounds. Such strongly female, domestic associations make it an ideal wife in folklore.

From entrances usually behind a bush or stump, it digs shallow burrows through soft, moist ground; emerges mostly at night due to poor eyesight, and is remarkably guileless. These rambling tunnels, with a roof plastered with packed clay and a floor of dry leaves and grass, include a nest chamber. Active all year, it continues to tunnel through deep snow. During flood, however, it swims out to find refuge at the highest elevations.[3]

An intensive herbivore, it delights in young fruit trees and fresh farm crops in new fields so that it quickly becomes a nuisance near human cultivation. It will scout for food by climbing saplings as much as 15 feet tall, trimming back side branches with its teeth to leave gripping stubs. Later, it will cut down the tree itself for food.

Members live dispersed, sometimes in scattered neighborhoods but never in colonies. Such habitat spacing is encouraged by a strong musky odor. They mate February to March. Females gestate a month, and have a litter of two to five pups, which are grey with large heads and closed eyes. They can be made into pets if confined outside in large enough enclosures to permit burrows, but they quickly die when held captive inside.[4]

The head is large, wide and low with small eyes, small ears and long

---

[1] Walter Dalquist, Mammals of Washington 1948: 367-369; Arthur Kruckeberg, The Natural History of Puget Sound 1991: 213-215; Ian Cowan and Charles Guiguet, The Mammals of British Columbia 1978.
[2] Ralph DeSola, American Wild Life Illustrated 1946: 57-60.
[3] Ralph DeSola, American Wild Life Illustrated 1946: 57-60.
[4] Walter Dalquist, Mammals of Washington 1948: 367-369.

vibrissae. The legs are short and heavy, but the forefeet are small and handlike; the hindfeet are large and powerful. The claws of both forefeet and hindfeet are long and strong. … The feet are pink. [5]

The animals are most abundant near springs, streams and damp places, although they are not aquatic. The tangled jungles of deciduous trees and shrubs that grow in ravines and stream valleys of the Puget Sound area present optimum habitat. … Small streams flow through some burrows. … [One] nest was composed of the leaves and stems of bracken [ferns] laced together with grass and fine twigs. [6]

Although principally nocturnal, mountain beavers are not infrequently active by day, especially in the fall. At this season they harvest food and spread it on logs to dry. The cured hay is removed to their burrows for nesting material and food. … In winter they eat such evergreen shrubs as salal (*Gaultheria shallon*) and Oregon grape (*Berberis nervosa*). They also eat the bark of trees, especially that of the willow (*Salix*). Under cover of snow, in the mountains, they burrow to some extent and pack excavated earth in snow burrows. The melting of the snow in the spring reveals the earth core, six to eight inches in diameter and two to four feet long. Several such earth cores were forked, showing that part of the earth had been pushed into a branching burrow. [7]

The mountain beaver holds its food in its forefeet, squirrellike, when it eats. Its food consists of the leaves and bark of woody plants and entire herbs, including roots. The mountain beaver is the only mammal so far as known that eats the bracken fern. It feeds on the branches of coniferous trees, including Douglas fir, red cedar, and hemlock. Such thorny species as blackberry, black-cap and devil's club are eaten. The odiferous skunk cabbage and the stinging nettle are on its bill of fare. A list of its food would include most plants found in its habitat, and we know of no species that it refuses as food. … [8]

It undermines roads and trails and defiles springs and streams. Control is simple for the animals readily enter steel traps set in their burrows. [9]

Its burrows can have up to a 19 inch diameter, with separate chambers for nest, offal, and food,

… surrounded by fan-shaped earth mounds and pathways; in very wet areas, a "tent" of sticks covered with leaves and fern fronds erected over burrow entrances; in late summer, "hay piles" of ferns and other vegetations up to 2 feet high on logs

---

[5] Dalquist 1948: 367-69.
[6] Dalquist 1948: 367-369.
[7] Dalquist 1948: 367-369.
[8] Dalquist 1948: 367-369.
[9] Dalquist 1948: 367-369.

or ground.[10]

Baseball-size balls of stone or clay [they] encountered in digging, which the animal occasionally gnaws upon to sharpen its teeth and used to close off nesting or feeding areas when vacated.[11]

In all, mountain beavers eat and act much like humans. Natives relied on bracken fern roots as a major food, along with other roots and berries. Nettles and devil's club are important medicines, and nettle fiber was once woven into nets. Evergreen wood was carved into a variety of tools. As competitors for the same resources, natives and mountain beavers would have frequently observed each other and recognized their common bonds.

---

[10]   John Whitaker, The Audubon Society Field Guild to North American Mammals 1980: 367.
[11]   Whitaker 1980: 368.

Appendix C: Northwest Anthropological Research Notes 25 (2): 139-154. (1991)

ON THE INDIAN TRIBES INHABITING THE NORTH-WEST COAST OF AMERICA
John Scouler, London
Reprinted from Ethnological Journal, A Magazine of Ethnology, Phrenology, and Archaeology
Vol. 1, pp. 228-252; London; 1848.

[Editorial comment: As part of the continuing effort of NARN to reprint old, obscure, or difficult to obtain sources, we are presenting Scouler's work. Because no clear copy was available it has been entirely reset rather than photo-reproduced. Starting below it is printed exactly as the original (except for line and page lengths) including idiosyncratic spelling and punctuation without the use of sic. The original page numbers are in [brackets] except for 228 which is presented as in the original. No editorial comments have been made concerning the various other authors, place names, tribal names, linguistic groups, or details concerning Scouler with the hope that an article based on this work will be forthcoming from among our readers. r.s.] {page #s of the NARN are within <angle brackets>}

(228)
ON THE INDIAN TRIBES INHABITING THE NORTH·WEST COAST OF AMERICA
By JOHN SCOULER, M. D., F. LS.
Read before the Society, 29th April 1846.

The ethnography of the tribes inhabiting the north-west coast of America, although far from being so well known as that of the Indian races to the east of the Rocky Mountains, has of late made considerable progress. In addition to the materials scattered through the works of the older voyagers, much valuable matter is to be found in Baer's recent work on the Russian Settlements on the north-west coast; and, in the Proceedings of the Geographical Society, I have published a very extensive series of Vocabularies of Indian Languages, collected by Dr Tolmie, which have been illustrated, and made the subject of comment by Dr Latham, in two communications, read before the Ethnological Society. In the following observations it is my intention to attempt a classification of the various tribes found between Behring's Straits and the Columbia River, and included between the Rocky Mountains and the Pacific Ocean. As all our more authentic information respecting the more northern tribes of Esquimaux and Koluschians, have been derived from Wrangel's communications to Baer's work, it will not be necessary to enter minutely on that part of the subject. In attempting this synopsis of the Indian tribes of the north-westward, we have to premise that it is merely an attempt, and one which will necessarily be subject to much correction. The number and names of the tribes is very imperfectly known; and, in many cases, we have no specimens of their language to enable us to fix their place, and often the indications of travellers are so vague, and even <140> contradictory, that their statements only produce perplexity. The following is, therefore, to be considered rather as an exhibition of what is known on the subject, than as a complete monograph. The distinction, however, between facts and probable inferences has been carefully observed.

With respect to the tribes inhabiting the Russian territory, [229] it may be remarked, that we find there three very distinct families of the human race brought into intimate relationship, and each retaining its own peculiarities. We find the Esquimaux to the north and west, the Koluschians, on the sea-coast, to the south, and, in the interior, the Carriers and other tribes of the Athabascan family, extending eastward toward Hudson's Bay, and spreading southward along the western side of the Rocky Mountains to the head-waters of Frazer's River. Notwithstanding the contiguity of these three families or groups, and that they have interchanged several words of their respective vocabularies, the distinction between them in language, manners, and modes of living, is very apparent, so that there is, in general, little difficulty in ascertaining to which of the three families a tribe belongs. Thus the Esquimaux of Greenland and Kodiac, although thousands of miles apart, have more dialectic affinities than the Kodiacs have with their neighbours, the Kenai or Koluschians. There is nothing more remarkable than the pertinacity with which even small tribes of Indians adhere to their language, retaining it, as Mr Gallatin observes, to the last moment of their existence. The difference of customs, as, for example, between a fishing and a hunting tribe, also tends to prevent intercourse, and thus keep languages distinct. Mr Dunn informs us, when speaking of the tribes situated around Puget's Sound, that "the coast tribes and those of the plains observe a marked aversion to mutual incorporation, and confine themselves to distinct localities; the plain tribes not approaching the Sound, and the tribes bordering on the Sound not extending their roamings into the plains." In the same manner, the Athabascan and Esquimaux races, in the northern regions, carry on a perpetual warfare. We also find, among the Indian races to the east of the Rocky Mountains, that amalgamations of dialects rarely, if ever, take place; their organization into tribes, and the necessity of preserving the full extent of their hunting-ground causes repulsion, not union, and is favourable to perpetual hostilities. It will be seen, in the course of this paper, that a different social condition has tended to obscure the marks of dialectic distinctions in certain tribes. [230]

1. Esquimaux. -- The ethnography of this race is now well known, and requires no illustration here. Extending from Greenland to Aliaska {Alaska}, they speak everywhere the same language, with dialectic variations. They inhabit the most northerly parts of the new world, and even part of the icy coasts of the old. The Esquimaux tribes, Inhabiting the north-west angle of America, appear to have been the most numerous portion of the race, in proportion to the extent of country which they occupy, and, at the same time, the most social and civilized. This may be accounted for by the milder climate of this region, by far the most temperate of any occupied by the Esquimaux, from its numerous islands, inlets, and peninsulas, which multiply, in a comparatively small space, an extensive line of seacoast adapted to their mode of life. The Esquimaux of this region display much industry and ingenuity, and carry on an extensive intercourse among themselves as well as with the Koluschians, and even with the inhabitants of the Asiatic coast. In this part of America the Esquimaux are divided into numerous small communities, whose names and places of residence are to be found in Baer's work, where much information may be obtained respecting them.

2. Athabascans. -- This family of Indians is not numerous in proportion to the extent of country which it occupies, but is interesting from its positions amidst so many distinct families, and occupying very nearly the whole breadth of the American continent. The Athabascans are

everywhere separated from the sea-coast by the Esquimaux; and towards the Mississippi River they become conterminous with the Algonquin race. To the west of <141> the Rocky Mountains, the Athabascans, under the names of Tacullies or Carriers, occupy the country called New Caledonia; but have nowhere reached the sea-coast, from which they are cut off by the Esquimaux, Koluschians, and other tribes. The Athabascan tribes are separated from the Ichthyophagous tribes of the coast by repugnance arising from difference of mode of life, or by natural barriers. To the north, the Athabascans inhabit the head waters of the streams which flow into the Pacific, and thus come into hostile contact with the Esquimaux. [231] Further south, they are cut off from the Koluschian and other sea tribes by the range of mountains which runs parallel to the coast, and from which they extend eastward to the Rocky Mountains. It would appear, that, to the north and west; the Tacullies or Athabascans rarely approach within 100 miles of the coast. Tribes of the Athabascan family occupy the country about the sources of the Salmon River, Frazer's River, and the northern tributaries of the Columbia. The *Nagailers* or Chin Indians, who speak the same language as the Tacullies, and are consequently Athabascan, come in contact with the Bellichoola on Salmon River, and with the Atnas or Noosdalums on Frazer's River. In the interior, they descend as far as Flat Bow Lake, where their neighbours are the *Kootanie* and Flatheads.

An inspection of the vocabularies of the languages spoken on the north-west coast, will aid us in defining the limits of the Athabascan family. If we examine the languages spoken from Observatory Inlet to the Columbia, we find they possess very few Athabascan words, the mountain barrier having obstructed the intercourse between the fish-eaters of the coast and the Athabascans of the interior. On the other hand, on the north and south, where no such defined barrier separates the different races, we find in the vocabularies evidence of a more frequent intercourse. In the dialects of the northern and continental Koluschians, we find a good number of Athabascan words; and the Kenai may probably be considered as rather Athabascan than Koluschian. In like manner, we find Athabascan words in the Kleketat and Shahaptan, as tribes speaking those languages form the southern frontier of the Athabascan race.

3. The Koluschians. -- The narrow portion of sea coast extending from Mount St Elias to the Columbia River is remarkable from being inhabited by Indians whose manners, physical features, and even intellectual and moral characters, differ considerably from those of the other Indians, whether of North or South America. The northernmost of these families may be called the Koluschian, and consist of many small tribes, of which we have attempted to give a tolerably complete enumeration. [232]

1. Ugalenzi. A small tribe, dwelling in winter to the east of the Island of Kodiac, and during summer at the mouth of the Copper River.
2. Atna. Living on the River Atna; distinct from the Atna of M'Kenzie.
3. Galzani, or Koltschani. Living to the north and east of the Atna River.
4. Kinai. Inhabiting the vicinity of Cook's Inlet.
5. Inchulukhlaites. Inhabiting the vicinity of the River Chulitna.
6. Inkalites. Inhabiting the vicinity of the Rivers Kwichpack and Kuskowim.
7. Sitkans. Inhabiting King George the Third's Archipelago.

8. Cheelkaats. Inhabiting Lynn's Canal, and neighbourhood. <142>
9. Tako. Inhabiting Point Salisbury and Snettisham.
10. Stikine. Inhabiting Prince Frederick's Sound and Stikine River.
11. Tunghaase. Inhabiting the island of Revilla Gigedo.

The territory occupied by the Koluschian family may be defined as including the islands and the shores of the mainland, from Cook's Inlet to the *Stikine* River. In the northern part of the Koluschian territory, the limits become undefined, from the intermixture of tribes of different lan~ages in the same country. Thus we find an Esquimaux tribe, the Tschugassi, inhabitmg the peninsula between Cook's Inlet and Prince William's Sound. The Inchulukhlaites and Inkalites, although Koluschians, live still farther north, amidst tribes of Esquimaux. Another cause of perplexity is, that in the six tribes first named in the table, we find in their vocabularies so many Athabascan words as to indicate an intimate intercourse with the Carriers. In the Kinai vocabulary, for example, the number of Athabascan words is so great, as to render it probable that they belong rather to that family of Indians than to the Koluschians, and that, to use a geological expression, they form an outlying portion of the Carriers. The more southern tribes, Nos. 7, 11, are [233] unquestionably Koluschian, speaking dialects of the same language, which is much freer from all Athabascan or Esquimaux intermixture. The Koluschian family, as we have defined it, includes the Tunghaase of Dr Tolmie, the Sitkans of the Russians, and Tchinkitane of Marchant.

4. Chimmesyan. -- In the present state of our knowledge, the Chemmesyans must be classed by themselves, as speaking a distinct language as peculiar as that of the Koluschians, with which it has had remote affinities.
The following table will exhibit the limits of this family and the principal tribes which speak the Chimmesyan language: -
1. The Naaskaak. Inhabiting Observatory Inlet.
2. The Chemmesyan. Inhabiting Dundas's Island and Stephen's Island.
3. Kitchatlah. } Inhabiting Princess Royal Islands.
4. Kethumeesh. }
5. Haidah. -- This well defined family comprehends the various tribes inhabiting Queen Charlotte's Island, including the *Skittegats, Maasets, Cumshewes,* &c. Besides the inhabitants of Queen Charlotte's Island, the Kyganie tribe, inhabiting Kyganie Bay, and the southern extremity of Prince of Wales' Archipelago, belong to the Haidah family.

6. Haeeltsuk. -- The Haeeltsuk tribes occupy the mainland and islands from Hawkesbury Island, and Millbank Sound to Broughton's Archipelago, inclusive, with the opposite coast of the Continent, and also the northern parts of Quadra and Vancouver's Island. The geographical position of the Haeeltsuk, will be best exhibited by the following table of tribes, and their places of residence.
1. Hyshalla. Inhabiting Hawksburg Island.
2. Hyhysh. Inhabiting Cascade Canal.
3. Haeeltsuk. } Inhabiting Millbank Sound.
4. Esleytuk.   } <143>

5. Weekenoch. Inhabiting Fitzhugh's Sound.
6. Nalatsenoch. Inhabiting Smith's Inlet.
7. Quagheuil. Inhabiting Broughton's Archipelago.
8. Tlutla-Shequilla. Including Northern extremity of Vancouver's Island.
9. Leequeeltoch. Inhabiting Johnston's Strait. [234]

7. Bellichoola. -- This family comprehends but a small number of tribes, speaking, however, a peculiar language. They live on the Salmon River and Dean's Canal, where they were visited by M'Kenzle on his journey to the Pacific Ocean. The small vocabulary collected by M'Kenzie, leaves no doubt, as Dr Tolmie and Dr Latham observes, that the Indians found by M'Kenzie at Friendly Village, belongs to the Bellichoola tribe.

We have classified the Koluschians, Haidah, Chimmesyans, Bellichoola, and Haeeltruk, as distinct families of Indians, and the distinction will hold good even if their languages should be proved to belong to one general tongue, of which they are respectively modifications. The languages of any of these tribes is unintelligible to the others; but, at the same time, the number of words common to them all induce us to suppose, that, with more copious vocabularies, many affinities might be detected and discrepancies removed.

8. Kawichen. -- The following tribes belong to this family: -
1. Commagsheak. Gulf of Georgia, Northern Part.
2. Kawichen. Gulph of Georgia, Southern Part.
3. Quaitlin. Frazer's River.
4. Noosdalum. Hood's Canal.
5. Squallyamish. Puget's Sound.
6. Atnas.

The table of tribes speaking the Kawitchen, and of their habitations, indicates the extent of country over which the language prevails. It extends along the shores of the Gulf of Georgia on the mainland, opposite Vancouver's Island, and south to Puget's Sound, where it approaches the Cowlitch River. Dr Tolmie has supplied three vocabularies, those of the KaWltchen, Noosdalum, and Squallyamish, which appear to be so many dialects of the same original language; the Squallyamish, however, exhibiting the greatest amount of variation. The Atna Indians of M'Kenzie are, as Dr Latham suggests, a branch of the Kawitchen family, and have for neighbours the Athabascans.

9. Nootkans.
    1. Naspatle; 2. Nootkans; 3. Tlaoquatch; 4. Nit- [235] tenat.
       All inhabit the western shores of Vancouver's Island.
5. Classet. Inhabit Cape Flattery.
6. Queenioolt. Inhabit Queenhithe South of Cape Flattery. <144>
7. Chikeelis. Inhabit Chikeeli Bay and River.
8. Cowlitch. Inhabit Cowlitch River.
9. Tilhalumma. Inhabit sources of Chikeeli River.

The relations of this important family, as well as its geographical limits, are very difficult to ascertain, especially as there is much confusion in the vocabularies and relations of the tribes inhabiting the Lower Columbia. If all the above mentioned tribes belong to the Nootkan family, it occupies a very extensive region, including the STeater part of the western and southern shores of Vancouver's Island. On the mainland It extends south to the Columbia River, and occupies the greater part of the region between Puget's Sound, the Cowlitch River, and the Pacific. As this extensive range is given to the Nootkan family for the first time, it is necessary to distinguish what is ascertained from what amounts only to a considerable degree of probability. We have many vocabularies of the Nootkan language by Cook, Mozino, Dr Tolmie, and Jewitt, who remained a captive at Nootka for several years. A comparison of these vocabularies leaves no doubt that the first four tribes in the preflxed table belong to the Nootkan family. We have, unfortunately, no vocabulary of the Classet language; but I have reason to believe that the Classets and Tlaoquatcb can understand each other, and if so, the former belongs to the Nootkan family. The chief difficulty is with the last four tribes mentioned in the list. Dr Tolmie merely says, that they speak the Chikeeli, but gives no further information respecting them. The reasons for supposing the Chikeeli tribes are allied to the Nootkan family are as follows: -- At the mouth of the Columbia River, especially on the south side, we find several tribes, hereafter to be mentioned, who use the Cheenook language. Above these tribes, and ascending to the falls of the Columbia, we find Cathlascans also speaking a peculiar language. Of the tribes on the north side of the river, between the [236] Cowlitch, Puget's Sound, and the sea, we have apparently no vocabularies, although the country is occupied by well-known tribes of Indians. It is not, however, upon this negative argument that we place the Chikeeli tribes in the Nootkan family. While residing for several weeks among the Indians of the Lower Columbia, I collected a small vocabulary of the language, and of the phrases essential for carrying on some conversation with the natives. A comparison of this language, spoken by the Chikeelis, with the Tlaoquatch vocabulary of Dr Tolmie and the Nootkan ones of Mozino and Jewitt, prove that it has very great affinities with the Nootkan.

		COLUMBIA.
Plenty	Aya, Tlaoquatch	Haya
No	Wik, Nootkan	Wake
Water	Tchaak, Tlaoquatch	Chuck
Good	Hooleish, do.	Closh
Bad	Peishakeis, do.	Peshak
Man	Tchuckoop, do.	Tillicham
Woman	Tlootsemtn, do.	Clootchamen
Child	Tanassis, do.	Tanass
Now	Tlabowieh, do.	Clahowiab
Come	Tchooqua, do.	Sacko
Slave	Mischemas, Nootka	Mischemas
What are you doing?		
	Akoots-ka-mamok, Tlaoquatch	Ektamammok
What are you saying?		
	Au-kaak-wawa, Tlaoquatch	Ekta-wawa

Let me see	Nannanitch	Nannanitch
Sun	Opeth, Nootka	Ootlach
Sky	Sieya, do.	Saya <145>
Fruit	Chamas, do.	Camas
To sell	Makok, do.	Makok
Understand	Commatax, do.	Commatax

The vocabulary here given proves that there is a very considerable affinity between the tribes of the north part of the Lower Columbia and the Nootkans of Vancouver's Island, and is the evidence on which we have ventured to place the Chikeelis in the same group as the Nootkans.

10. Cheenooks. -- The Cheenooks inhabit the lower part of the Columbia, near the sea, and from thence extend along the coast, probably until they reach the Umpqua tribes on the river of the same name. The chief tribes are
    1. Cheenooks. Inhabiting the south bank of the Columbia.
    2. Cladsaps. Inhabiting the sea-coast near Point Adams. [237]
    3. Kellamucks. Inhabiting the Kellamuck River, and south of the Cladsaps.
    4. Cathlamuts. Inhabiting the south bank of the Columbia above the Cheenooks.

11. Umpquas. -- Lewis and Clark have given the names of many Cheenook tribes which live on the bays and streams entering the Pacific, and extending towards the Umpqua river. Their names It is unnecessary to repeat. We will merely state, that beyond them, and on the Umpqua and Clamet rivers, we find the Umpqua Indians, of whom we know very little, except that they speak a very distinct language, and are therefore entitled to form a separate family.

12. Cathlascans. -- The Cathlascans inhabit the banks of the Columbia, from the Falls down to Wappatoo Island, and also the lower part of the Multrumah or Willamud river. The Cathlascans are divided into many little tribes. Their chief place of resort is Wappatoo Island, a low but fertile tract, which resembles the Lizerias of the Tagus. The alluvial and overflown parts of the island abound in a species of *Sagittaria*, resembling the *S. sagittifolia*, but remarkable for producing at the root a tuber of the size of that of the artichoke, which it very much resembles in flavour, and forms an important article of food to the natives of the Lower Columbia.

As in the case of the northern tribes, the families which we have called Kawitchen, N ootkan, Cheenook, and Cathlascan, may form a group by themselves, and the recurrence of the same words in several of the vocabularies, induces us to suppose that the differences will be reduced as our knowledge of the ethnography of the Oregon improves.

13. Shahaptan.
    1. Kliketan. Inhabit the tract between Fond Ner Percees, Mount Rainier,
        and the Falls of the Columbia.
    2. Shahaptans or Ner{z} Percees. Inhabit the southern branch of the Columbia,
        and spread over a great extent of country.
    3. Wallawalla. <146>

4. Cayoose. Inhabit the Snake River from its mouth to [238] its junction with the Salmon River, and the intermediate country.

5. Peloose. Inhabit sources of the Spokan River.

Of the numerous tribes inhabiting the upper tributaries of the Columbia, there are probably many who should be included in the Shahaptan family, but who, in the absence of vocabularies, cannot be placed in the table with any degree of certainty. That the Kliketat, Wallawalla, and Shahaptans, speak the same language, although with dialectic variations, is undoubted; and the vocabulanes in the appendix, perhaps the most accurate we possess of any Oregon languages, exhibits both the affinities and divergences. It was drawn up by the Rev. Cornelius Rogers, who has resided as a missionary among the Nez Percees, and is thoroughly versant in their language. The Peloose and Cayoose Indians may also be referred to this family without much risk of error. The first live on the Wallawalla and Columbia at their junction, the second to the west of the Ner Percees. The Shahaptan tribes occupy a very extensive territory, extending from Mount Rainier south to Ford Ner Percees, at the junction of the great northern and southern tributaries of the Columbia, and including the extensive country included between them.

14. Okanagan. -- This family is placed to the north and east of the Shahaptans. The language is spoken at Fort-Okanagan and in the upper part of Frazer's River. As Dr Latham conjectures, it is probable that the Salish or Flatheads belong to the Okanagans. The Rev Mr Parker says, they are a branch of the Shahaptans, and speak the same language, but the scanty vocabulary we possess is in favour of Dr Latham's opinion. The affinities of the following tribes are uncertain, although they must be referred either to the Shahaptans or Okanagans: -- the Spokans, who live on the Spokan river, the Coeur, and Alenes, and Ponderas, who are a numerous tribe living to the north of Clarke's River. The Cootanies on the M'Gillivray River, according to Mr Parker, speak a peculiar language, and beyond them we have the Athabascan Carriers. [239]

15. Kalapooiah. -- We possess vocabularies of two dialects, of this family, the Kalapooiah and Yamkallie. The language is spoken beyond the sources of the Willamut River, in the extensive plains in that quarter, and separated by the range from the Cheenook and Umpquas.

16. Shossoonies. -- The Shossoonies, Snakes, or Diggers, who reside in the mountains and deserts to the south of the sources of the Columbia, are the only remaining family to be noticed, as the tribes inhabiting California, from the sources of the Rio Colorado southward, are too little known to afford materials for description. In the absence of complete vocabularies, we only know that they form a family apart, having no affinity with the Shahaptans or Kalapooiah. The Shossoonies are, perhaps, the most miserable Indians on the whole continent, except the inhabitants of Terra del Fuego; and in their arid deserts their condition, as described by Captain Fremont, is more like that of the Hottentots, or the natives of New Holland, than of American Indians. Their chief subsistence, when fish is not to be found, consists in a scanty supply of game, lizards, and small mammifers, and such roots as the country affords.

Their chief vegetable food consists, according to Captain Fremont, of the roots of a thistle, the *Circium turgenianum* of the *Anethum graveolens*. The *Camas camassia esculenta*, and a species of Valerian, *V. eduli*. It is on such scanty fare that the Shossoonies subsist amidst their rocks and deserts.

In the preceding synopsis, it has been attempted to exhibit as complete a view as possible of the various tribes inhabiting the northern coast of America, from the Polar Seas <147> to the Columbia. The extreme difficulty of the task, and the toil of collecting information scattered in minute portions through a great variety of works, will, it is trusted, be taken as an apology for any errors which may have been fallen into. Were we to construct an ethnographical chart of the north-west part of America, and compare it with the excellent one which Mr Gallatin has given, illustrating the distribution of the Indian tribes east of the Rocky Mountains, nothing would appear more striking than the great variety of languages spoken in the narrow district included between the Rocky [240] Mountains and the Pacific, contrasted with the few but wide spread dialects, spoken between Hudson's Bay and the Gulf of Mexico. Unwilling to introduce premature generalizations, we have estimated the number of distinct languages at sixteen. Although the number will probably be considerably reduced by subsequent investigations; the Okanagan may be perhaps united to the Shahartan and the Haidah, with the Koluschian; but after all such reductions, the number 0 distinct languages spoken to the west of the Rocky Mountains, will be far greater, in proportion to the surface of country and population, than it is to the east, between the mountains and the Atlantic. The territory occupied by the Algonquin race alone exceeds the whole extent of the Oregon territory. In the south of the United States, however, we have something analogous to the population of the west coast, for there a great number of small tribes are found speaking distinct languages, and having little affinity with each other. The creeks and the jungles of that part of country appear to have afforded an asylum to tribes expelled from their ancient abodes. On the east of the Rocky Mountains the wide diffusion of particular languages depends in part on the nature of the country. Subsisting almost exclusively by the chase, each tribe required a great extent of country; few natural barriers existed to prevent dispersion, and the sanguinary nature of Indian warfare left no resource to the vanquished but the alternative of flight or extermination. In the history of the Irriquois confederacy, we have a picture of this desolating warfare in which even the harsh mercy of slavery was refused to the vanquished.

Among the natives of the north-west coast, the features of the country, intersected by mountain ranges, or broken up into islands, rendered the tribes more sedentary; while, at the same time, it permitted, and even from the diversity of its products required, some degree of commercial intercourse. Under such physical conditions, and where the modes of obtaining food varied with the character of the country, extensive conquests were impossible; the energetic Haidah of Queen Charlotte's island could not, even if conquerors, abandon at once their mode of life as fishers, and change themselves [241] into hunters if they penetrated across the mountains, and occupied the country of the Athabascans. This circumstance is unquestionably favourable to the production and preservation of a variety of dialects, although it is by no means a proof that they were not originally derived from a common source. When, to ascertain this, we compare the different vocabularies, we find a source of perplexity which does not occur to any thing like the same extent among the languages spoken to the east of the mountains. In the Irriquois, Cherokee, Sioux, and Algonquin, we find very few words common

to all or to any two of them; the term expressing numbers, the common objects of nature, articles of indispensable necessity or of family relationship, are perfectly distinct. In the languages of the north-west coast, ~n the contrary, there seem to be an equal balance of divergences and resemblances; the same words reappear in the most remote languages, and these frequently numerals or other terms of the first necessity. The similarity with respect to numerals, may be at once seen on inspecting the vocabularies published in the Proceedings of the Geographical Society. <148>
The following instances will explain the same fact: -

    Man, Tillicham, Columbia River: Boy, Tehileque, Carrier.
    Woman, Shewat, Koluschian; Aiat, Shahaptan.
    Water, Tchuk, Nootkan; Tshush, Walla walla.
    Child, Munna, Bellichoola; Mumunna, Kawitchen.
    Child, Tillcoole, Chimmesyan; Tool, Cheenook.

The source of strange confusion, so to speak, appears to depend on the following circumstances. The Indians of the northward possess a very different natural character from that of the eastern tribes; they are more sedentary, of a milder nature, their wars are far less cruel, the prisoners are usually detained in a state of mild slavery, and ultimately incorporated into the conquering tribe; and this circumstance alone will tend to produce an intermixture of dialects. Another modifying cause results from the extensive commercial intercourse carried on between even very remote tribes. Baron Wrangell has given an interesting account of the active trade carried on, from time immemorial, among the tribes from Behring's Straits to Queen Charlotte's Island, and even [242] to Nootka; Dr Tolmie has given valuable information respecting the fairs held at Naas, where the Koluschians, Haidah, Chimmesyans, and Haeeltzuk, interchange commodities.

    Previous to the arrival of Europeans, when the use of iron was unknown, copper was an article of great value, and the traditions concerning it prove its former importance; and also a commerce in articles constructed from this metal. Wrangell informs us that the Northern Atnas of the Copper River were famous for the fabrication and commerce in knives and daggers of copper. The tradition of the Chippewyans, recorded by M'Kenzie, that their ancestors came from the west, from a country abounding in copper, may probably refer to their intercourse, by means of the Carriers with the Atnas of the Copper River. According to Mr Dunn, the Cheelhaats of Lynn's Canal were, like the Atnas, famed for their copper, which they wrought with great dexterity. In this country, he says, great quantities of virgin copper are found, some of it is worked into a kind of shield, two feet and a-half long and one broad, with figures of men and animals expressed on it. The labour and ingenuity expended in working these shields gives them a great value. One of them is estimated as worth nine slaves, and is transmitted as a precious heirloom from father to son. The tradition of the Nootkans, as related by Meares, bears upon the same point. An old man entered the bay in a copper canoe with paddles of copper; and thus the Nootkans acquired a knowledge of the value of that metal.

    Another article of commerce, or rather the circulating medium of the country, was the hyaqua shell {dentalia}, which was a still better substitute for money than the courie of the east. These hyaquas were sorted according to their sizes, and afterwards strung together always to the number of fOrty. The mode of estimating their relative values was very ingenious and simple. If the string of forty hyaquas made only a fathom they were of small value; if thirty-five made a fathom, the shells were of greater size and worth, and, of course, five remained over, and when ten remained in excess, such a string of hyaquas was worth many beaver skins. These hyaquas are obtained at Nootka and De Fucas Straits, but so much value [243] was attached to them that they found their way to Oonalaska and the Columbia River. ThIs shell money, both from its limited supply, its durability, and facility with which its value could be expressed in numbers, and its portability, was far superior to the coccoa money of the Mexicans. This commercial intercourse must have {been} intended to produce some assimilation among the idioms; and, accordingly, we find that most exchangeable articles have the same name in Koluschian and Haldah, although the languages are, in other respects, very different. The practice of kidnapping and selling slaves must have had a similar tendency. <149>

Another cause of variation is the dialectic differences which grow up in distant tribes speaking the same language, leading to differences of pronunciation which the stranger cannot detect.

In the Wallawalla and Shahaptan vocabularies, appended to this paper, we see that, even in Indian languages, such variations follow certain rules. According to the excellent remarks of Mr Rogers, one form of the subjunctive ends in *tah* and *nah*, in Wallawalla it is always *tahna*; the Wallawalla substitute *sh* for the Shahaptan *k*, as in tshusk for scush; the Wallawalla substitutes *n* for Shahaptan *l*, as wanaka for walasa. Mr Rogers also adds, that the same word often varies considerably in signification; and hence another cause of difficulty in judging of affinities from imperfect vocabularies. Another observation by Mr Rogers, points out another cause of variation, of which I know of no other instance among Indian tribes. He informs us that the Cayoose Indians have an entirely distinct language of their own; but they have long since adopted the Nez Percee as their national tongue, and only a few of the old people retain a knowledge of their original language. If this circumstance be fully establlshed, it throws much light on the causes of variation in the Oregon languages, and indicates a much more fleXible disposition than is usually found among Indians. The smallest tribe, in the south of the United States, retained its language with the most obstinate tenacity; and the barbarous Otomis retained their uncouth language for centuries amidst the more polished languages of Mexico. With our present imperfect knowledge of the [244] languages spoken in the north-west coast, all attempts at ethnological classifications will remain imperfect, more vocabularies must be constructed, and the old corrected, before we can trace the affinities and migrations of tribes, the study of whose dialects constitutes all their history.

The researches of American philologists, especially Du Ponceau and Gallatin, have shewn, that, however different the words may be m Indian languages, the same grammatical structure pervades them all. From Canada to Chili, we find similar forms under a great diversity of words. The principles of M. Du Ponceau have been found applicable, with one exception, to all the hitherto examined languages of America, and it is an interesting inquiry to ascertain whether the languages of the north-west coast afford confirmation, or exceptions, to so extensive a generalisation; unfortunately the materials are not abundant, as It is far more difficult to obtain a grammar than a vocabulary. The only grammar of an Oregon language, which we are acquainted with, is a manuscript one of the Shahaptan or Nez Percee, drawn up by the Rev C Rogers, and which affords a short but perspicuous view of the peculiarities of that wide-spread tongue.

The only consonants used in Shahaptan are *h k l m n p s t w*. The letters *b d f g r v z* so often absent in Indian languages, are only used in Shahaptan, when pronouncing foreign words. They have, however, several sounds unknown to English as *ph* aspirated *lk, tkt, shk*.

Like the other American, or in short, all barbarous languages, the Shahaptan is rich in words indicating every variety of object, but poor in general terms, like the Malayan dialects, where there may be twenty names for gold, but none for metal. It is apparently to the same poverty of general ideas, that the pronouns and verbs, with their definite and general plurals, and vast variety of inflexions, indicating every minute particular of time, place, or motion, are very unfit for the discussion of moral topics. They resemble the technical language of botanists, expressing with rigorous precision, the form and properties of bodies, but unfit for any kind of speculative discussion. The distinction of bodies into animate [245] and inanimate, which pervades the Algonquin, and exists, although in a minor degree, in many American languages, has not been hitherto detected in dialects of the Oregon. Although not immediately connected with the subject, it may be mentioned that this distinction of bodies into animate and inanimate is not peculiar to some tribes in <150> North America. It appears to exist in the Peruvian where also animate objects are divided into rational and irrational. In the rational and irrational divisions, the sex is expressed by words equivalent to male and female, but these words are different in the two classes of nouns.

We have now to offer a few remarks on the physical appearance, intellectual character, and social institutions of the Indians of the north-west coast of America. Even if we exclude the Esquimaux, we find there is a considerable variety in the physical features of the north-west Indians. The Haidah and Koluschians differ greatly from the Chenooks and Cathlascans of the Columbia; and the Shahaptans and Kleketat differ from both. The northern tribes are of a pale complexion and are not darker than the Portuguese or Italians, while the complexion of the Columbian Indian is deeper, although not so much as the Irriquois of Canada. The features also of the northern tribes are more prominent, they have broader cheek-bones. The Koluschians are of middle stature, but strong made, with broad nose and great cheek-bones, and in all respects strongly marked features. The Cheenooks are of small stature, with crooked legs, from sitting so long in their canoes, with flat nose and large nostrils, but their features are less prominent than in the Haidah and Koluschians. The Kleketat and Flatheads are of a fair complexio~ tall stature, well made, and active. The peculiarities in the form of the cranium have been mentioned in a paper on the Oregon Indians, published in the Transactions of the Geographical Society.

The intellectual and moral characters of the Indians on the west coast are very different from those of the Indians east of the Mountains. From the nature of their pursuits the Oregon Indians have a more extensive range of ideas, and are less inflexible in character than the other American [246] tribes. The western Indians are imitative and docile; and instead of the hard-heartedness of the Irriquois, the ferocity of the Carib, or the implacable cruelty of the Brazilian, the Oregon Indians are comparatively humane, the custom of scalping is unknown, prisoners taken in war are rarely put to death after the excitement of the contest has subsided, and they are never exposed to lingering tortures. Those probationary tortures by which the young men were initiated into the rank of warriors, and of which, as practised by the Mandians, Mr Catlin has given so entertaining an account, are unknown to the west of the Rocky Mountains.

There is, however, a very considerable variety of psychological character among the tribes of the north-west coast. The northern tribes of Koluschians, Haidah, and Bellichoolas are, in point of skill and ingenuity, far superior to the Cheenooks and Cathlascans. The mechanical skill and imitative ingenwty of the northern Indians as displayed in the construction of their canoes, houses, fishing Implements, as well as in their ornamented daggers, pipes, and masks, has attracted the notice of all civilised visitors. The elaborate carvings of the Haidahs is equal in skill to any thing we find displayed by the Mexicans, and shews how small an amount of civilisation might suffice for the construction of the monuments of Chiapa or Yucatan. A very curious instance of the imitative powers of the northern Indians is related by Mr Dunn. The Bellichoolas of Millbank Sound were struck with admiration on the first sight of a steam boat, and undertook to construct a vessel on the same model. In a short time they had felled a large tree, and were constructing the hull out of its scooped trunk. Some time after the rude steamer appeared. She was from twenty to thirty feet long, she was black with painted ports, was decked over, and the paddles painted red, and Indians under cover to turn them round. She was floated triumphantly, and went at the rate of three miles an hour. The introduction and general cultivation of the potato without the aid of European lessons or example, is a remarkable instance of the docility and industry of the Haidah, and they not [247] unfrequently sell from five to eight hundred bushels of them at the annual fair at Naas. <151>

The Indians of Nootka are not equal to the northern tribes, but are superior to the Cheenooks and Cathlascans of the Columbia, who are the least energetic, and at the same time the most cowardly and licentious of all the inhabitants of the north-west coast. If inferior in some degree to the northern tribes, in as far as regards dexterity and mechanical skill, the tribes of the interior, such as the Flat-Heads, Cayuse, and Shahaptans, are by far the first in moral character. The desire for religious even more than for intellectual culture, and the strong, although untutored, devotional feelings, are pleasing phenomena in the Indian race, in general so untractable. This favourable account of the Flatheads and allied tribes, does not rest on the evidence of the missionaries alone, but is the opinion of all who have travelled among them. They are described as polite and unobtrusive. Even the children are more peaceable than other children, and although hundreds may be seen together at play, there is no quarrelling among them. They nave learned to observe Sunday, and will not raise their camp on that day; they also spend a part of it in prayer and religious ceremonies. The chief assembles them to prayer in Which they all join in an occasional chorus. He then exhorts them to good conduct. These customs were adopted before the arrival of Christian teachers among them.

The religion, or rather superstitions, of the Indians of the north-west coast, do not appear to differ greatly from those of the tribes to the east of the Mountains. The supposed simplicity of the Indians creed, as well as their equally imaginary eloquence, have been the subject of much vague speculation, founded on inaccurate observations. As an instance of the vagueness with which the customs of the Indians are sometimes described, it may be mentioned, that a very respectable writer, in speaking of the Cheenooks, alludes to assemblies around the council fire, taking up the tomihawk, and displaying the scalps of their enemies, although such customs were unknown in the Oregon territory. [248]

In like manner, when we hear the term Great Spirit so often used in speaking of Indian superstitions, we are ready to suppose that such an expression conveys the equivalent idea to the Indian which it does to ourselves, and that their faith was a simple natural theism. This, however, is very far from being the case. The religion of the Indian is merely a kind of fetichism, consisting in charms and incantations. In the narrative of Tanner, who lived from his childhood among the Indians, and whose faithful and detailed narrative is so different from the speculations of certain writers, we find that the religion of the Indian is merely a system of fetichism similar to that which once prevailed among the Finns, and is found at the present day among the people of Siberia. Among the Indians east of the Mountains, the fetiche, under the name 0 medicine bag, is well known, and consists merely of some object supposed to be possessed of mysterious powers. Along with this, there is excitement produced by fastings, incantations, and dreams. On the north-west coast the system is similar; and in a former paper, to which allusion has been already made, there is an interesting account by Dr Tohme of the superstitions of the Haeeltruk. In the Oregon territory, the term medicine-man is more appropriate than it is to the east of the Mountains; for, on the Columbia, the chief influence is derived from expelling diseases by means of charms and mystic ceremonies.

Connected with the religion of these Indians, their mode of interment deserves notice. It is remarkable, that the simple and natural process of committing the body to the earth, is rarely practised by the American Indians. Among the ancient Peruvians, the body was wrapped up in mats, and interred in a sitting posture, the same posture in which the dead are represented in the picture writings of the Mexicans. On the north-west coast, the body is sometimes placed in a box, and deposited in the crevices of the rocks, or put into a canoe, and raised upon props, where it dries, and becomes a mummy, and so remains until the body and the canoe fall into decay. The custom of burning the body, although uncommon, was practised among the Carriers of New Caledonia. Mr Dunn informs us, that, like the people of [249] Hindostan, they used, until lately, to burn their dead, a <152> ceremony in which the widow of the deceased, although not sacrificed, was obliged to continue beating the breast of the corpse until it was consumed on the funereal pile. Instead of being burned, she was obliged to selVe as a slave the relations of her deceased husband for a series of years, during which she wore around her neck a small bag containing a portion of the ashes of her husband. At the end of the allotted time a feast was held, and she was declared at liberty to cast off the symbols of her widowhood.

Another curious custom, of which, however, we have found as yet only obscure notices of its existence on the north-west coast, is what has been called the totem, among the Algonquins, among whom the institution exists in perfection. According to this institution, an Indian tribe or nation is divided into various clans or families, each supposed to have a common descent, bearing, as an emblem or surname, the appellation of some animal or other object, which, among the Algonquins, is called the totem of the clan. Individuals among the Indians cannot marry within their own clan, but must seek a wife in a clan bearing another totem; and hence marriages into a close degree of consanguinity are effectually prevented. The female children in many tribes follow the totem of the mother, while the males follow that of the father. This system appears to be very general among the Indians, and even in other barbarous nations; and we find traces of it among the Indians of the north-west coast. The Cheenooks generally seek for wives among the Chiheelees, and vice versa; and thus Indian women may be found in places very remote from the abode of their parents. Among the Koluschians and northern tribes, there is the division of the dog and raven clans, with numerous subdivisions. This system existed in South as well as North America. Thus Piedrahita, in his History of New Grenada, notices its occurrence among the Panches, a tribe inhabiting that country. He says, "No casaban los de uno pueblo con muger alguna del, porque todos se tenian por hermanos, y era sacro sancto para ellos e impedimento de parentesco pero era tal su ignorancia, qui si la proporia hermana nacia en deferenti pueblo, no escusaba [250] casarse con ella el hermano." The existence of this institution appears to have produced the very curious peculiarity of Indian languages noticed by Mr Gallatin, that the women use different words from the men to express family relationships. In some Indian languages this peculiarity penetrates even deeper into the language. Among the Moxas of South America, the women and the men use different pronouns in speaking to each other of things relating to each other. The Kobang of the Australians appears to be the very same institution as the totem of the Algonquins; and it would be interesting to know if similar peculiarities pervade their language.

	Shahaptan.	*Wallawalla.*	*Kleketat.*
Man	Nama	Winsh	Wins
Boy	Naswae	Tahnutshint	Aswan
Woman	Aiat	Tilahi	Aiat
Girl	Piten	Tohauat	Pitiniks
Wife	Swahna	Asham	Asham
Child	Miahs	Isht	Mianash
Father	Pishd	Pshit	Pshit
Mother	Pika	Ptsha	Ptsha
Friend	Ukstiwa	Hhai	Hhai
Fire	Ala	Sluksh	Sluks
Water	Tkush	Tshush	Tshaush
Wood	Hatsin	Slukas	Slukuas
Stone	Pishwa	Pshwa	Pshwa
Ground	Watsash	Titsham	Titsham
Sun	Wishamtuksh	Au	Au
Moon		Ailhai	Ailhai
Stars	Witsein	Haslu	Haslo
Clouds	spalikt	Pashst	----
Rain	Wakit	Sshhauit	Tohtoha
Snow	Maka	Poi	Maka
Ice	Tahask	Tahauk	Toh
Horse	Shikam	Kusi	Kusi
Dog	Shikamkan	Kusi Kusi	Kusi Kusi
Buffalo	Kokulli	Musmussin	Musmussin
Male Elk	Wawakia	Wawakia	Winat
Female Elk	Taship	Tashipka	Winat
Grey Bear	Pahas	Wapande	----
Black Bear	Jaka	Saka	Analmi
House	Snit	Snit	Snit

<153>

Gun	Timuni	Tainpas	Tuilpas
Body	Silaks	Waunokshash	----
Head	Hushus	Tilpi	Palka
Arm	Atim	Kamkas	----
Eyes	Shillm	Atshash	Atshash [251]

	Shahaptan.	*Wallawalla.*	*Kleketat.*
Nose	Nathnu	Nathnu	Nosnu
Ears	Matsaia	Matsiu	----
Mouth	Him	Em	Am
Teeth	Tit	Tit	----
Hands	Spshus	Alla	SPt
Feet	Ahwa	Waa	Waha
Legs	Wainsh	Tama	----
Mocassens	Ileapkat	Shkam	Shkam
Good	Tahr	Skeh	Shoeah
Bad	Kapshish	Milla	Tshailwit
Hot	Sakas	Sahwaih	Sahweah
Cold	Kenis	Kasat	Tewisha Kasat
Far	Waiat	Wiat	Wiat
Near	Keintam	Tsiwas	Tsa
High	Tashti	Hwaiam	Hweami
Low	Ahat	Smite	Niti
White	Naihaih	Koik	Olash
Black	Sunuhsimuh	Tshimuk	Tsimuk
Red	Sepilp	Sutsha	Sutsa
Here	Kina	Tshna	Stshiuak
There	Kuna	Kuna	Skone
Where?	Minu?	Mina?	Mam
When?	Mana?	Mun?	Mun?
What?	Mish?	Mish?	Mish?
Why?	Manama?	Maui?	----
Who?	Ishi?	Skiu?	Skiu?
Which?	Ma?	Mam?	----
How much?	Mas?	Milh?	Milh?
So much	Kala	Kulk	Skulk
How far?	Miwail?	Maal?	----
So far	Kewail	Kwal	----
How long?	Mahae?	Maalh	----
To long	Kohae	Kwalk	----
This	Ki	Tshi	Tshi
That	Joh	Kwa	Skwa

<154>

I	Su	Su	Suk
You	Sui	Sui	Suik
He, she, it	Ipi	Ipin	Pink
We	Nun	Nama	Nemak
Ye	Ima	Ena	Imak
They	Ema	Ema	Pamak
To go	Kusha	Winasha	Winasha
To see	Hakesha	Hoksha	----
So say	Heisha	Nu	Nu
To talk	Tseksa	Siniwasa	Sinawasa
To walk	Wenasa	Winashash	----
To read	Wasasha	Wasasha	Wasasha
To eat	Wipisha	Kwatashak	----
To drink	Makosha	Matshushask	----
To sleep	Pinimiksha	Pinusha	----
	Shahaptan.	Wallawalla.	Kleketat.
To wake	Waksa	Tahshisask	Tahshasha
To love	Watanisha	Tkeshask	Tkehsha
To take	Paalsa	Apalashask	----
To know	Lukuasa	Ashakuashash	Shukuasha
To forget	Titolasha	Slakshash	----
To give	Inisha	Nishamash	----
To seize	Inpisha	Shutshash	Wanapsha
To be cold	Iswaisa	Sweashash	Iswais
To be sick	Komaisa	Painshash	Painsha
To hunt	Tukuliksa	Salaitisas	Nistewasa
To lie	Mishamisha	Tshishkshash	Tshiska
To steal	Pakwasha	Pakwashash	Pakwasha

[252]

D

Appendix D
ORIGINAL TABLE OF CONTENTS

FIGURES

PLATES

D

TABLES

(32)

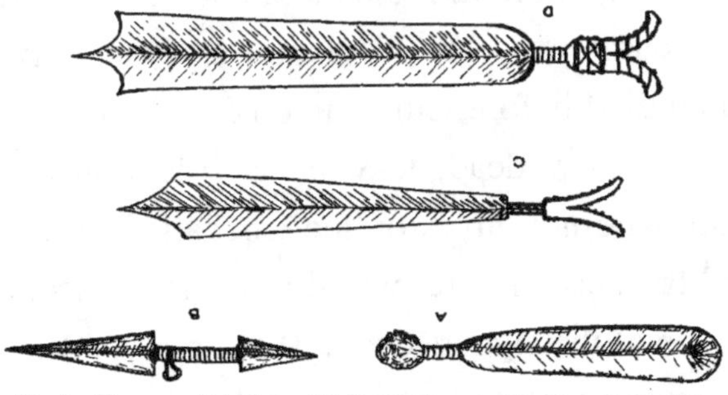

Fig. 2. Weapons. (A) Club; (B) Double dagger; (C) Short blade; (D) Long blade. After Lewis and Clark (Thwaites, *Original Journals*).

Appendix E ~ Depositions

#10 Samuel Mallet 76 @ 1906 to Charles McChesney BIA
#14 Howard Cultee 20
#15 Mary Wagner 76
#16 Catherine George 76
#18 Joseph Cultee 37
#33 Mrs Howard Cultee 38
#64 Isabel Bertrand 62
#100 Esther Mallet [Luscier] 60

Statement No. 10.

State of Washington, *Pacific County, ss*:

Samuel Mallet, of Bay Center, being duly sworn, deposes and says he is 76 years of age and born at Bay Center, and belongs to the Waukikum tribe of Chinook Indians.

I knew Cumcumley, a Lower Chinook Indian and one of the signers of the 1851 treaty. He died nearly forty-two years ago. Cumcumley had 5 children, 4 of whom died before Cumcumley did. One daughter survived him, whose name I do not now remember and who died about two or three years after Cumcumley died, and without issue, aged about 15 years. Cumcumley lived at the month of the Columbia River, near where Fort Columbia now stands, on the Washington side of the river.

I knew Kulchute, a Lower Chinook Indian and one of the signers of the 1851 treaty. He died of smallpox before Cumcumley's death. Kulchute had two wives and three children; both wives and two of the children died before Kulchute died. The daughter who survived Kulchute was named Tah-shuck, who is now dead, leaving as sole issue and heirs one son and one daughter, viz, Edward Smith, who now lives on the Chehalis Reserve, Oakville, Wash., and his sister, Maggie Smith, now Mrs. Joseph Pete, who lives same place. I knew Ahmoosamoose, a Lower Chinook Indian and one of the signers of the 1851 treaty, who is now deceased, leaving as sole heirs two sons and a daughter, as follows: Jack Abmoosamoose, who is dead, unmarried and without issue; Joseph Ahmoosamoose, who has since died, leaving a daughter named Kate, who is now alive and married to a man named John Walkowsky, and lives near Oysterville, Wash. The daughter of Ahmoosamouse was named Looks, and she is dead, leaving as issue two sons named Joe and Hank Hyasman, both of whom live at Granville, Chehalis County, Wash.

I knew Quewish, a Lower Chinook Indian, and one of the signers of the 1851 treaty. He is dead, and did not leave any children surviving him, but left grandchildren. One grandchild, whose name I do not now remember, married and left surviving her a daughter named Sallie, who is now dead. She was married and left surviving her a son named Matthew John, who now lives at Georgetown, Wash., and a daughter named Caroline, who is now Mrs. George Charley, and lives at Georgetown, Pacific County, Wash. Another grandchild of Quewish is named Joseph Narcotta, whose whereabouts I do not now know. He went to Victoria, British Columbia, several years ago, and I do not know whether he ever married or is now alive. Another grandson named Jones is dead, leaving surviving him as issue and sole heir a son named Paul Jones, who is now living at Bay Center, Wash. I knew Selahwish, a Lower Chinook Indian, and one of the signers of the 1851 treaty, who is dead. He had children, but they are all dead and without issue or heirs. All the children died in youth.

I knew Wahkuck, a Lower Chinook Indian, and one of the signers of the 1851 treaty, who died about thirty years ago without issue, but he left surviving him as sole heir a sister, whose name I can not now remember, who is also dead, leaving as sole issue and heir a son named James Julius, aged about 55 years, who now lives at Oakville, Chehalis County, Wash. I knew Chakinpon, a Lower Chinook Indian, one of the signers of the 1851 treaty. He is dead. He had children, who are also dead, and I know of no issue or heirs. I knew Huckswelt, a Lower Chinook Indian, one of the signers of the 1851 treaty. He is deceased, and left as sole heirs his wife, now named Catherine George, aged [25] about 60 years, living at Bay Center, Wash., and one daughter and two sons. The daughter's name is Josephine Hawk, now married to Fred Pope, at Granville, Chehalis County, Wash. One son is named Adam Hawk, and lives at Granville, Chehalis County, Wash., and the other son is named John Hawk, and lives at Bay Center, Wash.

I did not know Kahluckmuck. I knew Schoo, a Lower Chinook Indian, one of the signers of the 1851 treaty. He is dead, without issue and without heirs, as far as I know. I knew Tychawin, a Lower Chinook Indian and one of the assignors to the 1851 treaty. He is dead. He had children, but they are all dead, leaving no issue or heirs — all died of smallpox. I knew Narcotta, a Lower Chinook Indian, signer to the 1851 treaty. He was a grandson of Quewish, deceased. [See Quewish, above.] I knew Yahmants, a Lower Chinook Indian, and one of the signers of the 1851 treaty. He died fourteen or fifteen years ago. His wife and children are all dead, leaving no issue. The wife and all the children died before Yahmants did. Yahmants had a sister named Kahmuck, who was alive in 1851 and left surviving her at her death a daughter named Julia Lussier, who is now deceased, leaving as issue and heirs Alex. Lussier, of Bay Center, Wash.; Sterling Price, of Portland, Oreg.; Mrs. George Pryor, of Nema, Wash., and other children whose names I do not now remember.

I knew Kaase, who is dead. He was a Lower Chinook Indian and one of the signers to the 1851 treaty. He left no issue or heirs to my knowledge. I knew Wahqueon, a Lower Chinook Indian and ore of the signers to the 1851 treaty. He is dead and his wife is dead, and there is no issue. He had a sister who survived him named Willegas, who is now dead, leaving as sole heir a son named Samuel Jackson, who now lives at Bay Center, Wash., about 21 years of age. I knew Seekumtyee, who is dead. He was a Lower Chinook Indian, one of the signers to the 1851 treaty. His wife is also dead and they left no issue. Seekuintyee had a sister, who is dead and left as issue and sole heir a son named John Cliff, who now lives at Hnmptulips, Chehalis County, Wash., and who is the only heir I know of Seekumtyee. I knew Kadock, a Lower Chinook Indian, and one of the signers to the 1851 agreement. He had children, but they all died before he did, and he has no issue or heirs now alive to my knowledge.

I knew Yahwisk, who is dead. He signed the Lower Chinook treaty of 1851. His wife and children are all dead, but one of his sons, named Tyee John, who is dead, left two children, named John and Sampson. John John lives at Georgetown, Wash., and is about 40 years old. Sampson John lives at Oyhut, Chehalis County, Wash., and is over 40 years of age. I knew Elaspah, who is dead. He was a Lower Chinook Indian. He died unmarried and without issue. He had brothers, but they died without issue. He had no sisters, and there are no heirs to my knowledge. I knew Chacolitch, who is dead, and he left no issue or heirs. He was a Lower Chinook Indian. I knew Jack Wonio, a Lower Chinook Indian, who was alive when the treaty was made in 1851. He was a relative of Yahmants, deceased; and Jack Wonio died about ten years ago, leaving as issue and sole heir one son, named Henry Jack or Jackson, who is about 30 years old and lives at Bay Center, Wash. I know Herbert Petit, of Ilwaco. He is a Lower Chinook Indian. His mother is a Lower Chinook, and his father was a white man. Herbert was alive when the 1851 treaty was made.

I know Julia Kussel, who lives in Ilwaco, Wash. She is a Lower Chinook woman. I do not remember her mother's name. Julia was alive in 1851. Her mother was a daughter of a niece of Yosick. Julia Russel had a sister named Mary Ann Bouten, who lived at or near Ilwaco, and has other relatives alive there, I think. Catharine McCarthy, living at Ilwaco, Wash., is a descendant of the Clatsop Indians. Catharine was married to a man named Brown, who is dead, and Catharine's mother was related to Chenob's sister.

I knew Totillicum, who was a chief of the Kathlamet band, alive and one of the signers of the 1851 treaty. He died about thirty-five years ago. He had a number of children, but they died without issue. Totillicum had four brothers and two sisters, all of whom died before Totillicum did, except Klow-sum, who has since died, leaving as sole heirs the following: Samuel Mallet, male son, living at Bay Center, Wash.; Elizabeth Klowsum Springer, daughter, living at Bay Center, Wash. James Mallet, deceased, son of Klowsuin, deceased, who died about twenty years ago, leaving a son named Jason Millet, who lives at Tokeland, Wash. I did not know John, one of the Kathlamet treaty signers. I knew Kaisht, a Kathlamet Indian chief, who was alive in 1851. He is dead, without issue or heirs. I knew Sahoho, a Kathlamet Indian, who was alive [26] in 1851, but who has since died. He had children, but they are all dead, without issue or heirs, to my knowledge.

I knew Moses, who was alive in 1851, but has since died. He was a Kathlamet Indian.

He left no issue or heirs. I knew Kalup, who was Klowsuin's son and my half brother, same father but different mother. He is dead, without issue, and the only relatives of his now alive are Samuel Mallet, half brother, Bay Center, Wash.; Elizabeth Klowsum Springer, half sister, Bay Center, Wash.; James Mallet, deceased, half brother, and who left as sole issue and heir a son, Jason Millet, Tokeland, Wash. I knew Wakotsuck, who is dead. He left no children or heirs. He was a Kathlamet Indian and one of the 1851 treaty signers. I knew Twilts, also Scotchlecbie, who were both chiefs of the Clatsop Indians; both are dead, without issue or heirs, to my knowledge.

SAMUEL MALLET (his x mark).

Sworn and subscribed to before me at Bay Center, Wash., this 2d day of January, 1906.

CHAS. E. McCHESNEY,
Supervisor of Indian Schools.

STATEMENT NO. 14.

STATE OF WASHINGTON, *Pacific County,* ss:

Howard Cultee, of Bay Center, Wash., being duly sworn, deposes and says he is 20 years of age, and a Clatsop Indian descendant.

My father was Charles Cultee, who died about nine years ago, aged about 60 years. He was a full blood Clatsop Indian. My grandfather was named [28] Kularsen, who was my father's father, and he was a Clatsop Indian; alive in 1851 when the treaty of that year was made, but has since died, leaving as sole issue and heir my father. I have one brother named Joseph Cultee, who lives at Bay Center, Wash., who, with myself, is the sole heir of my father and grandfather. My mother died when I was very small boy.

HOWARD (his x mark) CULTEE.

Sworn and subscribed before me at Bay Center, Wash., this 2d day of January, 1906.

CHAS. E. McCHESNEY,
Supervisor of Indian Schools.

STATEMENT NO. 15.

STATE OF WASHINGTON, *Pacific County*, ss:

Mary Wagoner, of Bay Center, being duly sworn, says she is about 48 years of age.

My father's name was Kulhalah, a Clatsop Indian, who was alive in 1851. I have no brothers, sisters, aunts, or uncles alive, and no descendants of them now alive, and I am the sole heir of my father Kulhalah.

MARY WAGONER (her x mark).

Sworn and subscribed before me at Bay Center, Wash., this 2d day of January, 1906.

CHAS. E. McCHESNEY,
Supervisor of Indian Schools.

Note. — Mary Wagoner is reported to have been a captive and slave to the Clatsop Indians. However this may be, she is part Indian.

McC.

STATEMENT NO. 16.

STATE OF WASHINGTON, *Pacific County*, ss:

Catherine George, of Bay Center, Wash., being duly sworn, deposes and says she is about 78 years of age and belongs to the Wheelapa band of Chinook Indians.

My maiden name was Catharine Was-se-quah. I have been married twice; first time to Tom Hawks, or Huckswelt, a Lower Chinook Indian chief, who was alive in 1851 and one of the signers of the treaty of that year. He died about twenty years ago, aged about 60 years, and left surviving him, myself, Catherine George, his widow, and our children, as follows: John Hawks, son, 50 years old, Bay Center, Wash.; Adam Hawks, son, 45 years old, Granville, Wash.; Josephine Hawks Pope, daughter, 33 years old, Granville, Wash., who are his sole heirs. I am now married to an Indian named Wynooche George.

I have no brothers or sisters. I have a half-sister, named Catherine Dawson, living at Bay Center, Wash. I knew Cumcumley, who died many years ago, and he was a chief of the Lower band of Chinooks. He had five children, all of whom are dead, and there are no issue or heirs of his now living. I knew Kulchute also, who died before Cumcumley died. There were two Kulchutes, both Lower Chinook Indians, and they were cousins. The elder Kulchute died without any issue or heirs surviving him. The younger Kulchute, who was also alive in 1851, left surviving him one daughter named Tahshuck, who is also dead, leaving as sole heirs one son and one daughter, viz. Edward Smith and Maggie Smith Pete, both of whom reside on the Chehalis Reservation, Oakville, Wash.

I knew Ahmoosamoose, a chief of the Lower band of Chinook Indians, alive in 1851, but who is now deceased. He left three children surviving him and who are his sole heirs, viz. – Joseph Ahmoosamoose, son, who is dead and left surviving him a daughter named Kate, now Mrs. Kate Walkowsky, and she lives near Oysterville, Wash. Another son was named Jack, who is dead without issue. Ahmoosamoose also left a daughter named Looks, who is also dead, leaving as issue two sons, named Joe and Frank Hyasman, both of whom are now living at Granville, Chehalis County, Wash. I knew Quewish also, who is dead. He was a Lower Chinook Indian, alive in 1851. No children [29] survived him, but at the time of his death he had grandchildren, as follows: Wahpoayn, who is now dead, leaving as sole heirs Caroline, a daughter now living at Georgetown, Wash., and married to George Charley, and Mathew John, son, now living at same place. Narcortta, who is also dead, leaving as issue and sole heir Joseph Narcotta, whose whereabouts I do not now know. Jones, who is dead, leaving a son named Paul Jones, living at Bay Center, Wash., his sole heir. I know of no other heirs of Quewish.

I knew Selahwish, who is dead. He had two children, but they never married. Selahwish had a sister named Cahlast, who is dead also, leaving a daughter named Ellen, who is dead alsoi leaving two children as sole issue and heirs, viz. Archie Pallard, who lives at Altoona, Wash., and Adelaine, now Mrs. James, living at Bay Center, Wash. I knew Wahkuck, a Lower Chinook signer of the 1851 treaty. He died without issue. He had two sisters who survived him as sole heirs. One of the sisters died without issue and the other left as sole issue and heir a son named James Julius, now living at Oakville, Chehalis County, Wash. I do not remember the name of James Julius's mother. I knew Chakinpon, who is dead. He had children who are also dead, and I know of no issue or heirs now alive. I did not remember Kahluckmuck. I knew Schoo, a Lower Chinook chief who signed the 1851 treaty. He is dead and all his children are dead, and there are no heirs.

I knew Tychawin, who is dead. He had children, but they are all dead and without issue. All died of smallpox. I knew Narcotta, who was a grandson of Quewish, deceased. [See Quewish,above.] Yahmauts died about fourteen years ago. He had a wife and children who died before he did and without issue. He had a sister named Kahmuck, who was alive in 1851 and left surviving her as sole heirs a daughter named Julia Lussier, one named Mary Pettie, and Isabel Betrand, all of whom are, or were recently, alive. Julia Lussier I am told died a few years since and she left as issue and heirs several children, as follows: Alex. Lussier, who lives at Bay Center, Wash.; Mary Ann Lussier, now married to Louie Duchene and lives as [at] Skamokawa, Wakiakum County, Wash.; also Mary Lussier, who lives somewhere in Oregon; also Lulu Price, who is married to George Pryor and lives at Nema, Wash., and Sterling Price, who lives at Portland, Oreg. There are no other heirs of Yahmauts now alive.

I knew Kaase, who is deceased. He left no issue, and his wife died before he did and there are no heirs to my knowledge. I knew Wahqueon, a Lower Chinook chief also, and he is dead. His wife is dead, and there was no issue. A sister survived him, named Willegas, who is dead, leaving as heir a son named Samuel Jackson, who lives at Bay Center, Wash., aged about 21 years. I knew Seekumtyee, who is dead. He was also a Lower Chinook Indian and one of the signers of the 1851 treaty. His wife is dead and; all his children are dead and there was only a sister who survived him and who was his sole heir, and her name was Ahkiack, who is now dead. She had a son named John Cliff, who lives at Humptulips, Wash., about 40 years of age, and who is the sole surviving heir of Ahkiack and Seekumtyee. I knew Kadock, who is dead. All his children died before he did, and there are no heirs living.

I knew Yahwisk, and he is dead and his wife is dead. He left surviving him as sole heir his son, Tyee John, who is also dead and who left surviving him as sole heirs his sons, Johnny John and Sampson John. Johnny lives at Georgetown, Wash., and Sampson lives at Oyhut, Wash. There are no other heirs of Yahwisk, deceased. I knew Elaspah, who is dead. He died unmarried and without issue. He had brothers, but they died without issue. He had no sisters, and there is no heir. I knew Chacolitch, who is dead. He was never married and left no issue, and there are no heirs.

NOTE. — All the foregoing were signers to the Lower Chinook treaty of 1851. I knew Elaspah's father, who was a Lower Chinook Indian and was alive in 1851 when the treaty was signed. His name was See yak que kak, who left surviving him besides Elaspah, his son, a brother named Whah sa quah, who is dead, leaving a daughter (being myself), Catherine George, and another daughter (my half-sister), Catherine Dawson, now living at Bay Center, Wash., as his sole heirs.

I knew Mooyahuts, who was a Lower Chinook woman, alive in 1851 when the treaty was made, who is now dead and left as her sole heir her son, Jack Pisk, who died about twenty years ago, leaving as issue and sole heir one son named Henry Pisk, who is about 30 years of age and lives at Bay Center, Wash. There is no other heir alive of Mooyahuts, deceased. I knew Totillicum, who was a chief of the Kalhtamets, who is dead. He had a number of children, but they are all dead. He had a brother named Klowsum, who [30] survived him and was his only heir. Klowsum is also dead, and his heirs are Samuel Mallet, Elizabeth (Klowsum) Springer, and Jason Mallet, grandson, all of whom live at Bay Center, Wash. There are no other heirs of Totillicum, deceased. I did not know John. I knew Kaisht, who is dead. He was not married and died without issue — no heirs. I knew Lahoho, who is dead, and he has no issue or heirs now alive. I knew Moses, who is dead, and he has no issue or heirs now alive.

I knew Kalup, who was Klowsum's son. He is dead and had no children, and the only persons surviving him as relatives are his half-brother, Samuel Mallet, and half-sister, Elizabeth (Klowsum) Springer, and Jason Millet, son of his half-brother. James Millet, deceased, all of whom live at Bay Center, Wash. I knew Wakotsuck, who is dead and left no children or heirs — all are dead.

Clatsops. — I knew Tostow, who is dead, a Clatsop Indian chief, who was alive in 1851. He left surviving him as issue and sole heirs a son and a daughter. The daughter's name is Kate Tostow, who is now alive and lives at Skipanon, Oreg. I think she is married. Her son is dead. His name was Baker and he died without issue, and Kate is the sole surviving heir of her father, Tostow, deceased.

I knew Colata, who is dead. He had seven children (five are dead, having died unmarried and without issue). Two daughters are now alive, one named Grace Swawa, living at Tillamook, Oreg., and the other named Filly Cotata, unmarried, and lives at Garibaldi. Tillamook County, Oreg., aged about 40 years. Filly is the older sister. I knew Twilts, a Clatsop chief, who is dead, and there is no issue or heir to my knowledge. I do not remember Tickahah. I knew Washington, who is dead, and his wife is dead. A son, named Joseph Lane, survived him as issue and sole heir. Joseph is dead, leaving as sole heirs [sic] his wife, Jennie, now Jennie Williams, living at Bay Center, Wash., and son, James Lane, of Tokeland, Wash., aged about 21 years, and also a daughter named Louisa Lane, who is dead, and left surviving her a daughter named Nina Robb, married and living at Tokeland, Wash., also. I knew Skotchlechie, a Clatsop chief, who is dead, and his wife and children are all dead — no issue and no heirs alive.

I kmew Dunkle, who is dead. He left two children, Joseph and Mary Dunkle, who live at Nehalem, Oreg. I knew Winawox, a Clatsop, who is dead, and his children are all dead — no issue or heirs alive. I do not remember Hulleh. I knew Waucakie, a Clatsup, who is dead. He had one daughter, who died without issue, and there are no heirs now alive. Rob Silackie is a Clatsop Indian, alive, at Georgetown, Wash., whose father and mother were both Clatsops, who died about fifty years ago, bunt were alive when the 1851 treaty was made. The father's name was Queanequah. I do not now recall the mother's name.

I know Joseph and Howard Cultee, of Bay Center, who are Clatsops. They are sons of Kularsen, who was alive when the 1851 treaty was made, and he was a Clatsop Indian. I do not know any of the Tillamook Indians. I knew Wahmaskie, who was a Lower Chinook woman, who died about thirty-five years ago, aged about 55 years. She left as issue a son named Dixie James, now living at Bay Center, Wash., and also her husband, James Huckquist, now living at Bay Center, Wash., aged about 80 years.

CATHERINE GEORGE (her x mark).

Sworn and subscribed to before me at Bay Center, Wash., this 2d day of January, 1900.

CHAS. E. McCHESNEY,
Supervisor of Indian Schools.

STATEMENT NO. 18.

STATE OR WASHINGTON, *Pacific County*, ss:

Joseph Cultee, being duly sworn, says he is 37 years of age and lives at Bay Center, Wash.

My father was Charles Cultee, and he was a Clatsop Indian, and he died about nine years ago, aged about 60 years. He was alive in 1851 when the treaty of that year was made. My father's father was Kularsen, a Clatsop Indian, who was alive in 1851, but has since died. My mother died about twenty-seven years ago and my father and grandfather left as sole issue and heirs myself and my brother, Howard Cultee, of Bay Center, Wash.

JOSEPH CULTEE (his x mark).

Sworn ad subscribed to before me at Bay Center, Wash., this 3d day of January, 1906.

CHAS. E. McCHESNEY,
Supervisor of Indian Schools.

STATEMENT NO. 33.

STATE OF WASHINGTON, *Pacific County, ss.*

Mrs. Howard Cultee, of Bay Center, Wash., being duly sworn, deposes and says she is 38 years of age and that her maiden name was Lena Pete, and that she is a descendant of the Lower Band of Chinook Indians on my mother's side.

My mother's name was Kahlalto, a Lower Chinook woman, who died about fifteen years ago, aged about 40 years, and Tyee John was my mother's father, and he was a Lower Chinook, who died about four years ago, who was alive when the 1851 treaty was made. My mother has two other children alive and who are my sisters. Their names are Sallie (Pete) George, married and living at Bay Center, Wash., aged about 30 years, and Lizzie (Pete) Hays, married and living at Tokeland, Wash., aged about 25 years. We are all great-grandchildren of Chief Yosick, of the Lower Chinook Indians.

My father was named Heside, or Pete, and he was a Lower Chinook Indian, who died six years ago, aged about 43 years; and he was a son of Wetoolisk, a Lower Chinook Indian, who died many years ago, but was alive in 1851, when the treaty of that year was made.

MRS. HOWARD (PETE) CULTEE (her x mark).

Sworn and subscribed to before me at Bay Center, Wash., this 2d day of January, 1906.

CHAS. E. McCHESNEY,
Supervisor of Indian Schools.

Mrs. Lizzie Hays, of Tokeland, Wash., having had read to her the foregoing affidavit of her sister, Mrs. Howard Cultee, solemnly swears the same is true.

I am 22 years of age.

LIZZIE (PETE) HAYS.

Sworn and subscribed to before me at Tokeland, Wash., this 3d day of January, 1908.

CHAS. E. McCHESNEY,
Supervisor of Indian Schools.

Mrs. Sally George, of Bay Center, Washington, having had read to her the foregoing affidavits, solemnly swears the same are true.

I am 28 years of age.

SALLY GEORGE (her x mark).

Subscribed and sworn to before me at Buy Center, Wash., this 3d day of January, 1906.

CHAS. E. McCHESNEY,
Supervisor of Indian Schools.

NOTE. — As the result of inquiries I learn that Kahlalto was not alive in August, 1851. Chief Yosick, of the Lower Chinook Indians, died before 1851.

McC.

STATEMENT NO. 64.

State of Oregon, Multnomah County, ss: [52]

Mrs. Isabel Bertrand, of North Front and Hull streets, Portland, Oreg., being duly sworn, deposes and says she is 62 years of age, and was alive when the treaty of August, 1851, was made. My father was a white man and be is dead.

My mother's name was Elmermach and she died in 1880, aged 60 years, and she was a Lower Chinook Indian woman. I am a Lower Chinook Indian descendant. I had four sisters, who are dead, and who, with their heirs, are as follows: Mrs. Lafferty, who has no children alive, and she is dead without issue. She died in March, 1905, aged 77 years. The next sister was Julia Price, who is dead. She died two years ago, aged 73 years. Julia was married twice, once to Lussier, a white man, who is dead, and once to a man named Price, a white man, and the issue of these marriages are Alex. Lussier and Mary Ann Lussier (now Mrs. Duchene), and Emily Lussier (now Mrs. Cashel), who lives 6 miles above Astoria, near Burnside, Oreg., and Mrs. George Pryor, and Sterling Price, who are all alive. My next sister was named Catherine Pilcier, who is dead, and she has four children alive, who are named Edward Pilcier, who lives at Spokane, Wash.; Minnie Pilcier, now Mrs. Minnie Kelly, who lives at Spokane, Wash.; Matilda Pilcier (now Matilda Jones), who lives in Portland, Oreg., foot of Nineteenth street, and Elsie Tellier, now Mrs. Ludington, who lives same address in Portland. My other sister, who is dead, left no issue. My sister who is alive is named Mary Petit, and she lives at Ilwaco, Wash.

MRS. ISABEL BERTRAND (her x mark).

Sworn and subscribed to before me at Bay Center, Wash., this 7th day of January, 1906.

CHAS. E. McCHESNEY,
Supervisor of Indian Schools.

STATEMENT NO. 100.

State of Washington, *Pacific County, ss*: [69-70]

Mrs. Esther Millet, of Bay Center, Wash., being duly sworn, deposes and says she is about 60 years of age.

My maiden name was Esther Wa-wha-ho-wa, and I am a Kathlamet Indian descendant. My father was Wa-wha-ho-wa, and he was a Cowlitz Indian, and he is dead. My mother was Karmlele, who was a Kathlamet Indian woman, who died about forty-nine years ago, aged about 45 years. I have no brothers. I have no sisters. I have half-brothers and half-sisters, but they are of a different [70] mother, my father having been married before he married my mother to a Cowlitz Indian woman, and they are not heirs of my mother.

ESTHER MILLET (her x mark).

Sworn and subscribed to before me at Bay Center, Wash., this 9th day of April, 1906.

CHAS. E. McCHESNEY,
Supervisor of Indian Schools.

Charles E McChesney House of Representatives 59th Congress Second Session Document No 133 Rolls of Certain Indian Tribes in Oregon and Washington. December 1906
Began 8 Dec 1905 > 15 November 1906

Charles E McChesney
Supervisor of Indian Schools
P78 1107 38th Ave Portland, Oreg

p12 15 Nov 1906
Pawhuska Okla

Index

ACCULTURATING AMELIA ~ Round Valley 1937 California
ALASKA EDGE ISLAND ~ Siberian Yupiks of St Lawrence Island
ALLIED MOUNDS ~ Touching the Earth, Modeling the World, Reaching the Sky
ANIMAL PEOPLE ADVENTURES ~ Native North American Tribal Stories
AT BAY ~ Cultures Converging through Southwest Washington   > 5
BALLARD BULWARK ~
CHACO ECHOES ~ Pervasive Keresan Priesthoods
CHACOKIA ~ Chaco, Cahokia, Cities & Ceremonies ~ Bundles & Blood Lines Centuries Ago
CHINOOK CONCERNS ~ Emma Millett Luscier, Isabella Bertrand, Verne Ray
CIRCLING FOUR CORNERS ~ Re-Viewing Native American Indiens   > 10
CROSSING ~ LINES: An Educational Memoir of Native North America
DEL-AWARE ~ Lenape Legacies
DELAWARE INTEGRITY ~ Rituals, Removals, Reforms by Lenape Indiens
DISCLAIMING TREATIES I ~ Puget Tribes 1927 Testimonies
DISCLAIMING TREATIES II ~ Puget Tribes 1927 Testimonies   > 15
ELDERS' DIALOG ~ Ed Davis & Vi Hilbert Discuss Native Puget Sound Language, Culture, & Heritage
EVERGREEN ETHNOGRAPHIES ~ Hoh, Chehalis, Suquamish, and Snoqualmi of Western Washington
FEDERAL FISH FILES ~ Swindell 1942 Treaty Rights Report
GEORGE GIBBS NORTHWEST ARRAY ~ Full Reports, Place Names, Word List, Artifact Names, and Guide
GRASSROOTS JANET ~ Advancing Salish and Traditional Cultures   > 20
HERMAN HAEBERLIN REGAINED ~ Anthropology and Artifacts of Puget Sound 1916-17
HERSTORY NW ~ Women Upholding Native Traditions
INDIEN ~ ETHNOGRAPHY: Cultural Traditions of Native North America
INDIEN ~ ETHNOLOGY: Grounded, Gendered, Meaningful Cultural Traditions
LESCHI IN LOVE ~ A Novel of Native Puget Sound > x2   > 25
MARCO MUCK MASKS ~ Frank Cushing on Marshes and Mounds
MINTER BAY ~ Land, Lore, Loss, and Lucre in the South Salish Sea
NATIVE MET HOW ~ Improving Posterity
OLD LUKH ~ A Novel of Native Puget Sound Daily Life, Places, and Stories
OVER THE FALLS ~ Sdoqwalbixw Survivance Surrounding Seattle   > 30
PACIFIC PLATEAU PORTRAYALS ~ People Places Ponderings
RAY'S ARRAY ~ Raymond D Fogelson's Works
RIGHTING NATIVE PLACES ~ Adventures in Northwest Geography
SAHAPTINS STUDIES ~ Columbia River Plateau, Cora Du Bois, Homer Garner Barnett, Gerald Raymond Desmond
SDOQWALBIXW   > 35
SOUND SALISH STRAITS ~ Central Salish Sea Cultures
UNSETTLING SEATTLE ~ Arresting Local Talent and Academic Illiteracy
WRITING WORDS IN WARY WORLDS ~ World Wide Improved Spellings of Native America Languages

@ JONA Memoirs

RESCUES, RANTS, & RESEARCHES ~ A Re-View of Jay Miller's Writings on Northwest Indien Cultures ~ #9
TRIBAL TRIO of the Northwest Coast by Kenneth D Tollefson ~ #10   > 40
INTERWEAVING COAST SALISH CULTURAL SYSTEMS ~ Collected Works of Pamela Thorsen Amoss ~ #14

@ University of Nebraska Press

ANCESTRAL MOUNDS ~ Vitality and Volatility Crossing Native North America 2015
HONNE ~ The Spirit of the Chehalis 2015